Law, Liberty, and the Rule of Law

IUS GENTIUM

COMPARATIVE PERSPECTIVES ON LAW AND JUSTICE

VOLUME 18

For further volumes:
http://www.springer.com/series/7888

Imer B. Flores • Kenneth Einar Himma
Editors

Law, Liberty, and the Rule of Law

Springer

Editors
Imer B. Flores
Law School and Legal Research Institute
National Autonomous University
of Mexico (UNAM)
Mexico City, Mexico

Kenneth Einar Himma
University of Washington
School of Law
Seattle, WA, USA

ISBN 978-94-007-4742-5 ISBN 978-94-007-4743-2 (eBook)
DOI 10.1007/978-94-007-4743-2
Springer Dordrecht Heidelberg New York London

Library of Congress Control Number: 2012948783

Printed on acid-free paper

Springer is part of Springer Science+Business Media (www.springer.com)

I dedicate this volume to my wife, Hazel Blackmore, my sons, Ervin and Kevin, and my dear friend Roberto Salinas León.

–Imer B. Flores

I dedicate this volume to my wife, Maria Elias Sotirhos, my nieces, Angela and Maria, and my dear friend Icarus Tamagotchi Grabowski.

–Kenneth Einar Himma

Acknowledgments

Recognizing the intriguing nature of the changes underway in China, Imer B. Flores – jointly with Profs. Ofer Raban and Gülriz Uygur – proposed to the organizers of the XXIV IVR World Congress *Global Harmony and the Rule of Law* a Special Workshop on "Law, Liberty and the Rule of Law", not only because of the importance and transcendence of the subject matter itself but also due to its (in)appropriateness given the conference's location and the fact that 2009 marked the 150th anniversary of John Stuart Mill's celebrated *On Liberty* and the 100th anniversary of Isaiah Berlin's birthday.

In that sense, this volume grew out of a Special Workshop at the XXIV IVR World Congress *Global Harmony and the Rule of Law* in Beijing, China, in 2009, which drew more attention than originally expected: on the one hand, several scholars were interested and at the end 11 papers presented; and, on the other hand, Mortimer Sellers approached to offer the possibility of publishing them in the collection "Jus Gentium: Comparative Perspectives on Law and Justice". However, since Profs. Raban and Uygur had other previous commitments, Kenneth Einar Himma stepped in as co-editor. Similarly, since some authors were not in a position to submit their original papers for publication, as editors, we – Flores and Himma – decided to invite other scholars to contribute to the volume. We are indebted to the IVR for accepting the proposal and we are extremely grateful to all those who participated in the workshop and contributed papers to this volume.

Contents

Chapter 1
Introduction

Imer B. Flores and Kenneth Einar Himma

Revising the problems of the concept of the "rule of law" and its relationship to both law and liberty are the main aims of this volume. In fact, the concept of rule of law, like the concept of legitimacy, is a morally normative concept that expresses an ideal to which society and its governing institutions should, as a matter of political morality, aspire. For example, the notion of legitimacy applies to those governing institutions that are morally justified in coercively regulating the behaviour of citizens. For a state to be legitimate, as it has sometimes been put, is for the state to have a *moral right* to rule. Otherwise put, a legitimate state is morally justified not only in enacting restrictions or requirements pertaining to the behaviour of citizens (at least within the scope of its legitimacy), but also – and more importantly – utilizing the coercive enforcement mechanisms to increase compliance that might not be a conceptual feature of law but is a feature of every known modern municipal legal system.

Of course, just having a reasonably satisfactory theory of the concept of legitimacy tells us nothing at all about the content of the conditions that a state must satisfy in order to *be legitimate*. Getting clear on the concept of legitimacy is one thing; having a plausible *normative* theory of legitimacy is another. It is fair to say that there are not many disputes regarding the concept of legitimacy: the general idea is that the legal practices of the state, including the use of coercive enforcement mechanisms, are morally justified. But the normative theory of legitimacy remains deeply contentious: that is to say, it is deeply controversial, and there are many alternative theories of state legitimacy, what conditions a state must satisfy in order to have the property of legitimacy (i.e. to be justified in its legal practices).

I.B. Flores (✉)
Law School and Legal Research Institute, National Autonomous University of Mexico (UNAM), Mexico City, Mexico
e-mail: imer@unam.mx

K.E. Himma
University of Washington, School of Law, Seattle, WA, USA
e-mail: himma@wu.edu

I.B. Flores and K.E. Himma (eds.), *Law, Liberty, and the Rule of Law*,
Ius Gentium: Comparative Perspectives on Law and Justice 18,
DOI 10.1007/978-94-007-4743-2_1, © Springer Science+Business Media Dordrecht 2013

In contrast, it is not entirely clear exactly what the concept of the rule of law amounts to, which, of course, complicates efforts to arrive at an appropriate corresponding normative theory of the rule of law. For example, the rule of law is casually described in a number of different ways: rule by law and not people; no one is above the law – even the body that makes the rules; and the rule of law is a state of order created by law. One or all of these could be meant but it is not always clear how the term is being used in conversation or writing.

This is problematic for two reasons. First, having an adequate theory of the concept is important for its own sake as part of a comprehensive understanding of the nature of law and its various ideals. It is simply important, as an academic and practical matter, to understand as much as we can about the normative institutions that we create and have. Second, having such a theory would seem to be a prerequisite for developing a plausible account of the normative conditions for satisfying the ideal of the rule of law – and this is obviously necessary, as a practical matter, to improving our institutions to conform to the moral norms that apply to them and ensuring that the state's practices satisfy the norms of political legitimacy. If we are working with a concept of the rule of law that is too narrow, we might be missing normative issues that are of critical importance in assessing our legal practices, from the standpoint of political morality. If too broad, we might be imposing normative requirements that are incorrect from the standpoint of political morality. Being clear on the concepts is a necessary condition for developing the substantive theories that help us assess our legal institutions.

As it turns out, just these two difficulties raise many different issues that must be resolved to produce a plausible comprehensive theory of law. Consider, for example, some of the issues that arise in the theory of legitimacy. There are very general theories that attempt to provide an adequate moral ground for just the institution of law. Social contract theories, for example, ground the legitimacy of coercive legal institutions on citizen consent, whether actual or hypothetical, explicit or implicit. Of course, many of these theories provide some substantive constraints on the functions of the state as well. John Locke, for example, took the position that people voluntarily place themselves under the coercive authority of the state by consenting to obey those laws so long as they respect certain natural moral rights.

But the inquiry does not, and certainly could not, stop there – even if one of these theories were clearly successful. The problem is that the level of abstraction is too high to provide sufficient guidance to courts and legislatures in enacting and adjudicating law. Thus, there are subareas in legal theory that, in essence, deal with more specific questions of legitimacy: the normative theory of criminal law (e.g. what acts may permissibly be criminalized?); of tort law (e.g. for what accidents might a defendant be permissibly be held liable?); of constitutionalism (which includes questions about judicial supremacy and constitutional interpretation); of civil procedure; of criminal procedure; of property; of corrective justice; of retributive justice; of distributive justice; and of many more areas of law.

There are also empirically descriptive theories of what, as a matter of fact, ground the specific rules and principles of these various areas of law. These are usually the subject of most articles that are found in law reviews. In such an article, the author is concerned with identifying the answer to a difficult legal question based on the history of the relevant legal rules and principles, which, of course, requires an analysis that is partly historical in character (it is also interpretive in character).

Sometimes the empirical and normative theories are conjoined, presupposing that what really *is* law is what *should be* law. For example, Ronald Dworkin famously argues that the law includes the moral principles that show the existing legal history in the best moral light (Dworkin 1986). Moreover, he argues in earlier work that judges typically decide hard cases by attempting to do exactly that – find the moral principles on which the relevant rules are based and decide the case on the basis of which rules express the most important values.

Indeed, it seems reasonable to think that satisfying the ideals associated with the rule of law is at least a *necessary*, if not a *sufficient* condition, for a state to be morally legitimate. Again, the problem of legitimacy is an enormously complicated problem; and it might be that a state might be morally legitimate even though it satisfies some but not all conditions that seem to define the properties of the legitimate state. Surely, there is some room for error in the lawmaking and adjudicative activities of the state. The legislature might, for example, unbeknownst to members, enact some unjust laws (from an objective standpoint) without thereby calling into question the state's legitimacy. But it is hard to imagine, given the importance customarily attributed to rule of law ideals, that a state could be legitimate without largely conforming to those ideals.

The topic of the rule of law, if somewhat more narrow than the more general topic of legitimacy, presents the same problems: (1) getting clear on the concept so that we have a better understanding of what the relevant norms might look like; (2) identifying the relevant norms that govern the rule of law in all the areas in which rule of law issues might arise – and as will be seen in this volume, these issues arise in a number of contexts that are somewhat unexpected; and (3) understanding the history of both the ideal of the rule of law and how it arose and has been applied in past legal systems and theorized by legal theorists from the past.

While it might look as though these three issues are distinct and independent, this is a mistake. The relationship among the three issues are related in a way that any proposed resolution of one issue might require addressing the other two issues. Surely, for example, the history of the ideal as it has evolved over time and expressed itself in legal practice will be relevant with respect to addressing the conceptual and normative issues that arise in connection with theorizing the rule of law.

Law, Liberty, and the Rule of Law is a collection of ten original essays on various issues involving the ideals that fall under the rubric of the "rule of law", including its relationship to both law and liberty. The contributors to the volume are internationally recognized scholars that hail mainly from the Anglo-Saxon, Continental Europe and Latin America academic circles, representing not only a distinct number of countries, including Brazil, Canada, Mexico, Poland, Turkey, United Kingdom, and United States of America, but also a diverse number of perspectives and methodologies.

As one might expect from the above, the essays in the book include articles covering each of the three issues above, and in most cases touch on more than one issue – approaching the issue in what the editors believe is the correct way to theorize the rule of law. Hence most essays concerned themselves to some extent with conceptual issues that attempt to identify the conceptually essential properties of the rule of law (even when that is not the principal concern of the essay). Just as there are conceptually essential properties for being a bachelor (one of them being that a person is unmarried), one would expect there to be conceptually essential properties of the rule of law. These properties might not be essential "come what may", as our linguistic practices and ordinary intuitions that constitute *our* concept may change; but we are looking for those that are essential given our existing linguistic practices and ordinary intuitions.

Recognizing the hotly contested nature of the concepts, most of the authors of the essays in this volume devote ample space to carefully explaining what they intend by the various relevant concepts. While the various authors agree on a number of issues involving them, they disagree on others, taking care to make explicit their assumptions. This is important because the assumptions they make condition the direction in which they go on the other issues with which their essays are primarily concerned. Accordingly, it is not necessary to attempt to arrive at a definitive analysis of the concept of the rule of law in this introduction, as the authors do an exceptional job of situating their views among the wide diversity of conceptual views expressed in the essays in the volume. In fact, given the diversity of the conceptual views in the essays, it would detract from the project of the volume to try to impose any set of particular conceptual commitments on the essays because any set might fit some but not all essays in this volume.

Even so, it is worth briefly discussing some of the differences in accounts of the concept of the rule of law. Some theorists maintain that the concept of the rule of law is principally *formal* in character and correspond to ideals that define formal constraints on the rule of law. Examples of such explications of the concept include the view that the rule of law is governance by rules properly enacted by an authorized body and applied consistently to everyone, including those who enact them. The idea here is that people are governed by rules and not ruled by people. On this view of the rule of law, the ideals expressed may include certain procedural norms for regulating subject behaviour.

Others believe that the concept of the rule of law has to do with *substantive* matters of legal content. On this view, the ideals expressing the rule of law involve certain moral restrictions on the content of law – restrictions of a particular kind that conform to the specific conceptual characteristics of the rule of law. For example, the Equal Protection Clause of the Fifth and Fourteenth Amendments might, on such an analysis, satisfy the ideals associated with a substantive account of the concept of the rule of law.

Finally, and further complicating the issues, is that some theorists maintain that the concept of the rule of law has both formal and substantive elements. Because there is so much disagreement on the content of this somewhat underdeveloped concept, discussion and dialogue can be difficult to understand when the conceptual presuppositions are not made clear, as is all too frequently the case in published essays on the topic. Indeed, one recurring theme on the conceptual issue in the volume is whether the concept is best characterized as formal or substantive.

For this reason, it is best to allow the authors to define their own conceptual views in the process of arguing for a particular thesis. Conceptual issues are not generally best assessed by the substantive results they produce. For example, just knowing that it is a conceptual truth that a bachelor is an unmarried adult male tells us little, if anything, what sorts of substantive norms govern how they behave and how they should be treated. Likewise, though somewhat more contentious, questions about the nature of law – i.e., the content of the concept of law – do not, as a general matter, seem to have much by way of practical results. Indeed, critics of conceptual jurisprudence frequently point out that nothing of substantive or practical value seems to turn on such matters. According, for example, to Richard Posner (1997, 3):

> I grant that even if the *word* 'law' cannot be defined the *concept* of law can be discussed; and that is after all Hart's title, though he uses the word 'definition' a lot. Philosophical reflection on the concept of justice has been a fruitful enterprise since Plato; for that matter, there is a philosophical literature on time. I have nothing against philosophical speculation. But one would like it to have some pay-off; *something* ought to turn on the answer to the question' What is law?' if the question is to be worth asking by people who could use their time in other socially valuable ways. Nothing does turn on it. I go further: the central task of analytic jurisprudence is, or at least ought to be, not to answer the question 'What is law?' but to show that it should not be asked, because it only confuses matters.

But if Posner is correct about the substantive payoff of conceptual theorizing about the nature of law, a similar view is simply not true about conceptual theorizing about the rule of law. One reason that conceptual theorizing about the nature of law does not help much in our legal practices is that our pre-theoretical understanding of the nature law is good enough for us to find authoritative statements of law: authoritative reports of statutes and cases are trivially easy to find. This, however, does not seem to be true of the rule of law. Although there are pithy pre-theoretic formulations about what it is, these formulations are sufficiently vague that it is hard to get a handle on how they apply except in perhaps the most obvious of cases. Couple that with the fact that these casual formulations differ, and it becomes all the more difficult to ascertain what normative standards are associated with the concept of the rule of law.

This helps to explain why most of the essays in this volume are at least partly concerned with the conceptual issues. The conceptual questions addressed here are vital to addressing the normative questions; if we do not understand the conceptual assumptions being made or do not share them, we cannot understand the positions they take on the other issues or their reasons.

To understand each essay primarily concerned with a normative issue, we must understand the underlying assumptions about the concept, something the authors in this volume realize and address for the reader. Likewise, the historical questions addressed in some of the essays are vital to addressing the conceptual and normative questions – even if, as the editors believe, the contributions are valuable simply in virtue of what they contribute to the body of the literature pertaining to the history of political, moral, and legal theorizing about the rule of law.

The volume opens with an essay by Courtney Taylor Hamara precisely on "The Concept of the Rule of Law", which among other things introduces the debate by pointing out to the paradoxical and problematic nature of the concept of the rule of law. On the one hand, there is apparently an agreement in the sense that this so frequently used and politically weighty ideal is among the most important ones; but, on the other hand, it actually stimulates so much disagreement to the extent of being considered as an essentially contested concept. Moreover, Hamara advances the claim that more not less conceptual analysis of the external and internal coherence is required to facilitate meaningful and fruitful discussions on the rule of law.

Brian Burge-Hendrix, in "Plato and the Rule of Law", makes an important contribution both to scholarship on Plato and conceptual rule of law theory. He adroitly reassesses the legal philosophy of Plato, arguing that his work has been underappreciated and has much to contribute to contemporary debates in legal philosophy. Burge-Hendrix has a couple of specific concerns in this essay. The first is to show that Plato's philosophical methodology is one that has been adopted by many theorists in general jurisprudence; indeed, he argues that Plato has, albeit indirectly articulated, the foundation of a general jurisprudence. The second is to identify four different conceptions of the concept of the rule of law and shows that Plato's work in legal philosophy addresses all of them. As he states these conceptions in their broadest form, the rule of law can be construed as stating (1) an *existence condition* for an actual legal system; (2) a *practical constraint* on a legal system; (3) a *procedural principle* (or set of procedural principles); and (4) an *object-level practice* (i.e. a practice carried out by the officials of a particular legal system) whereby laws are *enforced* and enforcement is *justified* by reference to an implicit or explicit legal principle avowing the rule of law. Burge-Hendrix's discussion of each of these elements shows expertly how Plato's view engages those of contemporary theorists in general jurisprudence and on the rule of law and makes an intriguing case for Plato's relevance in general jurisprudence and rule-of-law theory.

Andrzej Maciej Kaniowski, in "Kantian Re-construction of Intersubjectivity Forms: the Logic of the Transition from Natural State to the Threshold of the Civic State", attempts to revitalize Immanuel Kant's theory of the republican polity. Kaniowski notes that Kant, like all mainstream theorists, supports the formation of an ethical commonwealth, and sharply opposes imposition of such a commonwealth by force: "Woe betide the legislator – says Kant – if he wishes to bring about through coercion a polity directed to ethical ends!" But he argues that the objection, however, is not only an opposition to the *method* of implementing a system based on norms of virtue; it is an objection to the attempt to mix the political polity with a polity based on principles of virtue or ethical ends. For Kant, the republic is necessary in order to conduct commonwealth in accordance with the absolute indications of practical reason and, according to him, has its foundation in the idea of "original contract". Accordingly, Kaniowski concludes the Kantian political theory of the polity remains vital to political theorizing in our times and, in addition, to the rule of law.

Two essays that are historical bear closer relationships to other issues. Brian H. Bix, in "Radbruch's Formula, Conceptual Analysis, and the Rule of Law", considers the work of a more recent theorist: Gustav Radbruch. Bix examines the relevance of Radbruch's view that unjust laws should not be enforced even though valid. He argues that the traditional understanding of this claim as a claim about the nature of law and legal validity does not neatly connect to discussions about the rule of law. Like Burge-Hendrix, he approaches the historical question by distinguishing different conceptions of the rule of law. He considers whether Radbruch might be more productively understood as a claim about the nature of law, rather than more narrowly as a prescription about how judges should decide cases. He notes the complex role of judges, observing that courts frequently apply (and see themselves as bound to apply) norms that *are not* valid within their legal system, and the courts also on occasion do not apply (and see themselves as bound not to apply) otherwise applicable norms that *are* valid norms within their legal system. Bix concludes that the better reading of the Radbruch *formula* is to construe it as a prescription for judicial decision-making rather than as a descriptive, conceptual or analytical claim about the nature of law. Accordingly, Bix's analysis touches not only on historical and conceptual claims, but also on normative standards regarding judicial decision-making, which he believes are conceptually distinct from normative standards governing the rule of law.

Two of the essays are primarily concerned with conceptual issues. First, Imer B. Flores, in "Law, Liberty and the Rule of Law (in a Constitutional Democracy)", considers, among other things, the relationship between the concepts and conceptions of law and the rule of law. Flores begins by arguing that the ideal embedded in the concept of the *rule of law* cannot be logically derived from merely combining the content of the concept *rule* with the content of the concept *law*. The *rule of law* has content that transcends both the atomic concepts of *rule* and *law* of which the more complex concept is constructed, as well as the formal assertion that *law rules*, regardless of its relationship to certain principles, including both *negative* and *positive* liberties. In that sense, he goes on to consider the relationship not only between the rule of law and concept of freedom by recalling the distinction between two concepts of liberty but also between the rule of law and *constitutional democracy*. Finally, Flores concludes that the tendency to reduce the *democratic principle* to the *majority rule* (or *majority principle*), i.e. to whatever pleases the majority, as part of the *positive liberty*, is contrary both to the *negative liberty* and to the *rule of law* itself.

Second, Gülriz Uygur, in "The Rule of Law: Is the Line between the Formal and the Moral Blurred", considers the issue of whether the standards defining the rule of law are moral standards or purely formal ones that derive from the necessary and sufficient conditions for the existence of a legal system. Uygur, similarly to Flores, identifies various conceptions of the rule of law, from Lon L. Fuller's idea of the rule of law embodying eight procedural requirement to more substantive conceptions relating to protecting human dignity, and attempts to determine whether these conceptions are moral or not. She identifies the features of these conceptions that seem to suggest the claim that the rule of law is on a blurred line between the formal and the moral. Having done this, Uygur argues that the rule of law cannot be separated from political ideals that give the concept of the rule of law its distinctive content. Of course, it is worth noting that there are both historical and normative considerations being discussed, but the issue of primary concern is conceptual: how to conceptually characterize the standards expressing the rule of law.

The remaining issues are largely concerned with normative issues pertaining to whether particular legal practices are consistent with rule of law ideals. Conrado Hübner Mendes, in "Political Deliberation and Constitutional Review", explores the idea that judicial review might be justified by the special *deliberative* nature of the function constitutional courts play in reviewing statutory enactments or common law rules. Mendes attempts to flesh out the content of the relevant concept of deliberative in order to identify standards that would guide courts in the exercise of this function such as to justify the practice of judicial review as consistent with the ideals governing rule of law. He considers, for example, the ideas of a deliberator as *public reasoners* and *interlocutors* through a broad survey of the literature on the role of courts in judicial review. Mendes concludes that judicial review cannot be justified solely on the strength of the court's role as deliberative and points the way to additional factors that are relevant with respect to the issue of the legitimacy of judicial review.

Tom Campbell, in "The Rule of Law and Human Rights Judicial Review: Controversies and Alternatives", argues that court-based human rights judicial review of legislation is in conflict with the fundamental principle of democracy that lawmakers should be accountable to its people. His analysis focuses on the interface between rule of law ideals and two related and relatively neglected critiques of human rights judicial review. The first part of the essay explains these two critiques: (1) *a (formal) rule of law objection*, that the bills of rights on which human rights judicial review is based are contrary to the principle that rules of law which courts are called upon to apply should be specific and clear as to what they require and permit, thereby reducing the accountability of elected governments, and (2) *a practical objection*: that human rights judicial review is largely ineffective in promoting human rights goals. In the second part of the essay, Campbell argues (1) that weaker versions of court-based human rights judicial review fail to meet either the rule of law or the efficacy objections, and (2) that is better "to institutionalise bills of rights as part of political constitutions involving mechanisms such as legislative review of existing and prospective legislation in order to promote and protect human rights in ways which are politically more effective and more in accordance with the twin democratic doctrines of the rule of law and the separation of legislative and judicial powers."

Kenneth Einar Himma, in "The Rule of Law, Judicial Supremacy, and Legal Positivism", argues that legal systems affording final authority to courts over the content of a constitution fall short of fully meeting the standards defined by procedural rule of law ideals. The problem, according to Himma, is that the rule of recognition in such legal systems affords the court with the legal power to bind other officials with objectively mistaken decisions (if there be such) about the content of the constitution. This means that, in contrast to procedural rule of law ideals, sometimes it is not the objective content of the law that governs citizens or legal officials; in such cases, it is the mistaken *subjective* views of unelected judges. Procedural rule of law means governance by law, and not by persons; but the doctrine of judicial supremacy seems inconsistent with this ideal. Nevertheless, it is crucial to note that, unlike Campbell, Himma does not take a critical stance towards the practice of judicial supremacy; rule of law ideals are only one component of a theory of political legitimacy by which judicial practice should be judged.

Juan Vega Gómez, in "Retroactive Application of Laws and the Rule of Law", argues that issues of retroactivity should be addressed by a two-stage process, the first dealing with a *formal test* of retroactivity and a second one that *involves issues of justification*. Vega Gómez believes that confusion occurs when problems of retroactivity are addressed only from the perspective of political justification. To avoid and resolve such confusions, he advocates approaching such problems in the two stages described above. The *formal test* is derived from Raz's idea of a formal conception of the rule of law; on this view, we must not confuse this formal conception with an idea that thinks that complying with the rule of law entails that the law in question is good law or, more specifically, necessarily promotes human rights; nor should it be thought that a formally retroactive rule necessarily is a bad law or fails to promote human rights. Accordingly, in this provocative essay, Vega Gómez argues that the retroactivity question requires both formal and substantive analysis.

As the editors hope is evident from this brief introduction that *Law, Liberty, and the Rule of Law* provides a welcome addition to the literature on the rule of law. Readers interested in the topic, no matter how specific their interests are, should find something of interest here. But the editors expect that readers will find value in all the essays not only on its own but also as a whole. In sum, the legitimate concern for the rule of law has increased substantially in the recent years as the number and variety of articles and books on the essence, nature, scope and limitations on this legal-political ideal demonstrate. However, the rule of law remains a multifaceted and deeply – and highly – contested concept. Hence, the book intends to promote: the discussion of its essence or nature, including its core principles and rules, and the necessity if at all of defining – and even redefining – the concept of rule of law; the revision of the proper scope and limitations of adjudication and legislation, which includes the problems not only of limiting legislative and executive power mainly via judicial review but also of restraining an active judicial law-making at a time of guaranteeing an independent judiciary capable of limiting the government but maintaining a balance of power; and, more generally, the deliberation on the relationship between the rule of law with not only human rights and separation of powers but also constitutionalism and democracy. This book provides valuable insights on the rule of law and themes that continue to occupy the attention of legal philosophers, as well of legal scholars, philosophers, political scientists, among others. Finally, we are extremely grateful to all the participants for their enthusiasm that made possible first the workshop and later this volume.

References

Dworkin, R. 1986. *Law's Empire*. Cambridge, MA: Harvard University Press.

Posner, R. 1997. *Law and legal theory in England and America*. Oxford: Oxford University Press.

Chapter 2
The Concept of the Rule of Law

Courtney Taylor Hamara

2.1 Introduction: Pervasive Disagreement in Rule of Law Discourse

It is undeniable that the "Rule of Law".[1] is an important political ideal. In fact, it has been called "*the most* important political ideal today" (Tamanaha 2004; Waldron 2008, 1). The concept is frequently invoked by politicians, the media and scholars in attempts to justify or condemn state actions, political decisions, or whole legal systems. As Jeremy Waldron writes: "Open any newspaper and you will see the "Rule of Law" cited and deployed – usually as a matter of reproach, occasionally as an affirmative aspiration, almost always as a benchmark of political legitimacy" (Waldron 2008, 1). While it might be going too far to say that the "Rule of Law" is *universally* accepted, it has indisputably achieved unprecedented support. As a testament to its current influence, despite supporting diverse ideologies, many heads of state from a variety of countries have expressed a commitment to and acknowledged the desirability of the "Rule of Law" including former American President George W. Bush, Robert Mugabe of Zimbabwe, President Mohammed Khatami of Iran, and Mexican President Vicente Fox Quesada (Tamanaha 2004, 1–2). This widespread support, in turn, has given rise to an unmatched rhetorical power. This term has the power to impress, persuade, convince, satisfy, legitimate and justify.

So what is the "Rule of Law"? What state of affairs does the term connote? What conditions must be present for a claim that the "Rule of Law" exists to be legitimate? In the interest of transparent and unambiguous communication, upon which the success of legal and political decisions often depend, and because of its current

[1] As Waldron (2008, fn 1) does: "I capitalize the term "Rule of Law" to distinguish it from the phrase "a rule of law" which may be used to refer to a particular legal rule such as the rule against perpetuities or the rule in the United States that the President must be at least thirty-five years old."

C.T. Hamara (✉)
McMaster University, Hamilton, ON, Canada
e-mail: hamaract@gmail.com

I.B. Flores and K.E. Himma (eds.), *Law, Liberty, and the Rule of Law*,
Ius Gentium: Comparative Perspectives on Law and Justice 18,
DOI 10.1007/978-94-007-4743-2_2,

prominence in legal and political discourse, it is essential that those involved in the discourse have a similar understanding of what the concept signifies.

Unfortunately, in its recent popularity, the "Rule of Law" has become a catch-phrase. As Richard Bellamy and Joseph Raz have noted, "some accounts of the "Rule of Law" use the term as a catch-all slogan for every desirable policy one might wish to see enacted" (Bellamy 2007, 54). The term is frequently accused of having no determinate meaning. Waldron has called it an "essentially contested concept" (Waldron 2002, 137), and Olufemi Taiwo has commented that "[it] is very difficult to talk about the "Rule of Law". There are almost as many conceptions of the "Rule of Law" as there are people defending it" (Taiwo 1999, 154). According to some, the "Rule of Law" is a metric for evaluating whether or not there is law in a given society (Kramer 2004, 172–222). On other accounts, it is the quality of the law that is evaluated (Finnis 1980, 270). Some scholars suggest that to claim that the "Rule of Law" exists in a given society says nothing of the value of law in that society (Kramer 2004, 172–222). Some think that it *is* a value, albeit not a moral value (Raz 1979, 210–32), while others regard it as among the highest of political ideals (Waldron 2008, 1). In fact, the only thing that seems to consistently garner *agreement* within "Rule of Law" discourse is that there is pervasive *disagreement* within "Rule of Law" discourse.

On a fundamental level, I find this to be a troublesome and undesirable state of affairs: there is no agreement about what the concept "Rule of Law" signifies, yet it is invoked incessantly by politicians, the media and scholars. I do not believe that well-informed, successful discussions and decisions are possible without effective communication, and the current pervasive disagreement about the "Rule of Law" has resulted in a discourse where participants are often talking past one another.

While undesirable, I do not think that this state of affairs is by any means *unavoidable*. The radical disagreement that currently surrounds the "Rule of Law" is evidence of undisciplined conceptual theorizing. In what follows, I sketch some basic methodological points about conceptual analysis, which have been overlooked by many current theorists engaged in "Rule of Law" discourse. In order to move towards a shared understanding of the "Rule of Law", it is necessary to re-evaluate the plethora of disparate theories and reconsider the concept in light of these considerations. The "Rule of Law" has become a powerful rhetorical tool in contemporary society, and we have a responsibility to clarify this concept, or at least narrow the scope of the disagreement, in order to ensure that our most important and salient political discussions and decisions have meaning and merit, not just force.

2.2 Increasing Consensus Through Conceptual Analysis

It is important for participants in any debate, argument or conversation to understand the terms of their conversation in (at least) similar ways for communication to be successful and meaningful. The problem with "Rule of Law" discourse has been that participants have often been using the term in very different ways, thus disabling meaningful communication. Philosophy is particularly amenable to the aim of clarifying, analyzing and reflecting upon concepts, and it is a suitable medium to employ in fulfilling our responsibility of bringing clarity to "Rule of Law" discourse. The "task of philosophy", according to Isaiah Berlin, is to reveal the way human beings think and to "discern the conflicts between [their use of words, images and other symbols] that prevent the construction of more adequate ways of organising and describing and explaining experience" (Berlin 1999, 10). The goal of conceptual analysis in particular is "improved understanding", according to Michael Giudice, who provides an outline of the first step towards clarifying concepts (Giudice 2005, 15–6):

> First [...] philosophical analysis of existing concepts or participant understanding aims at revealing confusion and disagreement, with the goal of clearing a way for the construction of more adequate theories or models with which to understand ourselves. Even if new or better concepts are not easy to find or develop, recognition of the limits or pitfalls of existing concepts is progress.

Though the concept in question may not be *easily* clarified, as Giudice points out, recognizing the existence of confusion or vagueness about its meaning is the first step to eliminating that confusion, and moving towards a situation where the concept can be meaningfully employed. Similarly, for Quentin Skinner and Joel Feinberg, "The goal of conceptual analysis [...] is thus to arrive, by way of reflecting on 'what we normally mean when we employ certain words', at a more finished delineation of what we had better mean if we are to communicate effectively, avoid paradox and achieve general coherence" (Skinner 1984, 199 fn 21; *cf.* Feinberg 1973). With the foregoing in mind, I would like to make some simple (and hopefully uncontroversial) recommendations for engaging in the conceptual analysis of the "Rule of Law". While each suggestion may seem almost trivial, there are a number of theorists who have not taken one or more of these points into consideration when theorizing about the "Rule of Law".

In order to begin to clarify the concept of the "Rule of Law", it is necessary to consider "what we normally mean" when we use that phrase. This requirement implicates an investigation of the current usage of the concept, and, since continuity exists with respect to the use of the term over time, an investigation of the historical usage of the term.

It is important to consider how a term is currently being used if, as Wittgenstein argued, the meaning of a word is its use in ordinary language. In other words, a word without a use has no meaning. Admittedly, as Stavropoulos points out, "actual usage is not, as it stands, *sufficient* for correct explication of meaning, as it is usually too unruly or haphazard, and may rest on incomplete understanding or be affected by general epistemic impediments" (Stavropoulos 2001, 81 – emphasis added). Language users have not come to a state of reflective equilibrium with respect to all of the concepts in their repertoire. If this was the case, conceptual analysis would be largely unnecessary. Investigating the current usage of a term is necessary to uncover confusion and disagreement, the first step towards improving clarity. Further, it is desirable for the concept in its analyzed form to maintain some kind of familiarity for average language users, since the overall goal of the analysis is to illuminate the "contents" of the concept and thereby improve communication and understanding. Stavropoulos continues (*Id.*):

> Actual usage sets limits [to the analysis of concepts]: the principle cannot fail to fit actual usage, except to the extent that it orders and ensures consistency of such usage. The principle

cannot introduce distinctions never made in the course of or entailed by actual usage, nor can it collapse distinctions actually made or entailed. Ambitious analysis therefore must track actual understanding.

Beginning with ordinary language use provides a good foundation for achieving the goal of conceptual analysis.[2]

2.3 The Rule of Law: Current and Historical Usage of the Concept

Though content of the concept seems elusive, if we consider the statements of politicians, journalists, people writing editorials and bloggers, it is possible to get a sense of the spirit in which the "Rule of Law" is currently used. In my introductory remarks, I observed that the "Rule of Law" is considered a political ideal and a desirable state of affairs. It is globally recognized that it sets a desirable standard for governments: there are attempts to implement it in developing countries through initiatives like the World Justice Project (http://worldjusticeproject.org/). It seems for the most part that it is understood as evaluating legal systems in a morally significant way. Regimes are criticized for violating the "Rule of Law" and praised for striving to achieve it. Decisions made and actions taken in accordance with the "Rule of Law" are seen as legitimate. In Waldron's research on the current state of "Rule of Law" discourse, he points to articles from *The New York Times*, *The Times* (London), *The Financial*

[2] I think that this is the appropriate place to begin despite some concerns that the reader may have at this point. First of all, a term may have different meanings in different contexts: "star" could mean a gravitational field of gases burning billions of miles away from the Earth; it could mean the shape, with four, five or more points; it could be understood as a pin-prick of light in the night sky; or perhaps one might think of an entertainer (musician or actor) as a star. Because a term might have a variety of current usages does not mean that this is not the correct place to begin collecting raw data. It simply means that the data will have to be sorted – and while this might be a harrowing task, its difficulty does not indicate that the wrong raw material has been considered.

There is also the possibility that individuals are not descriptive in their use of terms, but rather revisionary – it is meant to be used for some purpose. Therefore, the material collected may consist of data that is reported based on what individuals take to be the case from experience, but it may also consist of data that is constructed to serve a particular end. On this point, first of all, I think that instances of constructed concepts are likely to be much less prevalent that otherwise; average people are unlikely to be constructing their concepts to serve a particular purpose, especially if they see this understanding as at odds with the accepted understanding. It is more likely the case that it is scholars who revise concepts in this way – and, again, this is data that can be broken down and analyzed to determine whether or not it ought to be retained for the final analysis. If the conception on offer is so revisionary that it is miles away from ordinary usage, it may be discarded in the final analysis.

Finally the fact that many concepts are persuasive or evaluative does not cause any problems at this point. I think that it is important initially to collect a broad cross section of data to evaluate. The fact that some people might use the "*Rule of Law*" in a morally loaded way, such as the way we use *justice*, and that others might not use it in that way, but in a more descriptive way, such as the way we use *chair,* does not concern me at this point. These are problems to be addressed after the collection of such data.

Times and American case law to demonstrate that the "Rule of Law" is a benchmark of legitimacy (Waldron 2008, 1). This is evident even if you consider briefly some of the many things that have been said with respect to the United States' war on terror and treatment of detainees at Guantanamo Bay alone: "The "Rule of Law" has yet to be reinstated in the U.S. battle on terror. The problem started when the (Bush) administration rejected the Geneva conventions, which are intended to apply to every armed conflict in the world" (Barbara Olshansky quoted in "US builds…" 2006). Consider a second example (Michael Ratner quoted in "A mixed…" 2004):

> The Supreme Court has not closed the doors of justice to the detainees imprisoned at Guantanamo Bay. This is a major victory of the "Rule of Law" and affirms the right of every person, citizen or non-citizen, detained by the United States to test the legality of his or her detention in a U.S. Court

And a third (Ann Beeson quoted in "ACLU…" 2006):

> In the name of national security, the Bush administration has eroded the "Rule of Law" and the system of checks and balances in the United States, both fundamental principles in any democracy. In our America, we will not tolerate illegal spying or torture. The ACLU calls on the Human Rights committee to join us in our effort to hold the U.S. government accountable.

The message is clear: the "Rule of Law" is important, and its violation ought not to be tolerated. Overall, we seem to think that the "Rule of Law" is a good thing to have, and an ideal to aspire to.[3]

The current use of the "Rule of Law" just outlined, together with the importance of beginning conceptual analysis with current usage, calls into question the success of certain attempts to theorize it. While current usage is not the only criterion that Waldron thinks is necessary for both law and the "Rule of Law", his assertion that the "Rule of Law" is a political ideal is very much in line with it. This fact is unsurprising as Waldron makes explicit appeals to current understandings of the "Rule of Law" to provide a foundation for his theory. Matthew Kramer, on the other hand, offers a theory that seems to completely ignore current understandings of the "Rule of Law". He asserts that what he means by the "Rule of Law" is no more and no less than Lon Fuller's eight criteria of legality (Fuller 1969, 39), which can be used equally in the service of evil and the service of good. What is more, he argues that the "Rule of Law" has no necessary connection to morality insofar as the "freedom" it provides, might not actually obtain (Kramer 2004, 172–222).

John Finnis and Joseph Raz both offer nuanced theories of the "Rule of Law", and while it at first appears that Finnis's understanding is in line with current usage and that Raz's is not, upon further inspection it is possible to argue the opposite as well. While Finnis suggests that the "Rule of Law" is the name given to the state of affairs

[3] At this point, I am beginning to demonstrate that the "Rule of Law" is viewed as something of value by contemporary societies. However, does value entail *moral* value? I think in this case it does. First, acknowledgement of its desirability seems to be widespread, and people seem to think that without it, justice cannot be served (and justice is typically understood as a morally evaluative term). The "Rule of Law" has the potential to seriously affect the fundamental interests that people have, and in that sense it is morally relevant to their lives. Thank you to Professor W. Waluchow for bringing this point to my attention.

where the law is functioning as it ought to, namely in the service of the common good (Finnis 1980, 270), he also backtracks at one point and admits that the "Rule of Law" may be used in the service of self-interested and even evil aims (*Ibid.*, 273–4). However, his attempt to incorporate moral value into his theory of the "Rule of Law" demonstrates that he has taken into account a perspective at least akin to the current perspective, even if his theory seems to have problems with overall coherence. Conversely, at first it is difficult to read Raz as asserting anything but the neutrality of the "Rule of Law". Like Kramer, he seems committed to a view of the "Rule of Law" as a neutral tool. His example of the sharp knife has become infamous in arguments supporting such a conception. "Of course," he writes (Raz 1979, 225–6):

> [C]onformity to the rule of law also enables the law to serve bad purposes [as well as good ones]. That does not show that it is not a virtue, just as the fact that a sharp knife can be used to harm does not show that being sharp is not a good-making characteristic for knives. At most it shows that from the point of view of the present consideration it is not a moral good. Being sharp is an inherent good-making characteristic of knives. A good knife is, among other things, a sharp knife.

In other words, it is necessary that a knife is, to some extent, sharp in order to perform its primary function of cutting. However a sharp knife would be both an excellent knife for carving a turkey as well as an excellent choice for quickly bringing about the death of the neighbour's cat. According to Raz's analogy, the "Rule of Law" is a tool, morally neutral in and of itself, and can be used for both very good and extremely heinous ends. However, Raz does maintain that the "Rule of Law" is a value, albeit not a moral value, and in this way I think he tries to make room for understandings which link the "Rule of Law" to some desirable state of affairs.

It is important to consider not only current, but also the historical usage of a term as part of the initial stages of conceptual analysis. While it is true that concepts develop over time, it is also undeniable that if there is continuity of *use* over time, there is likely to be some kind of continuity with respect to how a term is used and understood. In the case of the "Rule of Law" there is a long and rich history to consider: the term has existed at least since antiquity when Aristotle debated the desirability of "the "Rule of Law" and not of men" in the *Politics* more than 2,000 years ago (2000, Book III). There are a variety of related themes that can be extracted from the discussions of the "Rule of Law" over the centuries, but most of them center on the idea that the "Rule of Law" is in some way the antithesis of the arbitrary use of power. Two streams of thought dominate the history of "Rule of Law" discourse: (i) the "Rule of Law", not of Man and (ii) the "Rule of Law" as formal legality.

In *Politics*, Aristotle, like Plato before him in *Laws* and *Statesman*, was concerned with outlining the way society ought to be set up and function in order to maximize people's ability to live well and achieve the good. This idea is also echoed later in the work of Cicero and St. Thomas Aquinas. Endorsing the "Rule of Law" is a crucial part of the social and political recommendations made by these philosophers, and, in particular, is meant to safeguard against the dangers of tyranny.

The "Rule of Law" is seen as desirable in this case since it is characterized as objective and in accordance with reason, and as such is contrary to the "Rule of Man", which is characterized as arbitrary and "subject to the unpredictable vagaries of [individual rulers]" (Tamanaha 2004, 122). To live under the "Rule of Law" "is to be shielded from the familiar human weakness of bias, passion, prejudice, error, ignorance, cupidity, or whim" which are associated with the "Rule of Man" (*Id.*). A sovereign or ruler who rules in accordance with the "Rule of Law" appeals to factors external to himself – existing rules, principles and reason – when creating legal norms and adjudicating disputes. A sovereign or ruler who typifies the "Rule of Man" does not appeal to factors external to himself, but only to internal factors such as his own needs, desires or predilections. Thus, it is evident how the rule of man might devolve into tyranny.[4]

---

[4] At this point it may be necessary to address one of the most important criticisms of this way of understanding the "Rule of Law". Aristotle, Aquinas, and Hobbes, among others, suggest that it is logically impossible for a sovereign to be limited by law, since the law depends on the authority of the sovereign and "for the plain reason that the law may be altered at the lawmaker's will" (Tamanaha 2004, 48). Further, laws do not exist, nor can they be applied without human interpretation and participation. Jean Hampton articulates this idea (Hampton 1994, 16):

> A rule is inherently powerless; it only takes on life if it is interpreted, applied, and enforced by individuals. That set of human beings that has final say over what the rules are, how they should be applied, and how they should be enforced has ultimate control over what these rules actually *are. So human beings control the rules*, and not vice versa.

So it seems that we can never escape the problems that derive from human involvement in law, which are intended to be circumvented by adhering to the "Rule of Law". According to Tamanaha, "the inevitability of such participation provides the opportunity for the reintroduction of the very weakness sought to be avoided by resorting to law in the first place" (Tamanaha 2004, 123). In other words, since we cannot escape the human element in law, it does not make sense to suggest that this way of understanding the "Rule of Law" is viable.

Aristotle was one of the first to identify this problem. He defined the sovereign as someone who was not himself subject to any other, and therefore thought that it was logically impossible for the sovereign to be limited by positive law. Aquinas took up this problem and while he agreed with Aristotle that it was logically impossible for the sovereign to be limited by positive law because the positive law was derived, in part, from the sovereign, he argued that the sovereign *could and should subject himself* to the law (Aquinas 1947, q. 96, art. 5). According to Aquinas, because there is no other human being suitable to pass judgment on the sovereign, he is therefore exempt from the law's coercive power. However, one reason for the sovereign to observe the dictates of law in Aquinas's time is that there is one who is competent to judge everyone including the sovereign: God. In contemporary society, the separation of powers also constitutes a limit on the exercise of power. However these are practical and not normative constraints on the sovereign.

The fact that human participation is unavoidable in law does not inevitably reduce the "Rule of Law" to the "Rule of Man", or mean that the "Rule of Law" is *prima facie* impossible. While sanctions add an extra element of assurance, it is not the case that they must necessarily exist in order for people to be persuaded to follow rules or principles. In *A Common Law Theory of Judicial Review: The Living Tree*, Wil Waluchow demonstrates that it is conceptually possible to talk about normative restrictions on a sovereign, even in the case where the executive, legislative and judicial responsibilities are assumed by one person. He points out that there is an important distinction to be made between *de facto* and *normative* freedom. It is true that a solitary ruler has *de facto* freedom to create and change rules and adjudicate according to her will. But having the *de facto* freedom to do so does not entail having *normative* freedom. If there are rules that pertain to her and limit her power, she does not have the *normative* freedom to break them if we can take a cue from Waluchow and H.L.A. Hart and accept the working definition that rules are "prescribed guides for conduct or action. They set general normative standards for correct behaviour or conduct" (Waluchow 2007, 32). So, while there may be limited ways of ensuring the existence of the "Rule of Law" by coercion or force, it is nonetheless possible despite the fact that human participation is inevitable.

One of the most significant aspects of this understanding of the "Rule of Law" is that the content or substance of the laws which promote the "Rule of Law" is restricted. Laws cannot have just any content and still contribute to the "Rule of Law" as is evident from the emphasis that philosophers from this tradition place on achieving the common good. The restraints they place on what can be law "properly so-called" are important because they identify which laws can contribute to the "Rule of Law". It might be useful to think of the "Rule of Law" (as opposed to the "Rule of Man") as an end, rather than a means. It is an end that can only be reached by adhering to certain content restrictions, among other things. Because of the nature of these content restrictions – the necessity of having an eye to the common good, being in accordance with right reason and moral principles – it is acceptable to say that in this sense, the "Rule of Law" is a moral ideal. It denotes a morally good state of affairs, rather than a morally neutral one.

The "Rule of Law" as rule by law or formal legality does not place content restrictions on rules and has therefore been called morally neutral; yet it is another way of understanding the "Rule of Law" as the antithesis of the exercise of arbitrary power. Both Waldron and Brian Tamanaha identify this sense of the "Rule of Law" as "favoured by legal theorists" and it is the conception held by the majority of post-Enlightenment legal theorists working on the subject.

This sense of the "Rule of Law" emphasizes the characteristics and the benefits of rules, where a law counts as a type of rule and the aim of rules is generally thought to be the guidance of human conduct. Recalling Lon Fuller's eight criteria of legality is useful here, as they provide criteria required of *all* rules with the capacity to guide. For instance, they must be public, prospective, understandable, and relatively stable (Fuller 1969, 39). There must be congruence between the rules as they are expressed and their application. This means, not only that individuals will be able to foresee what is expected of them, but also that the sovereign or government must operate in accordance with the rules that they set. Defined by these criteria, rules are able to provide predictability and certainty for individuals about what is expected of them and the consequences that will follow if they do not meet the requirements.

The "Rule of Law" in this second sense means the rule or governance of a community through the use of laws (rules), rather than by arbitrary or particular commands, which cannot provide standing guidance to individuals. This understanding of the "Rule of Law" has been articulated most clearly by F.A. Hayek, who writes (1944, 72):

> Stripped of all technicalities, [the "Rule of Law"] means that government in all its actions is bound by rules fixed and announced beforehand – rules which make it possible to foresee with fair certainty how the authority will use its coercive powers in given circumstances and to plan one's individual affairs on the basis of this knowledge.

Formal legality is desirable because when people have rules to structure their lives, their interactions with others and with the government, they are able to make plans, both short and long-term, around the existing rules. The ability to make plans is thought to be valuable because it allows individuals to exercise their autonomy, and by doing so contributes to their dignity as individual persons and potentially to their well-being.

In this way many theorists have argued that freedom does not exist without law. Without law, each is subject to the unpredictable impulses of others and the arbitrary whims of lawmakers and adjudicators. Hayek saw no freedom in such a way of life, nor did Montesquieu, who argued that "liberty is a right of doing whatever the laws permit" (1748, Book XI, s. 3). John Locke, one of the foundational figures of liberal theory, also understood freedom as requiring law. He writes (1689, Chapter 2, s. 23):

> Freedom of men under government is, to have a standing rule to live by, common to everyone in society, and made by the legislative power erected in it; a liberty to follow my own will in all things, where the rule prescribes not; and not to be subject to the inconstant, uncertain, unknown, arbitrary will of another man.

His articulation of what freedom requires is very much in line with the "Rule of Law" as formal legality.

One of the most frequently debated topics in "Rule of Law" discourse is whether or not the "Rule of Law", understood as formal legality, has any necessary connection to moral goodness. Above, I outlined the reasons that this sense of the "Rule of Law" is seen as desirable: the certainty and predictability associated with it provide for expressions of autonomy, and are related to dignity and well-being. It is even compatible with value and moral pluralism, which enables individuals to strive to achieve what each considers to be the good.

The same characteristics, namely the absence of content requirements, which enable formal legality to be compatible with pluralism, also enable it to be compatible with the aims of evil and iniquitous regimes. Because it makes no substantive demands on the content of legal rules, this understanding of the "Rule of Law" is "open to a range of ends" (Tamanaha 2004, 94). The fact that the "Rule of Law" as formal legality is open to being used in the service of a variety of ends, its moral worth has been seriously questioned. There are those, such as Joseph Raz, who argue that it is a virtue insofar as it entails an appreciation of the individual as an autonomous, rational being, who is capable of following rules, and that its necessary, though not sufficient, connection with good law makes it morally significant. On the other side of the argument one can maintain that formal legality is just as useful for the aims of an iniquitous regime as it is for the aims of a just one. There may be no interesting connection between the "Rule of Law" and morality if it is both a necessary condition for the effectiveness of good and bad laws alike.

Tamanaha offers yet another point of view on the moral neutrality of formal legality. He maintains that it is contrary to the long tradition of the "Rule of Law" (not of Man) which finds its motivation in the attempt to restrain the sovereign from tyrannical rule. According to Tamanaha, "such restraint went beyond the idea that the government must enact and abide by laws that take on the proper form of rules, to include the understanding that there were certain things the government or sovereign could not do" (*Ibid.*, 96). He recalls that the limits imposed by law historically had moral substance derived from shared customs and principles, Christian morality, right reason, and the good of the community. "Formal legality," he argues, "discards this orientation": the government can do anything that it desires as long as it enacts a legal rule first, in this way maintaining the "Rule of Law". Further, if the government decides to do something that is not currently legally permitted, it may change the law to allow for the desired action, as long as it meets the criteria that enable rules to guide the conduct of individuals.

Contemporary scholars have, in large part, been selective in their investigation into the history of the "Rule of Law" by focusing on accounts provided by one or two historical scholars to the exclusion of the others, or have overlooked the historical component completely. Though Kramer's work is compatible with an understanding of the "Rule of Law" as formal legality, the farthest back he goes when explaining what the concept means is a discussion of Lon Fuller's eight criteria of legality. His account does not provide evidence that the greater history was taken into account. Finnis's theory of the "Rule of Law" is not only commensurable with the "Rule of Law", not of Man conception, some of the theoretical work is so similar that it is evident that he has drawn upon the work of the ancient scholars and Aquinas in developing his theory of law and the "Rule of Law". His discussion of the common good and the "Rule of Law" as the appropriate end of law fits nicely in line with this historical trend. There is a small point of contention in Finnis' theory, surrounding whether or not he considers the "Rule of Law" to be an end or a means when he concedes that it might be used for illegitimate aims. While it is a confusing point in his theory, it is evidence that he also considered the formal legality trend in the "Rule of Law"'s history. Waldron's theory is rather problematic in terms of its ability to account for historical understandings of the "Rule of Law". While it is certainly not a theory of formal legality – Waldron is very interested in content and procedural restrictions on law – it is not a theory that is compatible with the "Rule of Law", not of Man trend either. The requirements Waldron outlines for law and the "Rule of Law" are very context dependent on modern Western liberal democracies. While he does suggest that norms ought to be oriented towards the public good, he also attempts to include in his conception more modern institutions of government such as courts and legislatures as we currently understand them – institutions that did not exist in the same way in ancient Greece or medieval Europe. In this way his account is both commensurable with and at odds with the "Rule of Law", not of Man. Still, there are others who seem to have taken account of even less. For example, Richard Bellamy argues that "in many respects, the "Rule of Law" is simply rule by democracy" (Bellamy 2007, 53). Such a claim seems to ignore important facts of the history of the "Rule of Law": the "Rule of Law" and democracy are two distinct concepts with distinct histories and we *use them* as distinct concepts, and many contemporary and historical societies which were not democratic made claims to and discussed the value of the "Rule of Law".

2.4 External and Internal Conceptual Coherence

Gathering raw material is not the end of conceptual analysis: it is only the beginning. Overall, the goal is to achieve something like reflective equilibrium with respect to a particular concept, in this case, with respect to the "Rule of Law". The raw materials – theory, history, and the understanding of individuals, among other things – do not always point to the same conclusion about what features make up the core of a particular concept. In fact, agreement between all of these sources is highly improbable. So it is unsurprising that in the case of the "Rule of Law" the raw materials do not point to one unified conclusion. It is important to appreciate, however, that because the analysis may be difficult due to the variety of material under consideration it does not mean that the wrong material is being considered.

As mentioned, not all of the raw material will point toward the same conclusion; fortunately, some of it can be discounted. The information gathered needs to be sorted and evaluated before it can be put together in a way that has the potential to illuminate the concept in question. There are at least two ways to evaluate raw material in the initial phase when it is being collected: discarding unconsidered opinions and making note of widespread ones. It is *prima facie* important to consider opinions which are widespread because it is important that the theorized concept be in line with participant usage as much as possible. It is also necessary to eliminate unconsidered opinions. An opinion may be unconsidered for a variety of reasons: for example, it may be based on little or no knowledge or it may be obviously incoherent. Giudice nicely summarizes the idea that while usage must be the beginning of conceptual analysis, there remains work for philosophers to do after the collection of material. He writes (2005, 11–2):

> In the explanation of concepts of social phenomena such as law, ordinary or participant understanding serves initially but only roughly to define the category or subject matter… Initial views […] give philosophers a point of departure but also a responsibility… Philosophers must also ask whether there are questions which participants have not thought about or perhaps are puzzled about…

By considering things that individuals (participants) have not, such as whether their conception is based on partial or false information, or if it is particularly uncommon or atypical, it is possible to eliminate some opinions from those that will ultimately contribute to the theorized concept.

Once the raw material has been initially sorted, it is logical to move onto the more rigorous analyses which make up the next phase of conceptual analysis. The concept in question ought to cohere with other related (external) concepts, and they may perhaps illuminate one another. It is also important to make sure the concept coheres internally: that some features believed to be necessary do not conflict with other necessary features of the concept. External conceptual coherence (or inter-conceptual coherence) is a desirable end of conceptual analysis where related concepts benefit from the illumination resulting from their comparison and contrast. To fully grasp a concept it is necessary to engage in an investigation of how it relates to and differs from others. According to Giudice, who is also taking account of social phenomena (*Ibid.*, 15):

> Philosophically-constructed theories may supply a better understanding of a social phenomenon by exploring its relations with other related phenomena… it is important not to collapse these important social phenomena into each other, but also that there are revealing distinctions and connections between these phenomena which contribute to a broad understanding of social life.

Thus, as Giudice points out, there are benefits to a coherent web of related concepts, and conversely, there are important drawbacks that occur when there is overlap or the collapse of two or more concepts. Giudice admits that "concepts which prove difficult to grasp on first thought are so often because the phenomenon they seek to explain or determine shares similarities and connections with other closely related phenomena" (*Ibid.*, 12). Indeed, the "Rule of Law" appears to share similarities and connections with many other social and political ideas, particularly law. Unfortunately, the intimate connection between the "Rule of Law" and law has created considerable confusion within "Rule of Law" discourse, and there has been an overwhelming tendency to significantly overlap and even collapse the two concepts. I suspect the reason for the collapse goes something like this: In order to determine what the "Rule of Law" is it is necessary to first investigate "law" since "law" is part of "Rule of Law", grammatically speaking. Once the concept of law has been developed, the "Rule of Law" may be derived, at least in part, from it. In other words the thought is that it is impossible to determine what the "Rule of Law" is without first grasping law *simpliciter*, since law appears to be one of the component parts of the "Rule of Law".

I think the enthusiasm with which the debates about the concept of law have proceeded over the last 50 years has contributed to the tendency to consider the "Rule of Law" as derivable from law, rather than considering the "Rule of Law" in its own right. There has been much investigation into the concept of law, and the concept of the "Rule of Law" seems like a natural place to attempt to apply some of the insights about law generally. Recall that many contemporary scholars are primarily concerned with the concept of law, and only derivatively concerned with the "Rule of Law". To reduce one concept to another is certainly not clarificatory in a way that enables communication and understanding; law and the "Rule of Law", like democracy and liberalism, are distinct ideas, and it does no service to the discourse to collapse them.

Waldron claims that there is "a natural correlation" between positivism and formalist conceptions of the "Rule of Law" and between richer concepts of law and the "Rule of Law" (Waldron 2008, 64):

> Conceivably the correlation could be shaken loose by an insistence that the concept of law and the "Rule of Law" are to be understood quite independently of one another.... Or we could imagine some positivist sticking dogmatically to [a positivistic concept of law], but acknowledging the importance of a separate Rule-of-Law ideal that emphasized procedural and argumentative values. But those combinations seem odd: they treat the "Rule of Law" as a rather mysterious ideal – with its own underlying values, to be sure, but quite unrelated to our understanding of law itself. It is simply one of a number of ideals (like justice or liberty or equality) that we apply to law, rather than anything more intimately connected with the very idea of law itself.

I think that Waldron is creating a false dilemma. The "Rule of Law" is an independent concept from, but not unrelated to, law. They ought to be *compatible*: neither identical nor unrelated. For my part, I do think that one can remain a legal positivist while acknowledging a more morally robust concept of the "Rule of Law". He ultimately concludes that law and the "Rule of Law" lie on the same spectrum: the same criteria are required for both, though the "Rule of Law" achieves the criteria to a higher degree. "Those who are familiar with the "Rule of Law"," he explains, "will have noted that what I have called the defining characteristics of law are also the most prominent requirements of that ideal" (*Ibid.*, 47). More explicitly, he states, "I believe that one can understand these two sets of criteria – for the existence of law and for the "Rule of Law" – as two views of the same basic idea" (*Ibid.*, 48). This is problematic. He does not introduce a *principled* distinction between the two concepts, and as a result, the "Rule of Law" and law are difficult to identify as distinct on his model. Is he guilty of *completely* collapsing law and the "Rule of Law"? Perhaps not due to his insistence that they lie at different points on the spectrum; but he has certainly overlapped the two terms to a significant degree, which makes it difficult to compare and contrast them. What is troubling is that Waldron seems to accept this overlap/collapse, and he is by no means the only scholar guilty of this kind of redundancy.

Kramer also admits to using his theory of law to inform his account of the "Rule of Law". While this is an acceptable place to begin, he goes too far and suggests: "[Many] of my analyses in support of legal positivism have aimed to show that the "Rule of Law" is not an inherently moral ideal" (Kramer 2004, 173). Unfortunately, he does not explain what the connection is between legal positivism and the "Rule of Law", and why analyses of positivism should shed any light on the moral composition of the "Rule of Law". Why must the neutrality of a theory of law extend to one's conception of the "Rule of Law"? What is more, the sum of the criteria which he calls the "Rule of Law" are synonymous with Fuller's eight criteria for legality: without which Fuller claimed *law* (not the "Rule of Law") could not exist. It is unclear why Kramer gives no account of his choice to make use of the Fullerian criteria of legality as the conditions for the "Rule of Law". If the "Rule of Law" is simply Fuller's eight criteria of legality for Kramer, then his conception of the "Rule of Law" seems to reduce to law *simpliciter*,[5] as Fuller's arguments in favour of these criteria aimed to demonstrate that the law cannot exist without them. By stipulating that Fullerian criteria of legality are synonymous with the "Rule of Law", Kramer effectively collapses the two concepts.

Finnis does the clearest job of maintaining two separate concepts. First of all, while he has a strict definition of what counts as law "properly so called," he admits that positive law *can* be created without considering the common good. However, such laws would not contribute to the "Rule of Law". The *telos* of laws which are created with an eye to the common good is the "Rule of Law"; it obtains when laws are being made and adjudicated as they ought to be. By inferentially identifying law as

[5] Kramer thinks that the "Rule of Law" criteria, though not moral in nature, are ones in terms of which legal systems can be evaluated, more or less instrumentally. He thinks that whether we have law and whether and to what extent the system which qualifies as law fulfils the "Rule of Law" criteria are two separate though related questions. However, I am unclear as to how these are separate questions if the criteria for law are the same criteria for the "Rule of Law". Perhaps, like Waldron, he intends for them to exist on a spectrum: law must fulfil a minimum of the criteria, while the "Rule of Law" strives to achieve the criteria more substantially. Still, I would like to see a principled distinction made between the two concepts. If the criteria are the same, what is to prevent us from saying the "Rule of Law" exists whenever law exists and vice versa?

a means, and the "Rule of Law" as an end, it is possible to see the distinction between the two concepts quite clearly.[6]

Internal conceptual coherence (or intra-conceptual coherence) focuses on one opinion, theory or conception of a particular concept and aims at a harmonious relationship among its constituent parts. In other words, theorists and philosophers desire to achieve a logical, orderly and consistent relation of parts whereby the whole concept or theory is intelligible. Testing for internal conceptual coherence is primarily reserved for more complex theories or models since simple opinions which lead to absurdity or are obviously incoherent are usually discarded at the first level of analysis as unconsidered opinions. Questioning the internal coherence of a theorized concept or model is what many scholars do when they are trying to refute another's position. It can take the form of questioning the truth of assumptions and premises, or demonstrating that the premises and assumptions lead to a conclusion not intended by the original scholar. For example, one might try to demonstrate that the premises lead to an absurdity, a contradiction, to a result the original scholar was not aiming to prove, or even to the antithesis of what he or she was trying to prove. Essentially when we test for internal conceptual coherence, we are looking for any defect that will be detrimental to a theory to the point that it must ultimately be discarded, or at least reconstituted. For example, a conception of the "Rule of Law" which suggests that it is a state of affairs where there are no lawmakers at all – perhaps to avoid the inevitability of subjective participation in and manipulation of law – is internally problematic. Because the existence of law depends upon the existence of some lawmaker, divine, human or otherwise, if there are no lawmakers then there can be no law.

An example of a contemporary theory where internal coherence is uncertain is that of Finnis.[7] Finnis's theory, while it takes into account a good deal of raw material, is possibly internally flawed because he seems to associate the "Rule of Law" both with means and ends. It is an end for Finnis insofar as it is the state of affairs which obtains when the law is functioning as it ought to – via general rules with the aim of supporting the common good of a community. However, if the "Rule of Law" is an end, then it cannot also be a means; it cannot be *used* to perpetuate iniquity. Again the reason this seems to be the case is Finnis's admission that it is conceptually possible, though he maintains that it is unlikely, that the "Rule of Law" can obtain in an iniquitous regime. If it can do that, it appears to be a means to an end rather than

---

[6] Before discussing internal conceptual coherence, there is an objection that I must consider: What if the "Rule of Law" and law actually do denote the same concept? I do not think this is much of a possibility considering the foregoing investigation. However, if it is the case, I think the burden of proof rests with those scholars who believe it. For such a position to be probable it must be argued for and the two concepts must not be collapsed without explanation. Thank you to Colin Macleod for bringing this possibility to my attention.

[7] Testing for internal coherence can be a long and meticulous process: scholars spend years trying to disprove the theories of their opponents! Here I will only be able to make some cursory comments on the flaws apparent in Finnis's theory.

an end itself. However, if Finnis means to suggest that having an eye to the common good will not always yield morally good state of affairs, then there is the possibility that the regime may not be morally good, while still having the "Rule of Law".

2.5 Conclusion

This essay was initially motivated by my desire to discover the meaning of the "Rule of Law". As a student of legal philosophy I felt compelled to investigate the meaning of this concept, particularly since it appeared, often without much explanation, in much of the theoretical literature that I had the benefit of studying. I also felt the need to understand the "Rule of Law" since its presence in contemporary law and politics continues to be pervasive. For me, these two motivations are undeniably related; I believe that gaining an understanding of the "Rule of Law" is critical: the theoretical discussions of it can and do play an important role in contemporary discourse. A concept such as this deserves careful consideration and it is important that we – scholars, politicians, and citizens – consider it carefully in order to facilitate meaningful discussions about it, the conditions that determine its existence, whether or not it is intrinsically valuable, and if it is a justifiable goal for societies.

So, what *is* the "Rule of Law"? One of the conclusions I have come to is that there is anything but an easy answer to this question.[8] Contemporary theorists provide no uniform answer; in fact, contemporary theoretical opinions on the "Rule of Law", though all provide valuable insights, are quite varied and thus are a confusing and difficult place to begin one's search. Contemporary scholars assert a variety of propositions about the "Rule of Law", many which are impossible to reconcile with one another. Though the indeterminacy that pervades "Rule of Law" discourse is undesirable because it inhibits meaningful communication between parties, it is not unavoidable. In order to sort through the chaos that is contemporary "Rule of Law" discourse, I have provided some standards and methods by which opinions and theories about the "Rule of Law" can be evaluated, and I hope that on this basis it is possible to begin refining and re-evaluating conceptions of the "Rule of Law". My suggestions will not bring about consensus, but they should nevertheless enable us to begin to engage one another on similar terms, and therefore in meaningful and fruitful discussions.

References

Aquinas, T. 1947. *Summa Theologica.* Available at: http://www.sacred-texts.com/chr/aquinas/summa/sum227.htm.

Aristotle. 2000. *Politics.* Trans. B. Jowett. Mineola: Dover Publications, Inc.

[8] My own conclusions about the content of the concept are beyond the modest scope of this article.

Beeson, A. 2006. ACLU calls on U.N. Human Rights Committee to hold U.S. Government accountable. *American Civil Liberties Union*, 13 March 2006. Available at: http://www.aclu.org/intlhumanrights/gen/24500 prs20060313 .html.
Bellamy, R. 2007. *Political constitutionalism: A republican defence of the constitutionality of democracy*. Cambridge: Cambridge University Press.
Berlin, I. 1999. The purpose of philosophy. In *Concepts and categories: Philosophical essays*, ed. H. Hardy. London: Pimlico.
Feinberg, J. 1973. *Social philosophy*. Englewood Cliffs: Prentice-Hall, Inc.
Finnis, J. 1980. *Natural law and natural rights*. Oxford: Clarendon.
Fuller, L.L. 1969. *The morality of law*, 2nd ed. New Haven: Yale University Press.
Giudice, M. 2005. The significance of contingent relations in the philosophy of law. PhD dissertation, Hamilton: McMaster University.
Hampton, J. 1994. Democracy and the rule of law. In *The rule of law: Nomos 36*, ed. I. Shapiro. New York: New York University Press.
Hayek, F.A. 1944. *The road to serfdom*. Chicago: University of Chicago Press.
Kramer, M.H. 2004. *Where law and morality meet*. New York: Oxford University Press.
Locke, J. 1689. *Second treatise of government*. Indianapolis: Hackett.
Montesquieu, Ch. 1748. *Spirit of laws*. London: Bell and Sons.
Olshansky, B. 2006. US builds new Guantanamo prison. *Breaking News*, 12 January 2006. Available at: http://www.breakingnews.ie/archives/2006/0112/world/cwmhsnkfgboj/.
Ratner, M. 2004. A mixed verdict on the terror war: Detainees have right to US courts, justices rule. *CNN.com*, 29 June 2004.
Raz, J. 1979. *The authority of law*. Oxford: Clarendon.
Skinner, Q. 1984. The idea of negative liberty: Philosophical and historical perspectives. In *Philosophy in history: Essays on the historiography of philosophy*, ed. R. Rorty et al. New York: Cambridge University Press.
Stavropoulos, N. 2001. Hart's semantics. In *Hart's postscript: Essays on the postscript to* The concept of law, ed. J. Coleman. Oxford: Oxford University Press.
Taiwo, O. 1999. The rule of law: The new leviathan? *Canadian Journal of Law and Jurisprudence* 12: 151–168.
Tamanaha, B.Z. 2004. *On the rule of law: History, politics, theory*. Cambridge: Cambridge University Press.
Waldron, J. 2002. Is the rule of law an essentially contested concept (in Florida)? *Law and Philosophy* 21: 137–164.
Waldron, J. 2008. The concept and the rule of law. *Georgia Law Review* 43: 1.
Waluchow, W.J. 2007. *A common law theory of judicial review: The living tree*. Cambridge: Cambridge University Press.

Chapter 3
Plato and the Rule of Law

Brian Burge-Hendrix

3.1 Introduction

My primary aim in this essay is to identify some possible avenues of discussion about Plato's legal philosophy and the modern concept of the rule of law. The notion of the rule of law is important to legal philosophy in all its forms and not only where topics of general jurisprudence are considered. Legal punishment, for instance, can be justified (or criticized) more straightforwardly without reference to its legal character: one could simply offer a moral justification (or criticism) of punishment in general. But to do only that would be to risk overlooking the characteristics of *legal* punishment, whose *institutional character* is a complicating factor in our moral analysis of it. Criminal punishment in our society has an official place within and is legitimately effectuated only by officials authorized by law, who themselves rely upon other officials to react to, discover, and prosecute perceived violations of criminal law. The entire legal system is thus implicated in the process of punishing crime, and *the* fundamental principle of legal systems is "the rule of law." Furthering our understanding of the rule of law will thereby sharpen our understanding of criminal law as a whole and criminal punishment in particular.

The example of criminal punishment highlights the relevance of the rule of law to this particular problem in legal philosophy. The issue of punishment also brings forth the appreciable value of Plato's philosophical reflections and arguments about law. Another aim of this essay is to elucidate some of the reasons for the fact that, in general, Plato is an underrated legal philosopher. It cannot be denied that Plato's work on *particular* legal problems and issues is worthy of serious consideration, yet it is perhaps contestable whether Plato's philosophy of law is, taken more

B. Burge-Hendrix (✉)
Department of Humanities, Quest University, Squamish, BC, Canada
e-mail: bbh@questu.ca

I.B. Flores and K.E. Himma (eds.), *Law, Liberty, and the Rule of Law*,
Ius Gentium: Comparative Perspectives on Law and Justice 18,
DOI 10.1007/978-94-007-4743-2_3,

broadly, of relevance to twenty-first century legal philosophy in the grand sense of "general jurisprudence." You would be hard-pressed to find, for instance, any current discussions of "the concept of law" where Plato is given a voice. His absence is, I think, an oversight on our part, one that acts to the detriment of our understanding of law, including the concept of law, and in particular the rule of law.

I have said that my primary aim is to identify the relevance of what Plato has to say about the rule of law. A secondary and related aim is to argue for Plato's relevance to contemporary legal philosophy more broadly. I now warn you of a consequence of these two goals: much will be said about the methodology of legal philosophy before anything is said about the rule of law as Plato understands it. Having done much work myself on methodological questions in legal theory, I can sincerely empathize with those of you who cannot help but bemoan their appearance in my discussion. Nevertheless, putting ourselves in a position to appreciate Plato's thoughts on the rule of law requires some consideration of the methodological suppositions whence Plato's legal philosophy develops itself. Plato has much to say about particular problems in legal philosophy, such as the justification of punishment, as well as much to say about more general or abstract issues, such as the rule of law – yet he generally connects these analyses together, and this characteristic refusal to confine his discussions to one level of analysis is worthy of consideration in its own right. So some methodological discussion is unavoidable.

My discussion will proceed, initially, by showing that the relative lack of Plato's direct influence on contemporary legal and philosophy is due in large part to contestable claims or presuppositions about his legal philosophy. While many of the accusations of irrelevance which have been made against Plato's political philosophy have been shown to be overstated, Plato's relevance to legal philosophy is still not fully recognized. This is a sad state of affairs, especially since Plato is perhaps most underrated by a group of legal philosophers whose own methodological disputes are leading them towards conclusions which Plato had long ago arrived at. In the second section of my discussion I shall move on to consider the rule of law itself.

3.2 The Place of Plato in Modern Legal Philosophy

While Simon Blackburn correctly notes that much of the western philosophical tradition "contains vehement rejections of Plato, rather than footnotes to him" (Blackburn 2008, 4), that is not the case with present-day legal philosophy, where Plato's work is, with a few notable exceptions, now largely relegated to footnotes. In a very recent compilation of essays on Plato's relevance to modern law, Richard Brooks, the editor, observes that "[t]o treat Plato seriously today seems audacious, since many of his political, epistemological and metaphysical views seem at worst outrageous and at best quaint" (2007, xiii fn). We need not consider a detailed genealogy of the waxing and waning of Plato's influence in legal philosophy to take note of a few claims against Plato's contemporary relevance:

1. Plato's legal philosophy, like all of his philosophical work, depends upon dubious metaphysical notions (*v.gr.* the theory of the forms);
2. The context of Plato's discussions renders his conclusions anachronistic; and
3. Plato is simply not a legal philosopher in the present-day sense.

A brief consideration will show that each of these claims can be contested. In some cases, they have less import than might first appear; in other cases, they are simply misleading or wholly incorrect.

3.2.1 Metaphysics

Does Plato's metaphysics require us to devalue his contributions to legal philosophy? In particular, does his theory of the forms force us to choose between, on the one hand, accepting his legal theory as one imbued with (to our modern eyes) empirically indefensible transcendental concepts or, on the other hand, as Plato-lite, "to be read regardless of our attitude to the heavy-duty metaphysics" (Blackburn 2008, 15)?[1] Fortunately, the claim that Plato's metaphysics renders his legal philosophy unpalatable is one of the easiest of the claims to set aside, for we are no longer bound to Neo-Platonist interpretations of Plato's legal and political philosophy.

Almost 25 years ago R.F. Stalley observed: "So far as logic, metaphysics and epistemology are concerned, the traditional *Republic*-centred view of Plato is now extinct, at least among English-speaking scholars" (1983, 2).[2] I suggest, then, that we can proceed apace with some degree of confidence that, with regard to Plato's legal philosophy, or at least the positions he sets forth in the *Laws,* it is not unwarranted to assume a considerable degree of relative freedom from the spectre of the Neo-Platonists' emphasis on the forms. Making that assumption, however, does raise some problems which we should at least take note of. First, it might commit us to the developmentalist camp of the developmentalist/unitarian divide in the interpretation of Plato's work as a whole.[3] Secondly, it might inadvertently lead us to inappropriately de-emphasize what I call Plato's *integrative approach* to legal philosophy.

[1] Blackburn is referring specifically to the *Republic*, but his turn of phrase seems equally applicable to the project of "lite-ifying" Plato's legal philosophy.

[2] Stalley (1983, 2) goes on to say: "Those trained in the analytic tradition of philosophy have found that they can learn as much, if not more, from late dialogues such as the *Sophist* as they can from those of the middle period. As yet there has been no corresponding change with regard to political philosophy… a re-evaluation of the *Laws* is overdue."

[3] *Vid. v.gr.* Melissa Lane's discussion of the chronology of Plato's dialogues (Lane 2005, 160).

The second problem is easy enough to avoid, but at this point I must admit to accepting the widely but not universally held belief that the *Laws* appeared in Plato's so-called late period. There is also a third problem that arises in particular from my emphasis on the *Laws*: I may be taking what was arguably meant to be a popular work to be more philosophical than it really is. Malcolm Schofield suggests that the *Laws* "offers an account of the transcendent moral and religious framework of political and social life, and the legal norms needed to sustain it, that is designed to be persuasive to citizens at large… without any particular talent for philosophy or experience of it" (2006, 18). With luck, the third section of this essay will show that, regardless of its ultimate philosophical weightiness in comparison to his other works, Plato's *Laws* provides material for consideration of Plato's legal theory which is of considerable significance to the idea of the rule of law.

3.2.2 Anachronisms

While Plato's metaphysics need not be a barrier to our understanding of his legal philosophy, it can be difficult to reconcile some of our own fundamental beliefs and considered moral conclusions with those held by Plato. Consider that, while Richard Brooks is clearly sympathetic to the notion that Plato *is* relevant to modern law, he himself finds it necessary to abstract away Plato's more "egregious beliefs" (Brooks 2007, xv):

> Of course, we moderns are not ready to simply adopt Plato's conclusions, partly because the conclusions he offers seem so offensive to modern thought… His acceptance of slavery, of the inequality of classes and peoples and of the rule over the producing classes, as well as his crude and radical proposals on eugenics and on the radical sharing of property, is unacceptable…

Such egregious moral conclusions are problematic not only because they are, to us, morally indefensible, but also because they suggest that the social, political, and institutional context which Plato is writing about is so different from our own modern context as to make his political and legal philosophy wholly anachronistic and so, for us, wholly unhelpful for understanding law. Yet we need not defend Plato's moral conclusions or beliefs, and in fact the tensions we encounter – between, for instance, what he has to say about law, the moral values he attributes to legal practices, and the moral presuppositions or conclusions he himself makes – may be helpful in critically assessing his legal philosophy.

There is course the danger of misrepresenting Plato's legal philosophy (or his political philosophy or any other aspect of his thought) by artificially separating it from his moral philosophy – but to do that would be to do wilful violence to his philosophical methodology rather than to disagree with his moral conclusions. We can disagree with Plato on matters of morality without resorting to charges of anachronism. Perhaps a more plausible version of the charge of anachronism (hence general irrelevance) would highlight the fact that the *institutional* structures of ancient

Greece are hardly identical with our own, and that, despite considerable historical, ideological, and rhetorical influence, the difference between Athenian legal institutions and our modern legal institutions is too extreme to permit any heuristic application of, for instance, Plato's conception of the rule of law to the rule of law as it is *for us*. By emphasizing the institutional differences a critic could argue that while Plato might have something to contribute to some debates in applied legal philosophy, such as the justification of criminal punishment, he cannot contribute to other debates, such as the role of the rule of law, because in the former instances the problem surfaces in the same way in all legal systems, while in the latter cases the institutional features of the particular legal system make comparison impossible.

The charge of institutional (rather than moral) anachronism is, it seems to me, a relatively insignificant one, at least as regards the rule of law. It relies on the presupposition that differences in institutional arrangements between legal systems reflect differences in the values and principles those legal systems instantiate. But in fact different institutional or practical arrangements sometimes instantiate the same principles or values, while at other times nearly identical institutional or practical arrangements instantiate different principles or values. This is clear with regard to the scope of criminal penalties. The existence of the death penalty in a legal system seems to have little to do with its structure and institutional arrangements. Canada and the United States have very similar institutions and practices as regards criminal law, but in one nation the most severe penalty for premeditated homicide is life imprisonment, while in the other convicted murders can be executed. Contrariwise, in American courts evidence obtained illegally is much more likely to be excluded in a trial, while in Canadian courts illegally obtained evidence is often usable in a prosecution.[4] Even at the most general level of political organization, institutional arrangements do not track principled commitments. Canada and the United Kingdom are parliamentary democracies, yet in the one judicial review is a pronounced feature of the legal and legislative system while in the other the principle of parliamentary supremacy carries much greater weight. While in the actual world principles of punishment and the degree of legislative authority do vary widely from place to place and time to time, that variance is not due to a simple correlation between, on the one hand, the content of those principles and, on the other hand, institutional structures and practices.

Plato's legal philosophy is not obviously susceptible to charges of anachronism and it ought not to be relegated to the history of ideas on that basis. Nonetheless, issues of historical interpretation and retrospective analyses arise whenever we attempt to learn from long-past philosophical work. We should be particularly careful not to induce anachronisms by attributing to Plato concepts or ideas he did not hold and methodologies he did not use. Malcolm Schofield, for instance, points out the

[4] The use of illegally obtained evidence is permitted by Canadian courts if its exclusion would "bring the administration of justice into disrepute", and it is not at all uncommon in a serious case for a Canadian court to make use of that clause.

while modern concept of the state is useful for the historical analysis it is not a concept which fully corresponds to what Plato and Aristotle had in mind when using the term *polis* (2006, 34). We should be equally careful, then, to recognize when historical contexts are relevant and to recognize when ideas and institutions, which might initially appear similar to our ideas and institutions, in fact turn out to be very different. Athenian democracy, to give just one example, is very different from modern representative democracy. To conflate the two types of political organization together is to invite significant misunderstanding and, importantly, to miss out on opportunities to engage with thinkers from the past. Thomas Brooks asks that we "recognize that Plato's critique of 'democracy' is a critique of 'Athenian democracy' and not democracy as we understand it today"; armed with that distinction, Brooks argues that "most, if not all, of his criticisms of democracy do not create specific problems for modern democracy precisely for this reason" (Brooks 2008, 2).

3.2.3 Plato and General Jurisprudence

The disparity between Plato's moral beliefs (*v.gr.* that slavery is justifiable) and our own fundamental moral beliefs does not prevent us from taking Plato seriously when he talks about politics or law; nor do the obvious dissimilarities between ancient Greek and modern political and institutional arrangements prevent us from engaging with Plato's claims and criticisms about very particular issues such as criminal punishment as well as very general projects such as the constitutional structure of a society. Yet one thing might stand in the way of a fuller appreciation of Plato's significance to modern legal philosophy: his contributions to general jurisprudence.

Modern legal philosophy, like most other subdivisions within philosophy, suffers from an overemphasis on specialization and compartmentalization. We have also, as philosophers have always done, struggled with the classification of various substantive, theoretical, and methodological philosophical positions. Intensive specialization within the modern academy can lead us to consider Plato when we address particular problems, such as the justification of criminal punishment, but ignore him when we pay philosophical attention to legal systems as a whole. Plato's absence from debates in general jurisprudence – debates about such things as the concept of law and the nature of legal authority – is especially lamentable because Plato himself prefigured an integrative practice of legal philosophy that is rapidly becoming, if it has not already become, the preferred methodological approach in general jurisprudence. Present-day legal philosophers cover a lot of ground. The wide scope and varied working materials of philosophical inquiry into law leads some legal philosophers to prefer the term "legal theory" since that label readily encompasses a multitude of scholarly disciplines, including sociology, economics, history, psychology, and anthropology, among many others.

It is not only the case, however, that we can investigate law from many descriptive and critical perspectives; it is also the case that we can consider law at many different levels. Some legal philosophers are concerned with problems at the level of individual legal subjects and their actions – the possible justifications for judicial punishment, for instance, or the character of legal reasons in terms of action theory. Other legal philosophers survey legal phenomena from a different perspective, aiming to understand its institutional characteristics, or to explicate its relation to modern democratic societies. Regardless of whether a legal philosopher is considering the relation of a particular kind of law or legal action to a particular kind of rational subject, or instead is concerned with the relation of legal systems to different constitutional structures, the complexity of law allows for very fine-grained legal-philosophical forays to complement and in turn to be enlightened by large-scale analyses of law in its grander modes. In large part, it is the breadth of philosophical inquiry into law which makes it so rich.

Given the current trend towards a very liberal view as to what constitutes legal philosophy and legal theory, it is peculiar that Plato is not a more prominent figure. His writings on law exhibit concerns which identifiably fall within the larger scope of legal theory. At no time does Plato consider law from a narrow perspective, unless it is to move on to a broader one; nor does he engage with issues of law's institutionality without relating them to particular legal subjects. Plato presents a rich and complicated picture of law, legal systems, and constitutions, and he connects all these to the individual as well as to society. If we apply the distinction between legal philosophy and legal theory, surely we must classify Plato as a legal theorist, which is to say that his philosophy of law makes reference to and use of sociological, psychological, historical, and other types of analyses. Of course, Plato himself would not use our twenty-first century vocabulary and topology of scholarly inquiry. He would likely see it as invidious and counter-productive to philosophical understanding. As capable as he was at distinguishing different types of "science", from his perspective philosophy could comprehend them all, and accordingly his philosophical disposition – indeed his philosophical conviction – aimed to integrate his analyses into a comprehensive whole. In this regard, at least, it seems undeniable that Plato is a general legal theorist *par excellence*.

3.3 The Rule of Law

In the previous section, I argued that Plato's legal philosophy is not undermined by his more egregious moral beliefs that from our perspective it is not anachronistic, and that in fact Plato's integrative approach is remarkably similar to that exhibited by modern analytical legal philosophers who aim to develop a general jurisprudence. If I am correct in arguing that Plato deserves as great a place in modern legal philosophy's more abstract debates as he has earned in their discussions of very particular problems – if Plato has merit as a legal theorist concerned with general jurisprudence – then we can expect that his legal philosophy will be of use in those debates. Let us, then, move on to consider the rule of law itself.

With regard to usage and plain meaning, the phrase "rule of law" is very much underdetermined. In the context of the history of legal and political philosophy, its emergence can be attributed (on grounds of influence if not originality) to Aristotle. Though Aristotle discusses issues related to the rule of law in much of his work, and there are many fine distinctions and nuances in those discussions well beyond the scope of this essay, the most general meaning and arguably most influential element of his account of the rule of law is reflected in Brian Bix's *A Dictionary of Legal Theory,* where Bix's entry on the rule of law identifies it as "a complex and contested ideal which can be traced back at least to Aristotle, under which citizens are to be 'ruled by law, not men'." (2004, 190). The belief that it is both possible and desirable to have a set system of enduring social organization – a constitution – where the ruling power comes from law rather than from individuals is the foundation of the modern rule of law in all its practical variants.[5]

In contemporary legal theory, the concept of the "rule of law" can refer to:

(1) An *existence condition* for an actual legal system…:

  (1a) that is used by legal theorists to identify actual legal systems and distinguish them from non-legal systems, and/or…;
  (1b) that is appealed to by the subjects of that system to justify the imposition of a legal system;

(2) A *practical constraint* on a legal system;
(3) A *procedural principle* (or set of procedural principles)…:

  (3a) used by legal theorists to *identify* legal systems, and/or…;
  (3b) used by legal theorists to *prescribe* the necessary practices of a legal system, and/or…;
  (3c) used by legal theorists to *evaluate*, from a critical moral perspective, the moral worth of a particular legal system;

(4) An *object-level practice* (*i.e.* a practice carried out by the officials of a particular legal system) whereby laws are *enforced* and enforcement is *justified* by reference to an implicit or explicit legal principle avowing the rule of law.

I shall call (1–4) *elements* of the rule of law because, on the one hand, any actual, real-world example of the rule of the law may incorporate some or all of the elements, and, on the other hand, any theoretical concept of the rule of law may incorporate some or all of the elements. In the following subsections, I shall proceed by first briefly discussing each of the elements of the rule of law and, where I am able, I shall identify whether that element is present in Plato's legal theory. I hasten to add that my aim is to identify possible avenues for future discussion rather than to make authoritative pronouncements about Plato's philosophical positions!

[5] That the desirability of the rule of law can be contested is, however, less obvious to us modern egalitarians than it is to Plato and Aristotle. Nonetheless, there are debates even within contemporary legal theory as to whether an iniquitous legal system is better than no legal system at all – that is, debates about the rule of law being necessarily superior to rule by any other means.

3.3.1 *The Rule of Law as an Existence Condition qua Descriptive Label (1a)*

As a theoretical matter, classifying a particular society as a legal society involves an implicit or explicit apprehension of the rule of law as an operative principle of organization in that society. Thus (1a): the rule of law is a *descriptive label* applied by legal theorists to particular societies so as to distinguish legal from non-legal societies. Thus the fundamental division in H.L.A. Hart's taxonomy of social organization is between so-called "primitive" societies "without a legislature, courts, or officials of any kind" where "the only means of social control is that general attitude of the group towards its own standard modes of behaviour" (Hart 1994, 91).[6] Where social control takes the form of explicit rules rather than general attitudes, and where those rules (according to Hart) are elaborated to include, besides primary rules of obligation, secondary rules of various types, we can identify a transition from "the regime of primary rules into what is indisputably a legal system" (Hart 1994, 94). So (1a) can be understood as the identifying mark of a community with a legal system. Communities lacking the rule of law in that sense are communities lacking a legal system.

Does Plato have his own version of (1a)? To my knowledge of Plato's *Laws*, nowhere does he distinguish between communities with legal systems and communities without legal systems in the way that Hart and other modern legal theorists do. It is important to note, here, that the sort of codified rules Hart and most all modern theorists have in mind are law in the narrow sense, *positive law*, rather than law construed more broadly, which might include divine law or objective moral law or any number of ideal *sources* of positive law which are not themselves to be considered (by positivists) to be law solely on account of not being set-out or posited as such. Nevertheless, Plato, like Hart, does seem to recognize that societies can exist without positive law. Consider the following passage from the *Laws*, where the Athenian stranger raises the problem of requiring knowledge of what good rule is in order to identify which communities are ruled well (Plato 1988, I, 639c):

> Take any community for which there is by nature a ruler, and which is beneficial when that ruler is present: what would we say about someone who praised it or blamed it without ever having seen it operating in a correct communal way under its ruler, but had always seen such social intercourse without a ruler or under bad rulers? Do we believe onlookers like these will ever have any worthwhile praise or blame for such communities?

The key phrase here is "social intercourse without a ruler." The Athenian stranger is comparing the evaluative perspective of someone who did not know how a

---

[6] Note that Hart does not consider "social control" to be the only means of control. Rather, social control is what we might think of as the "diffuse social pressure" that causes individuals to feel obligated to behave or refrain from behaving in certain ways. There are, clearly, more direct ways to direct behaviour, such as by means of force exerted by a tyrant, but that is not (for Hart) an instance of "social control." Note also that by "primitive" Hart does *not* mean morally deficient or in any sense inferior, except in regard to the (potentially but not necessarily better) development of more complex systems of social control involving rules, *v.gr.* legal systems.

particular activity could be instantiated as a beneficial communal activity – in this case the activity is that of holding drinking parties – because the evaluator had no experience of that activity "operating in a correct communal way." Such a person, lacking experience and knowledge of a well-ruled drinking party and a community in which such parties played a proper role, would not be competent to determine the true worth of drinking parties, any more than an evaluator ignorant of military knowledge who set out to evaluate the worth of an army whose general who lacked the art of generalship could arrive at a correct evaluation of armies. If we can understand "social intercourse without a ruler" to refer not only to human rulers but the absence of particular rules entirely (including, then, posited laws), and understand the "communal way" of social practices of that non-legal type as instances of what Hart calls pre-legal societies where there is no rule by law, but rather only diffuse social pressure acting to standardize behaviour, then we might identify in Plato an implicit distinction between legal and pre-legal or "primitive" societies.

Does it matter whether Plato's legal theory makes use of the distinction made by (1a)? Perhaps here we are either going to great lengths to inadvertently transform Plato's legal theory into a kind of legal positivism, which would be anachronistic and silly, or are making much of a small point. What certainly does matter is that a legal theory is able to distinguish between communal "custom" and positive law.[7] On that point Plato's legal theory is on safe ground, for even merely on the evidence of the passage cited above we can see that he was well aware of the possibility of both customary social norms and the imposition of positive law (whether by a good or a bad ruler).[8]

3.3.2 The Rule of Law as an Existence Condition qua Justification (1b)

(1b) is the element of the concept of the rule of law that is appealed to by the subjects of a legal system to *justify* the imposition of the legal system itself. Whereas (1a) was a descriptive label allowing for the classification of forms of social organization, (1b) invokes a moral claim. Note that (1b) is distinct from (4): the former is used to justify the imposition of a legal *system* with the counterfactual possibility in mind (*i.e.* that there could be a state of affairs where the system did not exist) while the latter is used to justify the imposition of the consequences of disobeying legal prohibitions or failing to obey legal duties on the grounds that the already existing legal system requires it.

(1b) amounts to an answer to the question "Is a legal system a moral necessity for our society?" So far as I am aware, whenever that question has arisen in a judicial or political context within a modern democratic state, the answer has been affirmative.

---

[7] I place scare quotes around "custom" because, as Hart observes, the term "often implies that the customary rules are very old and supported with less social pressure than other rules" (1994, 91).

[8] *Vid.* also Richard Kraut's discussion of the Greek word *nomos* (1984, 105–6).

Modern democratic states generally presuppose that a legal system is a necessary condition for their existence and also presuppose that the adoption of a legal system is at least morally justified if not a moral requirement. Unlike the practice of justifying the enforcement of particular laws, which is a practice that every prosecutor and judge in a modern legal system will eventually have to engage in, the need to justify the legal system itself is rarely encountered.

In Canada, however, legislative incompetence led to a constitutional crisis in which the Supreme Court of Canada did in fact have to assert that the rule of law – in the sense of (1b), namely the imposition of a legal system upon Canadian society – was not only a practical necessity but a morally good state of affairs. The crises came about when the Province of Manitoba failed to abide by the legal requirement that it publish its laws in both English and French. This requirement was absolutely fundamental to the validity of Manitoba's law, for the relevant section of the act which brought the province into existence "entrenches a mandatory requirement to enact, print and publish all Acts of the Legislature in both official languages and, thus, establishes a constitutional duty on the Manitoba Legislature with respect to the manner and form of enactment of legislation."[9] Unfortunately, the Manitoba Legislature wholly failed to publish its laws in any language but English for more than a hundred years, leaving the Supreme Court of Canada with no legal choice but to declare all those purported laws all to be "of no force and effect", which is the Canadian judicial system's way of saying that they were not and never had been law at all.

The consequences of the Supreme Court's ruling on the validity of more than a century's worth of Manitoba law could not be understated, and to its credit the Court put the matter very clearly and forcefully: "The conclusion that all unilingual Acts of the Legislature of Manitoba are invalid and of no force or effect means that the positive legal order which has purportedly regulated the affairs of the citizens of Manitoba since 1890 is destroyed and the rights, obligations and any other effects arising under these laws are invalid and unenforceable."[10] Faced with "a legal vacuum" the Supreme Court decided "to deem temporarily valid and effective" the clearly invalid decrees, and it justified this decision on legal grounds by noting that "[t]he constitutional principle of the rule of law would be violated by these consequences." This principle, as the Court saw it, "requires the creation and maintenance of an actual order of positive laws to govern society." Moreover, just in case the legal arguments were insufficient, the Court went on to appeal to practical necessity ("[l]aw and order are indispensable elements of civilized life"), quoted both John Locke and Joseph Raz, and rather testily pointed out that the preamble to the Canadian *Constitution Act (1982)* states in its very first paragraph that the principle

[9] *Reference re Manitoba Language Rights,* [1985] 1 S.C.R. 721.

[10] At another point in its decision the Court again stressed the severity and extent of a dire situation: "The situation of the various institutions of provincial government would be as follows: the courts, administrative tribunals, public officials, municipal corporations, school boards, professional governing bodies, and all other bodies created by law, to the extent that they derive their existence from or purport to exercise powers conferred by Manitoba laws enacted since 1890 in English only, would be acting without legal authority."

of the rule of law is one of only two ultimate principles presupposed by that Act, which is itself the explicitly recognized "supreme law" of Canada.[11]

In a nutshell: the Supreme Court of Canada, faced with the threat of a legal vacuum within an entire Canadian province, argued that under the circumstances it had a legal and moral obligation to impose the rule of law. Without the rule of law, Canada would have no constitution ("a purposive ordering of social relations"), and without that and the legal authority it provides, it would have no legal system ("an actual order of positive laws"). In the court's view, the alternative would be a morally unacceptable state of "chaos and anarchy."

Does Plato avow (1b) in his legal philosophy? Does he hold the position that without positive law, there would be anarchy and chaos, and so even a bad legal system is better than no legal system at all? That question brings forth the vexing problem of distinguishing between the ideal state and the practically achievable state. Consider the following passage in the *Statesman,* spoken by the Stranger and following from the point that the pure form of the art of government, if it should be actual at all, "will be found in the possession of one or two, or, at most, of a select few" (Plato 1983b, 293a3–4) of truly knowledgeable leaders (1983b, 293c5–d2, emphasis added):

> Then the constitution par excellence, the only constitution worthy of the name, must be the one in which the rulers are not men making a show of political cleverness but men really possessed of scientific understanding of the art of government. Then we must not take into consideration on any sound principle of judgment whether their rule be by laws or without them over willing or unwilling subjects or whether they themselves be rich men of poor men.

On this account, the true constitution ruled by true rulers with true authority has no requirement for rule by positive law, nor for the consent of the ruled. The Stranger's interlocutor, young Socrates, remarks that "the saying about ruling without laws is a hard saying for us to hear" (1983b, 293e6–7) and the Stranger characterizes the next stage of their discussion as dealing with "this question whether a good governor can govern without laws." (1983b, 294a4–5) Here the Stranger prefaces the discussion by seemingly acknowledging the practical necessity for positive law while disputing its claim to authority (1983b, 294a9–10):

> In one sense it is evident that the art of kingship does include the art of lawmaking. But the political ideal is not full authority for laws but rather full authority for a man who understands the art of kingship and has kingly ability.

Some of the objections Plato raises against supreme authority for positive law are clearly recognizable in modern legal philosophy (though in the *Laws* he advocates what Stalley calls the doctrine of the sovereignty of law). Positive laws, for instance, must be general, and the requirement of generality diminishes its worth in particular circumstances: "Law can never issue an injunction binding on all which really embodies what is best for each." (1983b, 294a13–b1) Modern legal theorists, not to

---

[11] The other principle, interestingly, is "the supremacy of God."

mention judges and legislators, freely admit that in many circumstances a *decree* or set of decrees suited to the particularities of a given situation (or very similar but not necessarily identical situation types) would be morally preferable to a generally applicable *law* (so long as we are considering only that particular situation or type of situation).

I shall say more about the modern view on the merits and demerits of the generality of positive law later and of its general or universal enforcement later, when discussing (4), where I bring forth a feature of modern legal systems which Plato would find to be utterly reprehensible: institutionalized discretion in the enforcement of existing law. At this juncture, however, I wish to focus our attention to the question of whether Plato would justify the imposition of a legal system on the grounds that a community is morally better-off with one than without one.

The simplistic answer is that Plato's political philosophy admits of an ideal about which his legal philosophy has nothing to say. The ideal city with true rulers and a true constitution does not require a positive legal order, so it follows (on the simplistic answer) that Plato would not avow (1b): the ideal city would have no absolute requirement for positive law because it is ruled by the best statesman or (small) group of statesmen. The more nuanced, and I think unavoidable, answer is that Plato may or may not see (1b) as a morally sound claim. Our reconstruction of his position, it seems to me, will depend on the weight we give to the *Statesman* and the *Laws* in comparison to the *Republic*. Does the *Republic* espouse a position which Plato later rejects, or can we interpret the *Republic* in light of its focus on an ideal which Plato saw as impossible to instantiate in actuality and/or saw as serving to mark our proper aspirations as opposed to our actual abilities? Perhaps (1b), which implies that a community with a legal order will always be in a morally better position than it could be without a legal order, could serve as a useful question with regard to the larger issue of developmentalism in Plato's philosophy.

I also note that all of what the Supreme Court of Canada said about the moral need to uphold a legal order in a society threatened by a "legal vacuum", and the moral necessity to avoid "chaos and anarchy" by instantiating a legal order where one is absent, is premised on the link between a free and democratic society and the rule of law. It is virtually inconceivable in modern political philosophy to have a democratic society without the rule of law, and so the value of a democratic constitution is closely tied to the value an efficacious legal order. In modern legal and political philosophy, arguments about the supposedly intrinsic value of the rule of law seem strained when placed within the context of a democratic society (where the principle of the rule of law seems to be a given) and yet seem wildly hypothetical when placed in another context (where the spectre of tyranny overshadows a careful understanding of the principle of the rule of law). Plato, though well aware of tyranny and democracy, did not carry the same historical baggage as we do. A closer consideration of his evaluation of non-democratic legal orders might be helpful for us when we consider (1b) more critically. In the *Laws* the doctrine of the sovereignty of law is applied more to constrain the democracy (the tyranny of the many) than to ensure the freedom we associate with a democratic constitution.

3.3.3 *The Rule of Law as a Practical Constraint on a Legal System (2)*

H.L.A. Hart's suggestion that *The Concept of Law* could be read as "an essay in descriptive sociology" incited considerable controversy among philosophers and sociologists. It began the movement, in analytical legal philosophy at least, towards legal theory rather than purely conceptually oriented legal philosophy.[12] It is fair to say that sociologists as a group did not take Hart's assertion as seriously as he might have liked, though there are exceptions. By discussing (2) my aim is to draw out some of the sociological or anthropological aspects of legal theory and to consider their relevance to both modern legal philosophy and Plato's legal philosophy.

The strongest tack to take in defending Hart's sociological aspirations is to highlight how, in *The Concept of Law,* Hart describes the move from a pre-legal society to a legal society, and why on Hart's account that transition entails the rule of law as a practical constraint on every such society and every associated legal system. Hart sees the rule of law as a practical requirement of a legal society and thus of a legal system insofar as: (i) the actual circumstances of human communities make a regime of positive law practically unavoidable if a community's customary norms are insufficient to keep order; (ii) most all human communities are too complex to be governed by customary norms alone; and (iii) the degree of social complexity which makes customary norms insufficient for an orderly, enduring society practically entails *laws about other laws* (or what Hart calls "secondary rules").

I am too inexpert to summarize what Plato has to say about (i) and (ii). It is possible that his wide knowledge of Greek and foreign cities and their constitutions, of which there were an astounding variety and each of which to modern eyes may appear in many respects far more vigorous than those that exist today, would allow us to gather useful anthropological data and further our sociological models of human communities. More likely, a careful analysis of the data available to Plato, of his presentation and interpretation of that data, and of the conclusions he draws from it all might give us some insight into the methodology of ancient anthropology and sociology.

Regardless, what is particularly interesting from the perspective of modern legal philosophy is Plato's apparent denial of (iii). The city he describes in the *Laws* is one of considerable complexity: its explicitly specified constitution comprises a set of elements no less complex than modern states, and the laws Plato provides for the city are many and varied, going into remarkable (to modern eyes) depth of detail. And yet *the entire system is effectively static as regards the laws themselves.* Plato does not appear to provide very little leeway for rules of change, nor does he explicitly specify any. As Stalley notes, Plato "makes legislative change so difficult as to be

[12] Others would trace the origins of this movement to the legal realists, both American and Scandinavian, but that movement had stalled long before Hart came on the scene. In any case, it is not as important to determine responsibility for the growth of legal theory as it is to recognize its contemporary significance.

virtually impossible" (Stalley 1983, 84). Though generally appreciative of Plato as a legal philosopher, Glen Morrow proffers a very severe criticism of Plato's legal philosophy because of the static character of law: "Another respect in which Plato's conception of the rule of law fails to meet a requirement regarded as axiomatic today is the absence of any theory or process of legislation" (Morrow 1941, 124). Setting aside Plato's more egregious moral beliefs, if there is anything in his legal philosophy that renders it truly anachronistic it is the comparative absence of what Hart calls rules of change – laws providing for the introduction of new laws, the withdrawal of old ones, and the change of portions of existing law. While the *Laws* provides for a hierarchical system of courts, and so enables the judicial review of lower-court judicial decisions, there is nothing like a conception of the judicial review of legislative decisions (though the role of the Nocturnal Council may be more pertinent to this matter than I have been able to discern).

In any event, if a descriptively accurate conception of the rule of law as it exists in modern societies should be coincident with an actual capacity on the part of every legal system to modify its laws *according to and by means of law* – a feature which most modern legal theorists do consider necessary and most actual modern legal systems seem to evince – then Plato's legal philosophy is, as Morrow claims, lacking an axiomatic element. If so, then my assertion that Plato has a credible claim to offering a legal theory capable at the level of a general jurisprudence is simply false, for it is evident that modern legal systems exhibit legislative change to a considerable degree. I am hesitant, however, to give up so easily, and I wonder whether there might be some corrective in Plato's philosophical views as a whole which allows for at least an implicit theory of legislative change. Legal positivists, following Hart, find some satisfaction in the facts of language's inescapable "open texture" and of the inevitability of unforeseen circumstances, two practical constraints on legislation which give rise to a constant need for the interpretation and "precisification" of law. I know nothing of Plato's philosophy of language, but I wonder whether it contains something capable of addressing the problem of legislative change.

3.3.4 The Rule of Law as a Procedural Principle or Set of Procedural Principles (3)

The distinction between so-called natural-law theories and all other types of legal theories, especially legal positivist theories, was, until recently, a distinction of considerable import in general jurisprudence. Of late, however, it is a distinction that is increasingly deemed to be misleading or irrelevant to the methodological positions upon which a modern philosophy of law might be founded.[13] It is not unfair to say

[13] As just one example of the irrelevance, sublimation, or transcendence of the distinction, consider Neil MacCormick (2007).

that for much of the previous century, many of the central debates in legal philosophy were sidetracked by arguments about the demarcation or boundary between natural-law theories and, usually, legal positivist theories. Legal theory progressed apace, however, despite the caricature of natural-law theories and the (often inapposite) accusation, directed by one legal theorist to another, that the other was a simple-minded natural-lawyer who insisted on a descriptively false (though perhaps, arguably, normatively preferable) connection between law and morality.[14]

One advance was the result of Ronald Dworkin's insistence that the legal practice of interpreting laws must be understood as making use of both rules and principles. That point, though not so radical a criticism as Dworkin and others held it out to be,[15] was fundamental to Dworkin's far more important claim that every legal system must, though "constructive interpretation", aspire to present itself in the best moral light possible – law must make itself the (morally) best it can be. Dworkin attributes to all legal systems a particular procedure for the internal practice of understanding and interpreting law, and in that sense uses this (supposedly) necessary function of legal systems to: identify their existence (3a); prescribe, as a practical matter, the necessary incorporation of this particular practice within all legal systems (3b); and so posit *within legal systems themselves* a constant practice of moral evaluation (3c).

Of course, not all legal philosophers agreed with the idea that the practice of interpretation, integral to every legal system, must necessarily aspire to moral perfection. Legal positivists have been especially critical of that view, for it seems clear that moral progress is far from a necessary result of the existence of a legal system. But Dworkin's idea does usefully highlight the *self-perception of a legal system* and the constraints on a legal system's existence which may arise from its *perception (in the sense of moral evaluation) by its subjects.*

Consider a fundamental claim made by Joseph Raz's legal theory: every legal system must sincerely claim authority (1979). It is important to note that Raz does not claim that every extant legal system is *justified* in its sincere claim to authority, nor for that matter does he claim that any actual legal system can correctly claim it. Rather, Raz sees the claim to authority as reflecting the fact that legal systems are creatures of a sort that must be at least capable in principle of being practical authorities. A rich literature has arisen from Raz's controversial accounts of authority in which various types of authority have been distinguished (*v.gr. practical* and *epistemic* authorities). Analyses of the relation of authority to reasons for action have further contributed to our understanding of legal systems as a result of the

[14] I eschew any discussion of that connection here except insofar as it has a direct bearing on Plato's legal philosophy.

[15] Suffice it to say that Hart, who was the primary target of Dworkin's avowal of the importance of the distinction between rules and principles, did not deny the distinction, nor modify his legal theory to take account of it in any significant way. In fairness to Dworkin, however, it must be said that his attacks on Hart had the salutary effect of intensifying legal positivists' understanding of legal positivism itself, and in that regard Dworkin is one of the influences for the development of "post-positivism."

efforts of Raz, his critics, and his defenders. Here I wish only to point out that Plato's philosophy can contribute to our understanding of the nature of reasons and of human authorities (*vid.* Hatzistavrou 2005); and, conversely, the fine-grained Razian contributions to action theory may yet further our understanding of Plato's accounts of knowledge, expertise, and in particular the role of knowledge and expertise within legal practices (both ideal and actual).

The second important advance resulting from the positivist–natural law debates in recent legal philosophy involves both the notion of an aspirational theory of law and the question of the extent to which human nature determines *a priori* the necessary features of a legal system. Here I am thinking of Lon Fuller's work on "the internal morality of law" (1969) and John Finnis' weighty tome *Natural Law and Natural Rights* (1980). For the sake of brevity, I shall confine my remarks here to Fuller's identification of a kind of "morality" and purposive activity with law, but a notable fact is that both Fuller and Finnis draw upon the social sciences to elaborate their views on law, thus recognizing that law is a topic whose philosophical consideration can be furthered by inquiry on a broad rather than narrow front.

Even those legal theorists who insist upon the potential for a wide and deep-ranging capacity on the part of legal systems for evil, and who accordingly deny that the rule of law is necessarily preferable to the "chaos and anarchy" so dreaded by the Supreme Court of Canada, nonetheless envision legal systems as subject to certain internal constraints. A legal system is not merely a bundle of decrees, but a complex rule system with some degree of internal logic. The pertinent question with regard to (3) – the element of the concept rule of law presented as a set of procedural principles – is the moral status of that internal logic.

Fuller offers a description of that internal logic which is premised on the distinction between what he calls the "morality of duty" and "the morality of aspiration." He identifies the aspirational morality as the one "most plainly exemplified in Greek philosophy" where it "is the morality of the Good Life, of excellence, of the fullest realization of human powers". The morality of duty, however, does not aim for human excellence; it simply "lays down the basic rules without which an ordered society is impossible, or without which an ordered society directed toward certain specific goals must fail of its mark" (1969, 5) Hence we can find "the closest cousin" of the morality of duty in the law, which must only secure the minimum conditions for human co-existence. Fuller's "procedural version of natural law" (1969, 97) met with considerable criticism, and in the long run most of his insights were either absorbed or explicated by more powerful legal theories that were readily able to accommodate them (*vid.* Hart 1994, 193–200).

One of Fuller's replies to his critics, however, has been taken aboard only relatively recently. Fuller inveighed against "the assumption that law should be viewed not as the product of an interplay or purposive orientations between the citizen and his government but as a one-way projection of authority, originating with government and imposing itself upon the citizen" (1969, 204). It is, I think, a profound failing of modern legal philosophy that we often inadvertently overlook or underplay the important fact that legal systems instantiate *reciprocal relationships* between the subjects of the system and those who legislate, adjudicate, or enforce it.

The import of the purposive character of that type of relationship is contestable, of course, but the mere fact of the existence of reciprocal relationships within legal systems is vitally important. Fuller and Finnis were heavily influenced by Plato and Aristotle – perhaps we can turn to ancient legal philosophy to retrace our steps so as to determine when and why law took on or appeared to take on a unidirectional character.

3.3.5 The Rule of Law as an Object-Level Practice of Enforcing and Justifying the Law (4)

The enforcement of the law on everyone and the associated practice of finding legal authority alone to be sufficient justification for such enforcement is the simplest and most readily identifiable element of the modern concept of the rule of law. When reference is commonly made to the rule of law without further specification, something like (4) is understood an actual or desirable practice on the part of the officials of a legal system. As the Supreme Court of Canada puts it, "law is supreme over officials of the government as well as private individuals, and thereby preclusive of the influence of arbitrary power." What Stalley calls the doctrine of the sovereignty of law is clearly stated by the Athenian in the *Laws* (Plato 1988, 715d1–9):

> I have now applied the term "servants of the laws" to the men usually said to be rulers, not for the sake of an innovation in names but because I hold that it is this above all that determines whether the city survives or undergoes the opposite. Where the law is itself ruled over and lacks sovereign authority, I see destruction at hand for such a place. But where it is despot over the rulers and the rulers are slaves of the law, there I foresee safety and all the good things which the gods have given to cities.

Morrow sees in the doctrine of the sovereignty of law a clear continuity with Plato's legal theory and modern legal practice: "Plato adheres very closely to that conception of the rule of law which is a cherished part of our political heritage. All the persons in his state, whatever their rank or condition, are subject to the ordinary laws of the state and are amenable to the jurisdiction of the ordinary courts" (Morrow 1941, 123).

There is, however, a quite startling difference between the letter and the rule as regards actual practice of the rule of law in most modern legal systems, one which makes Plato's doctrine of the sovereignty of law appear to be quite severe indeed. As a practical matter, in modern legal systems police and prosecutorial *discretion* largely alleviates a felt need to recognize that occasionally it is (morally) better to eschew legal enforcement. The public expect a degree of (what it takes to be) sensible discretion and the police officer or prosecutor who insists upon universal and strict application of each and every law is liable to cause considerable discontent among a citizenry otherwise supportive of the rule of law.

While the expectation of discretion in the enforcement of the law is commonplace in modern democratic populations, the popularity of that expectation may speak only to the degree to which we moderns have been become unruly, hence more in need of the doctrine of the sovereignty of the law than ever before. But discretion in the enforcement of the law can go beyond common expectations and become an explicit and authorized institutional feature of a modern legal system. For instance, in Canada it is a criminal offence to advocate or promote genocide. That offence exists despite the existence of the fundamental freedom of expression specified in the *Canadian Charter of Rights and Freedoms,* a constitutional document. The *legal existence* of the Canadian Criminal Code provision against inciting advocating or promoting is dependent on another section of the Charter which permits fundamental freedoms to be restricted by "reasonable limits prescribed by law as can be demonstrably justified in a free and democratic society." Yet the *political palatability* of the law prohibiting the advocation of genocide, in a modern democratic society where freedom of expression takes pride of place, can be fairly described as due to the institutionalization of prosecutorial discretion, insofar as the Criminal Code provision specifies that "No proceeding for an offence under this section [prohibiting advocating or promoting genocide] shall be instituted without the consent of the Attorney General." Here, then, we have an instance of explicit prosecutorial discretion of a type that would be anathema to Plato. What does this say about freedom of expression, modern democracies, and the applicability of Plato's legal theory?

3.4 A Final Topic for Discussion: Education

In conclusion, I want to draw attention to a feature of Plato's legal theory that has the potential to further our understanding of a function of law most modern legal philosophers pay no attention to whatsoever. One of the most complex problems in positivist legal theory is the status of moral criteria for legal validity. Some legal positivists, following Joseph Raz, hold that the existence of a law cannot depend on its substantive moral merits. Others, following Wilfrid Waluchow, argue that the specification of moral criteria for legal validity can be a feature of a legal system itself (rather than the permission for judges to exert an extra-legal power). The debate centres on the existence of explicitly posited moral-political rights such as the right to freedom of expression and equality before and under the law, and the contrary positions of exclusive and inclusive positivism in characterizing such rights as legal rights or as permissions for extra-legal reasoning are wholly at odds with each other. The way in which we resolve that opposition will go a long way to determining our view of the limits and power of positive law.

It seems to me that Plato has something to say about this debate, despite the fact that his legal theory is far removed from positivist theories of law. One of the main concerns of Plato's legal philosophy is the *educative function* of law and legal systems. This is a feature of his thought that permeates all his work; it is not confined to the *Laws* alone. In the *Crito,* for instance, Plato invokes the laws of Athens in personified form, and the personified Laws opine that "all our orders are in the form of proposals, not of savage commands, and we give him [the citizen] the choice of either persuading us or doing what we say" (1983a, 52a1–3). Laws, in short, have the capacity to *persuade* us. But what form does such persuasion take? Is it rational persuasion or merely a rhetorical appeal to irrational sentiments? Or, is it neither, but instead something in between, namely a moral exhortation to do what the law says?

It seems to me possible that in Plato's legal theory laws may do more than appeal to our emotions or exhort us to be better. In the *Laws,* the importance of the role prescribed for the Minister for Education, and the considerable amount of discussion Plato engages in to describe the merits of legal preludes, suggest that one of the primary functions of a legal system is to educate its subjects so as to make them better individuals and thus work towards the maintenance of a good society or the improvement of the already existing one. Education, for Plato, is not merely a matter of inculturation and habit – it is a rational activity directed towards becoming a better person.

If a legal system must be capable of educating its citizens (rather than simply indoctrinating or habituating them), as Plato's legal theory seems to require, then that requirement entails something about moral criteria for legal validity irrespective of Plato's belief in objective morality, for a legal system must be capable at least in principle of educating its subjects, and that process requires something beyond persuasion in the limited sense of securing agreement – it requires rational consideration and a rational dialogue within the legal system about the fundamental values of the state. The notion of law as facilitating a dialogue between legislators and courts has become a part of Canadian constitutional jurisprudence. The dialogue model is often used to describe and make sense of the give-and-take between legislators, whose laws are expected to respect and further the moral-political rights of Canadians recognized in the *Charter*, and courts, whose decisions are expected to further democratic decision-making while constraining it, again in light of the relevant moral-political constitutional rights. On that model, Canadian legislators and courts educate each other by furthering each others' understanding of what Fuller would call the requirements of the morality of aspiration, rather than merely the requirements of the morality of duty. But explicit within the legal dialogue in Canada is the understanding of the particulars of the morality of aspiration – the correct interpretation of the fundamental values of the state – is uncertain. Moreover, legislative acts and judicial decision often evince the kind of moral exhortation (perhaps even attempts at rational persuasion) we find in the form of the preludes in the *Laws*. The analogy may not hold, for several reasons,[16] but Plato's careful attention to the relation between law and education may have much to say about the presence of moral argumentation and discussion in modern democratic states where moral-political rights are entrenched in their constitution.

---

[16] *V.gr.* The preludes may be merely a form of unidirectional moral exhortation rather than a practice for inducing rational evaluation of the laws; the fact that the fundamental values of Canadian constitutional law are recognized to be uncertain may render them, from the perspective of Plato's legal theory, incapable of doing the work that Plato thinks laws must do; citizens may simply ignore the *Charter's* attempt to establish a legal-political context for the realization and specification of fundamental values through legal discourse, in which case the legal system does not educate its regular subjects however much its officials may contribute to their own collective intellectual progress.

References

Bix, B. 2004. *A dictionary of legal theory*. Oxford: Oxford University Press.

Blackburn, S. 2008. *Plato's republic*. New York: Grove Press.

Brooks, R. (ed.). 2007. *Plato and modern law*. Aldershot: Ashgate Publishing.

Brooks, T. 2008. Is Plato's political philosophy anti-democratic? In *Anti-democratic thought*, ed. E. Kofmel. Exeter: Imprint Academic.

Finnis, J. 1980. *Natural law and natural rights*. Oxford: Clarendon Press.

Fuller, L. 1969. *The morality of law*, 2nd ed. New Haven: Yale University Press.

Hart, H.L.A. 1994. *The concept of law*, 2nd ed. Oxford: Clarendon Press.

Hatzistavrou, A. 2005. Socrates' deliberative authoritarianism. *Oxford Studies in Ancient Philosophy* 29: 75–113.

Kraut, R. 1984. *Socrates and the state*. Princeton: Princeton University Press.

Lane, M. 2005. Socrates and Plato: An introduction. In *The Cambridge history of Greek and Roman political thought*, ed. C. Rowe and M. Schofield. Cambridge: Cambridge University Press.

MacCormick, N. 2007. *Institutions of law: An essay in legal theory*. Oxford: Oxford University Press.

Morrow, G. 1941. Plato and the rule of law. *Philosophical Review* 50(2): 105–126.

Plato. 1983a. Crito (trans. Grube, G.M.A.). In E. Hamilton and H. Cairns ed. *The collected dialogues of Plato: Including the letters*. Princeton: Princeton University Press.

Plato. 1983b. Statesman, (trans. Kemp, R.). In E. Hamilton and H. Cairns ed. *The collected dialogues of Plato: Including the letters*. Princeton: Princeton University Press.

Plato. 1988. *The laws of Plato*. Trans. T. Pangle. Chicago: University of Chicago Press.

Raz, J. 1979. *The authority of law: Essays on law and morality*. Oxford: Clarendon Press.

Schofield, M. 2006. *Plato: Political philosophy*. Oxford: Oxford University Press.

Stalley, R.F. 1983. *An introduction to Plato's laws*. Oxford: Basil Blackwell.

Chapter 4
Kantian Re-construction of Intersubjectivity Forms: The Logic of the Transition from Natural State to the Threshold of the Civic State

Andrzej Maciej Kaniowski

4.1 Introduction

Immanuel Kant,[1] would undoubtedly like people to conduct their commonwealth – *das gemeine Wesen* – in the form of a "society based on norms of virtue" (1910, VI, 94).[2] He even considers the formation of such an "ethical commonwealth" the task which the members of the human race must face and treats it as an order of reason. He warns politicians, using a dramatic tone, against attempting to bring such a polity by force: "Woe betides the legislator – says Kant – if he wishes to bring about through coercion a polity directed to ethical ends!" (1910, VI, 96). This objection, however, is not only an opposition to the *method* of implementing a system based on norms of virtue; to be exact, it is not merely a protest against violence. Kantian objection is more fundamental in nature – it is an objection to the attempt to mix the political polity with a polity based on principles of virtue or ethical ends. Any attempt to give priority to the latter, thus imposing such principles on a politically constituted polity (the only form of which – compatible with reason and worthy of acceptance – is, according to Kant, the *republic*), which can only occur under the conditions of a civic state.

Republic is necessary in order to conduct commonwealth in accordance with the absolute indications of practical reason, and has its foundation in the idea of "original contract". This form of polity constitutes a pattern of polity for all modern countries of the Western world; namely, the countries with a liberal-democratic political system. And, it is precisely this polity system, this political form of organizing and conducting

---

[1] Works of Immanuel Kant are quoted after the issue of the Prussian Academy of Sciences (with some exceptions) in my own translation.

[2] "[*E*]*ine Gesellschaft nach Tugendgesetzen*".

A.M. Kaniowski (✉)
Department of Philosophy and History, University of Lodz, Lodz, Poland
e-mail: maciek@filozof.uni.lodz.pl

I.B. Flores and K.E. Himma (eds.), *Law, Liberty, and the Rule of Law*,
Ius Gentium: Comparative Perspectives on Law and Justice 18,
DOI 10.1007/978-94-007-4743-2_4,

commonwealth that should be granted – as Kant stated – priority over all other forms of organizing a polity. This Kantian postulate is valid in our times.

To help us to understand this primacy of the republican polity, as well as the concept of original contract, which constitutes the basis of this polity, one should primarily reconstruct Kant's logic of reasoning: the logic of ascending from the most elementary forms of intersubjectivity to the most sublime form of commonwealth, from the standpoint of human finitude and limitations, namely "ethical commonwealth". Nevertheless, it is the republican form of commonwealth, rather than the most sublime one, that is of paramount importance. This study will present only one, yet crucial, aspect of this path, the culmination of which is a civic *state* with a public normative authority: a civic *polity*. In turn, the only form of a civic polity consistent with the principles inferred *a priori* from the concepts is a *republic*.

4.2 *A Priori* Versus Empirical Knowledge of the Forms of Intersubjectivity

Kant is familiar with different forms of human coexistence, *i.e.* various forms of intersubjectivity. He is also perfectly aware that various "propensities for community", which includes *feelings*, can constitute a "sensual" bond that connects people within these different forms of intersubjectivity. This way of perceiving intersubjectivity, through the prism of different "propensities for community" is an empirical way to comprehend intersubjectivity. It undeniably fulfils the premise that we are beings who belong to an empirical order, an order of sensible system of nature and, as such, we are creatures filled with feelings, emotions or inclinations. However, as we know (or at least, as Kant believes), it is not just this fact that determines our specificity and the dignity characteristic of man. It establishes our simultaneous membership in noumenal order of nature, *i.e.* the order in which we find ourselves as creatures capable of representing a supersensible order of nature – due to our rational power. Such an order can be constituted by means of our norm-giving will. Anthropology as a form of empirical knowledge, as presented in the *Anthropology from a Pragmatic Point of View* (1910, VII, 117–334), cannot tell us what forms intersubjectivity *shall* take. In order to satisfy our membership in a noumenal system of nature and in order to not merely describe the forms of intersubjectivity but to be able to identify those forms which *shall* occur, there is the need of a different knowledge, with a different attitude, namely not empirically but *a priori* proceeding knowledge.

4.3 Intersubjectivity Viewed in Terms of "State" and "Polity"

Kant does not (obviously) apply the notion intersubjectivity. In order to refer to various forms of intersubjectivity, he makes use of such concepts as "society" (*Gesellschaft*) or "commonwealth" (*das gemeine Wesen*). Kant characterises these different forms of "community" or forms of "commonwealth" by means of characterising "state" (*der Zustand*) and "polity" (*Verfassung*), which we deal or should deal with. What is that state and what is this polity? "State (*status iuridicus*) is [such] relation of the arbitrary will to the arbitrary will of others, by virtue of which everyone is capable of rights". Kant says that each such state must, in turn, be somehow constituted. It needs a form; a "polity" which is nothing else but the *state* which deals with the relationship of *combining* or *unifying* arbitrary will of one and arbitrary will of other. This unification (polity), can have a "purely objective" existence; it can exist "in the sense of the highest principle of possible states"; or it may be something "subjective", *i.e.* it may simply be "an act of arbitrary will" (1910, XXIII, 239). In other words, the polity (*i.e.* the state in which arbitrary volitions must be combined) may take one of two forms: (i) a state imposed by arbitrary will, which occurs in the form of *common will*, but this unification is then of subjective character; or (ii) it may have the status of an *idea* or *concept* of "combined arbitrary will", namely combined in a way which is completely unconstrained, yet, dictated by reason – such a unification would have an objective character.

4.4 Law and Freedom as the Fundamental Categories of Determining Intersubjectivity

These forms of intersubjectivity, which can be only determined by *a priori* proceeding knowledge, should primarily be taken into consideration. They also represent a major concern of Kant's practical philosophy. The thing that immediately hits the eye when looking at these Kantian insights is that these forms of intersubjectivity are perceived by Kant from a particular perspective; namely, from the perspective determined by two categories or two concepts: the concept of law[3] and the concept of freedom.[4] The latter is by no means merely a coincidence. Only by virtue of the freedom and ability to present the law, human beings belong to the noumenal system of nature. However, this means that any form of developing intersubjective relations is considered and classified in terms of mode of freedom and kind of law, which deal with, or rather, which we *are to deal* or *should deal with* in a case at issue.

In order to name and characterise these forms of human coexistence have to be explained firstly the modes of law and the kinds of freedom that can and must be discussed here. Likewise, it should be added that different modes and kinds of law and freedom determine these different states – understood as specific types of the relationship in which arbitrary volitions remain to each other. These states, in turn,

[3] The word "law" is used here deliberately in an ambiguous way, in order to cover both: the notion of "right", "entitlement" (*Recht*) and the notion of "norm" (*Gesetz*).

[4] "Freedom is in fact *ratio essendi* of moral law, while the moral law is *ratio cognoscendi* of freedom" (1910, V, 4fn).

demand to be manifested in a certain form of polity. They require such forming that arbitrary will of the one and arbitrary will of the other will be unified.

Let us start with "varieties" of freedom. Kant commences with the elementary "variety" of "authority" or "capacity" in terms of which freedom is rightly understood. He begins, therefore, with inherent freedom as a possibility to act; without freedom – perceived in an elementary way – it is not possible to imagine any other forms of freedom. These forms of freedom are derived by Kant from this very elementary concept of freedom by taking into account the conditions that must be fulfilled for a given pattern of freedom to be of a real character, rather than being merely a requirement of reason. From this basic concept of freedom, *i.e.* the possibility to act, reason leads us to conclude that this freedom could not be of viable character if my freedom did not match or, more precisely, if it did not harmonize with the same freedom of another agent by means of coercion exercised unilaterally, but it would rather harmonise while remaining "under the governance" of a certain norm, that is a rule which is superior in relation to our particularistic rules (*i.e.* the maxims of our actions) and it in the same way restricts my and your external freedom. Therefore, according to Kant, one's freedom – perceived as the possibility to act – should be interpreted in relation to the same freedom of others.

Of fundamental significance (determining the specificity of the whole Kantian thinking about "commonwealth" and therefore about intersubjectivity) is the awareness that the commonwealth is only possible under the conditions of certain frameworks. It distinguishes this thinking from all antagonistic concepts, glorifying conflict and struggle. The governance of this polity consists of nothing else but the unity of differing arbitrary wills under the rule of the common norm. Kant is, undoubtedly, fully aware of the existence of antagonisms and a clash of one arbitrary will with the other. The latter takes place on the empirical level, on the level of sensual system of nature, which we also belong to. However, due to our noumenal nature we have to look at ourselves as beings who are above those conflicts and struggles. This is the level at which it is feasible to imagine the conformity of arbitrary volitions. Without the existence of such a framework, where there is harmony between differing arbitrary wills, it is not possible to pursue one's own freedom. This freedom is conceived as the opportunity to pursue one's own life and one's own vision of prosperity. The conflict and the clash of particularities are inevitable. It does not mean, however, that we should not be able to provide a standard where opposing external freedoms remain in harmony. Going beyond the conflict, and ordered by reason, this harmony of external freedoms is only achievable under the rule of a particular norm. Furthermore, this norm is revealed to us by insight into the very concept of freedom and is, therefore, superior to this conflict and "sociability" (1910, VIII, 20).

Before going on to a brief characterization of "higher" kinds of freedom and, simultaneously, forms of intersubjectivity, it is necessary to explain areas of Kant's understanding of law. When referring to law, it is important to remember that the single word *law* covers both terms used by Kant: *Recht* and *Gesetz*, which are by no means synonyms (though in conceptual layer they are used by Kant as complementary concepts). The need to eliminate this ambiguity implies apt proposal to express the term *Gesetz* by the word "norm". The word *Recht* is ambiguous in German because it stands both for the system of regulations existing in certain conditions or juridical provisions as well as (or even primarily) for *entitlement*. On the one hand, there is a reference to that juridical order and to patterns of behaviour regulated by these provisions, passed by the relevant authority. On the other hand, there is a reference to "entitlement", which is understood very broadly. The latter can stand for entitlement, which has its basis in certain juridical regulations or norms, but also (or even primarily) an inherent entitlement based on "the norms dictated by reason" (*Vernunftgesetze*), *i.e.* on *dictamina rationis*.

4.5 The Basic Forms of Intersubjectivity in Natural State

Kant, as has already been noted, was aware of various forms of intersubjectivity existing on the empirical level. However, what interested him in particular were those forms of intersubjectivity which were called to be brought into existence by a norm-giving reason. Each of these forms is a certain embodiment of law (understood primarily as an entitlement but also as a norm) and freedom. How do these forms look like?

4.5.1 Fundamental Freedom and Its Rational "Adjustment"

Kant does not consider these forms in terms of time or history, but in a logical order which can also correspond to genetic order. However, this issue of correspondence is not essential at this time. What is crucial, on the other hand, is Kant's reasoning which leads from a situation where *one is somehow left to one's self with one's inborn entitlement to make use of one's external freedom*. In this situation, one is in fact left to one's self. However, reason can easily formulate the most general, the most basic norm that should govern this freedom. As Kant claims, reason derives this *a priori* knowledge from the very concept of freedom. This norm is as follows (1910, VI, 230):

> Right [or *legitimised*] action is every action which can coexist, in accordance with a certain universal norm, with the freedom of any [man], or it is [such action] that arbitrary volition of every [man] – in accordance with the maxim of that action – when complying with a certain universal norm, can coexist with the freedom of every [man].

This fundamental norm can also be expressed in the form of the following imperative: "act externally in such a way that the free use which you are making with your arbitrary volition, could – whilst adhering to a certain universal norm – coexist with the freedom of everyone". This imperative was derived from the concept of freedom and it is nothing else, as Kant believes, than the explication of the *elementary condition of compliance of the notion of freedom with one's self* and the latter condition is a restriction of freedom – understood as the arbitrary volition – by a requirement of compliance of the use made by man of his arbitrary will with the same use made by others from their arbitrary volition. Compliance to this imperative does not have to (unlike purely moral imperatives) result from regard for the norm expressed in the imperative. Therefore, it does not entail any "moral compulsion" to follow it. However, it carries another important detail conveyed to us by reason, namely, "in accordance with its idea, my freedom is limited to [acts feasible when meeting] these conditions and may also be actively limited to them by others" (1910, VI, 231). The first norm dictated by reason and concerning our freedom (what is meant by the latter, of course, is an external freedom, namely our arbitrary volition) is, therefore, a certain imperative peremptory information on a peculiar fundamental entitlement vested both in me as in my partner in intersubjective relationships; it is not only the entitlement to act but, above all, to resist someone who hinders the activity in accordance with the above principle. This is, in turn, equivalent to the legitimization to exert coercion upon him.

The abovementioned elementary form of intersubjectivity can be defined by the inherent entitlement to make external use of the possibility to act. Concurrently, it may be defined by awareness of the existence of an overarching principle, a particular norm which reason makes freedom subordinate to. One might say that, under this form, I know what conditions must be met when making use of external freedom. Besides the pressure that another person may exert on me (if he is strong enough to do that) or the coercion which I am entitled to exert due to the norm dictated to me by reason, there is nothing here that would guarantee the implementation of my innate entitlement. Additionally, there is nothing that would (with the exception of my reason) determine my right (understood as entitlement) and resolve the dispute concerning that right. Under these circumstances, everyone is one's own "rudder, sailor and ship", everyone is the judge for oneself, and the executor of one's entitlements. Such a situation is characteristic to natural state.

4.5.2 Acquisition and Its Principle – The Need for a Transition to Legal Status

The character of the abovementioned state is by no means changed by the second – next to the innate right of making use of external freedom – crucial fact that Kant focuses on when reconstructing the logic of forms of intersubjectivity: *i.e.* the need to deal with the use of external objects; the need to be in possession of something. In the case of this form of intersubjectivity, the object of arbitrary volition (that both arbitrary wills make a claim to) enters into the relationship between me and the other object of arbitrary volition. The conditions of exerting pressure on another person undergo a change in this situation. The condition of coercion, in a manner consistent with the norms of freedom, has (as its object of arbitrary volition) the same object that we took into our possession (1910, XXIII, 277):

> When it comes to having a particular thing – external in relation to me – I cannot in compliance with the norms of freedom exercise coercion against others in a different way than only

> when all others, whom I can enter into a relationship with, agree with me on this matter, namely only through the will of others reconciled with my will, it is only then in fact that I compel everyone – in line with norms of freedom – by means of their own volition.

In order for me to exert pressure on another person, in accordance with the norms of freedom, a change of conditions must exist. Their arbitrary will wishes, against my will, to: make use of my property; or, of the object of my arbitrary volition, I have to resort to a "united will of all"; or, as we might say, to "the will of all united with my own will". In other words, the will of those for whom the same thing is – or may be – the object of their arbitrary volition. What is needed, therefore, is to have and to acquire a reconciled arbitrary will. This follows the fact that "entering into possession", namely "acquiring" (*Erwerbung*) (which takes place at the level of developing the forms of intersubjectivity) imposes a certain obligation on others. It is a commitment "to do something or refrain from doing something", and it is manifested only at the moment of "entering into possession": "this obligation was not imposed on them prior to that act of mine" (1910, XXIII, 219), as Kant observes. Such an obligation may arise, however, only if the other party assumes such obligation: without *assuming* the obligation, we cannot speak about the existence of commitment; as Kant says: "there can be no commitment *vis-à-vis* anyone apart from the one that was assumed by this person itself" (*omnis obligatio est contracta*)". This means that "entering into possession", entailing the imposition of an obligation on the other, can take place in no other way than "through united arbitrary will of those who (by means of acquisition-entering into possession) create an obligation and conclude a contract with each other (*sich wechselseitig contrahiren*)" (1910, XXIII, 219).

The foregoing deliberations provide another imperative and another principle that should govern intersubjective relations. People inevitably enter these relations while an arbitrary will is unavoidably aimed at external objects and the need to acquire these goods or enter into their possession: "the primary principle (*Princip*) of any acquisition is the rule of limiting every (even unilateral) arbitrary volition by the requirement of compliance with possible universal unification of arbitrary volition [oriented] at the same object" (1910, XXIII, 219).

It is only under this form of intersubjectivity that the relations which people enter into among one another become legal relations. It is at that moment when a community is created. Thus it is a certain form of intersubjectivity in which legal or juridical regulation of both arbitrary freedom and the acquisition of these becomes indispensable.

4.5.3 Peculiar Duality of Legal State

Even though, by its very nature, it is of a legal character, this "acquisition", namely "entering into possession" of external objects, will be "temporary" in nature, rather than "peremptory" in nature (*vid.* 1910, VI, 256ff, 264ff, 267), until the principle of the abovementioned state becomes the principle which *actually* governs the reality: until the "legal status" (which for now is a deontic state) becomes reality. This state, that is legal in status, is a peculiar one in comparison to all other states and all other forms of intersubjectivity. In contrast to all other states, obtaining this state (or form of intersubjectivity) is a necessity which an external norm-giver and executor of this duty is entitled to enforce. In other words, even if we do not want to enter a legal state – whether it is us or someone else – according to a norm dictated by reason, we can be compelled to reach this state as much as we can compel the other to go to legal status.

Before we focus on a certain peculiarity of what is referred to as "legal status", we should briefly explain what is meant by the right when we speak of "legal status". This is, generally speaking, understood by Kant as "such a relationship between people which contains the conditions under which everyone is able to *exercise* their right [*i.e.* entitlement]" (1910, VI, 305fn). Right, conceived as entitlement, entails "being in the possession of arbitrary will of another person [standing for] [...] the possibility of inducing him in accordance with the standards [concerning] freedom by means of my arbitrary will to a certain action"; right can be therefore referred to as "an external property within causality of another person" (1910, VI, 271). When characterizing right, construed undoubtedly as the entitlement which corresponds obligation, Kant points out and firmly emphasises that this right applies only to a purely formal compliance between one and the other arbitrary will; thus, the wishes and needs, as well as the matter of arbitrary volition, remain outside the area of interest (1910, VI, 230):

> The concept of right [*i.e.* entitlement], in so far as it relates to the obligation corresponding with it (*i.e.* its moral concept) concerns, *firstly*, only the external and practical relation of one person towards another, as long as the activities of these people – as actions actually taking place (*facta*) may (directly or indirectly) exert influence on each other. *Secondly*, it does not stand for the attitude of arbitrary will [of one man] to the *wishes* of another (and thus also to its very need), as for example in activities defined as charitable or ruthless, but rather for the attitude to the *arbitrary* will of the other. *Thirdly*, in this mutual relationship of [one and the other] arbitrary will, we do not take into account the *matter* of arbitrary volition (*Willkür*), *i.e.* the aim which each of them wants to achieve together with the thing that s/he desires, for example, we do not ask whether someone can also have the benefit from the goods they are buying from me for trading purposes or not, we merely ask about the *form* of mutual relationship of volition (*Willkür*), as far as this volition is considered to be unencumbered and about whether the conduct of one of the two parties can be reconciled with the freedom of the other on the basis of a universal norm. Right is therefore a set of conditions under which the arbitrary will of one [man] can be reconciled with the arbitrary will of another, according to a certain universal norm [concerning] freedom.

The intersubjectivity that Kant refers to when speaking about legal state (about a certain relation that must take place as a necessity dictated by reason) is such intersubjectivity whose constitutive moment is a purely formally defined relationship of compatibility between differing arbitrary volitions. When looking from the perspective of deontic form of commonwealth (arising at this stage of its logical and rational reconstruction), feelings, sympathies, needs or goals of particular people, whose deeds are interdependent due to their mutual influence, remain irrelevant or they merely play a secondary role.

On the basis of a certain universal standard, the peculiarity of the legal status is the imperative to win the arbitrary will of the actors who mutually interact and is the dual character of this state. In other words, *de facto* exists in two forms. On the one hand, the legal status means the reconciliation of differing arbitrary volitions in accordance with a universal norm. As such, it entails the departure from natural state. On the other hand, however, an indispensable condition of departing from the natural state is to arrive at a specific reconciliation or unification of arbitrary will, namely, "a really universal unification carried out in order to establish norms" (1910, VI, 264). This fact, the unification due to the determination of norms, constitutes a hallmark of properly construed legal status, which is a real contrast to natural state. Opposition to this is civic state or, more precisely, legal-civic state.

4.5.4 Departing from the State of Private Law and Arriving at the State of Public Law (Explanation of Peculiarities)

The abovementioned peculiarity of this state (or rather its duality) was described by Kant in the penultimate chapter (§ 41) of the first part of *The Metaphysical First Principles of the Doctrine of Right*; a chapter dedicated to private law, with the title: "Transition from Property in Natural State to Property in the State of Law as such".[5] In order to identify this duality or peculiarity, it is necessary to reconstruct Kant's description of this (logical) transition.

Kant's point of departure is the abovementioned most general definition of legal status. According to this definition, legal state (*der rechtliche Zustand*) is "such a relationship between people, which includes the conditions under which the man is able to *exercise* right" (1910, VI, 305fn). According to the requirements of his metaphysical thinking,[6] Kant goes on to identify the formal principle which is constitutive for this state, *i.e.* to identify the "formal principle of this state being feasible". Considered in the light of "the idea of universally norm-making will", this principle is called "public justice". The principle of public justice, in turn, can be divided into three sub-principles, or rather we can speak of three components of public justice, distinguished by three modes (modalities) of "possession of objects ([understood] as the matter of arbitrary volition)" for the possession to "correspond to norm". These three modalities are as follows: *possibility* – when it comes to possession of things in compliance with norm; *reality* – when it comes to the same possession of things in accordance with norm; and finally, *the necessity* – when it comes to possession of things in compliance with norm. Accordingly, as Kant states, public justice "can be divided into *protective* justice (*iustitia tutatrix*), justice in

[5] In the translation of M. Gregor: "Transition from What Is Mine or Yours in a State of Nature to What is Mine or Yours in a Rightful Condition Generally" (Kant 1999, 450).

[6] What is meant by the above is a modern metaphysical thinking, applied to a specific area, namely to the sphere of *praxis*, that is to the question of commonwealth and the problem of human activity; it is by no means a coincidence that the lecture in law that is referred to is titled: *The Metaphysical First Principles of the Doctrine of Right*.

mutual acquisition [*i.e.* reciprocal] (*iustitia commutativa*) and *distributive* justice (*iustitia distributiva*)" (1910, VI, 306). A crucial, somewhat qualitative difference can be observed between the latter component of public justice and the first two components. This difference, however, only becomes visible and understandable in light of Kant's further argumentation. Here he continues on to analyse (while departing from the determination that state should be defined as a state which is not a legal status) which state should be considered as being in opposition to natural state. However, before we discuss these distinctions concerning non-legal state, as well as the one opposed to the natural state, we should indicate this crucial difference between the component of public justice, which referred to as distributive justice, protective justice and justice in mutual acquisition.

While differentiated due to "*possibility* (when it comes to possession of goods in compliance with norm)", what does protective justice consist of? In other words, what is actually determined by the norm which constitutes the precondition of protective justice? As Kant states, in the case of protective justice, the norm "determines only what conduct, by reason of its form is, looking from the inside, a *legitimate* behaviour (*lex iusti*)". In the case of the second component of public justice (namely, in the case of justice in *mutual acquisition*) norms (which similarly, as in the former case, guards a specific entitlement and ensures the possibility of exercising it by everyone) determine "what else, being the matter, shall also be subject to external normalization, *i.e.* what is [another] reason why the state of possession is [the state of possession] of a *legal nature* (*lex iuridica*)" (1910, VI, 306). As compared to the abovementioned forms of public justice, a very important difference becomes apparent with the transition to the third component of public justice. In the case of distributive justice, norms determine (1910, VI, 306):

> [W]hat particular ruling of the tribunal is in a particular case, in light of a certain norm (*unter dem gegebenen Gesetze*) adequate in relation to this norm, *i.e.* what is *valid*, final (*lex iustitiae*) and in such case the tribunal itself (*Gerichtshof*) is treated as the state *justice* and [when] one can ask – as the most important thing of all juridical cases – if the existence of such [*i.e.* state justice] can be spoken of or not.

While in the case of the first component, the norm itself determines the *form* of conduct only in relation to which it is *legitimate* (*recht*). In the case of the second component, the norm determines why the state of property, as a certain *matter*, may be of *legal character* (*rechtlich*); *i.e.* it meets the requirements to be externally subject to normative regulation. Finally, in the case of the third component of normative justice, the norm determines something that is placed at a qualitatively different level because it is placed at the level of a binding resolution (which is not necessarily valid or final) and a resolution of why "the ruling of the tribunal [issued] in a particular case is in the light of a particular norm adequate in relation to the latter"; in other words, why it is *valid or final* (*Rechtens*).

The specific character of this kind of public justice and peculiar implications, connected with the latter, are revealed as a result of Kant's use of the principle of opposites twice. However, the first opposition that Kant applies was *oppositum contradictorie.*[7] The second, *oppositum contrarie.*[8] That former opposition was used by Kant to determine non-legal state. Such state which is not legal is the one in which there is no distributive justice. This very state is defined as the *state of nature* (*status naturalis*). The second opposition, on the other hand, was applied by Kant in determining the state which should be opposed to the state of nature. Kant criticizes Achenwall's view according to which *social state* constitutes the opposition of the state of nature. It is not the social state which, according to Kant, could be reasonably referred to as an artificial state (*status artificialis*): placed in the antipodes of the state of nature – defined by Kant as such state in which there is no distributive justice. The state which constitutes actual opposition of the state of nature, is a civic state (*status civilis*), understood as a state of "community in which distributive justice rules". So it follows that we are indeed dealing with social state, with the community. But the factor that organizes this community is a special form of the principle of public justice – referred to as the principle of the legal state. As noted by Kant, the difference between this community and any other communities that may exist in the state of nature and can be "communities meeting the entitlements [of the members of this community]" (referred to in Kantian terminology as *rechtmäßige Gesellschaften*), lies in the fact that the norm requiring (in *a prioric* manner) participation in a given community does not apply to any of these communities. It is only the community in which distributive justice is the predominant one. Accordingly, participation in only this variant of "legal state" can be determined as a duty "of all the people who can enter into (even contrary to [their] own will) in legal relations with one another". Therefore, only this legal state may be referred to as "being a legal state as such" (1910, VI, 306).

If compared through the prism of three components, or three varieties of public justice, three of the abovementioned states (the state of *nature*, *social* state and *civic* state) can be classified as follows: "The first and second state can be referred to as the state of *private* law, and the third and the last one – as the state of *public* law" (1910, VI, 307). Kant emphasizes that in the case of the public law state, people are no more burdened with more responsibilities than those already imposed at the level of the private law: "the matter of private law is the same in both cases". The difference, however, is that "the norms of public law relate [...] exclusively to legal form of human coexistence (to the system), due to which these norms must necessarily perceived as public" (1910, VI, 306).

---

[7] *Oppositum contradictorie*, namely under the principle of contradiction, what can be also meant by the latter is the contradiction on the basis of *oppositum privative*, that is, on the basis of opposing, on the one hand, the lack which should not take place, on the other hand, property corresponding with this lack (*das Entgegengesetzte das nach Weise eines nicht sein sollenden Mangels und des entsprechenden Habens*) (*vid.* Schütz 2006, keyword: *oppositio*).

[8] *Oppositum contrarie* or *oppositum diametraliter*, namely oppositions on the basis of the greatest distance between two things in the same kind or species (*das Entgegengesetzte das nach Weise des größten Abstands zweier Dinge innerhalb derselben Gattung oder Art*) (Schütz 2006, keyword: *oppositio*).

This transition from private law to public law is, according to Kant, the postulate arising from the very private law in the natural state: "when remaining in a relation of inevitable coexistence with all others, you should depart from it [*i.e.* the natural state] and go to legal state, namely the state of distributive justice". According to Kant, the reason for such a transition "can be analytically derived from the concept of right (*Recht*) [being the entitlement that one has] in an external relation, [which constitutes] the opposition of [the concept] of violence (*violentia*) [in external relation]" (1910, VI, 307). This reason is clearly presented by Kant in § 42 of *The Groundwork for the Metaphysics of Law*. The reasons presented by Kant should be discussed in more details and thoroughly analysed.

The primary thesis in this paper is as follows: as long as the first party does not guarantee refrain from interfering in the subject of possession of the second party, the latter is also exempt from the obligation to refrain from interfering in the subject of possession of the former. The interpreter of this argument who assumes a different approach to Kant, and treats moral precepts, such as the Ten Commandments, as his point of departure could probably become indignant at this (alleged) exemption of this actor from moral obligation: for example, with the seventh commandment. This objection, however, may only present itself as justified on the basis of a particular pattern of thinking. For example, they believe intersubjective order is secondary to individuals, perceived to be equipped with the Decalogue, or having other strong moral backbone. On the basis of this thinking, external order and the behaviour of others seem to be irrelevant; the only thing which is crucial is to follow one's internal moral compass. It is on the basis of these moral actors that moral community is created. Legal provisions shall indeed be created, on account of those in whom this moral compass is defective and, therefore, must be either deterred by a system of penalties or subject to moral rehabilitation. Kantian thinking differs in this aspect. Kant foresaw the possibility of disposing a similar compass to the moral one: namely, reason. What has been pointed as a precondition of possession is mutual acceptance of this possession or ownership; Kant highlighted the principle which shall govern my conduct. At the same time, Kant was perfectly aware that the focal point, when determining the ethical basis of intersubjective relations, may not be sought in the moral properties of the individuals who enter into relations with one another, but in the normalization of these relations. These relations are dictated by reason according to the logic used in the formation of these relations; not so much through the individuals equipped with moral Decalogue, but through the interests that ensure others will not violently interfere in what does not belong to them. Thus, it is the internal logic of intersubjective relations which constitutes the source of intersubjective normative order. Although the latter will generally correspond to individual moral precepts (*v.gr.* with the seventh commandment), it does not have to be based on these commandments but rather on the norms dictated by reason. Such norms exist where the external freedom of one party corresponds with intersubjective relation of the other party.

The parties should, therefore, be interested in the transition from the state of private law to the state of public law. While remaining in the first state with one another, they remain in a state of "*äußerlich gesetzloser Freiheit*": a "freedom deprived of regulations in the external dimension" and, since they choose to remain in that state, "they do not act unfairly *vis-à-vis each other* if they fight with each other". As Kant notes, "[what] applies to one of them, shall also apply to the other, as if it was agreed between them" (1910, VI, 306). They do not act unfairly *vis-à-vis* each other because there are somehow in the state of "harmonizing" their arbitrary volition with each other. At the same time, however, Kant states that "what they do amounts to the highest iniquity by the fact that they want to live and remain in this state which is by no means a legal state, *i.e.* [it is such state] in which the ownership of no one is protected against violence [of others]" (1910, VI, 308).

Alongside the objection presented by Kant, a significant feature of this argument is that this "highest degree of iniquity" does not consist of a certain "wicked" deed *vis-à-vis* your neighbour. Generally, in this state, we cannot talk of individually committed wickedness. Instead, it rather consists of a refusal to join a deontic form of intersubjectivity. Moreover, this iniquity is not committed by the individual but by all those who do not intend to undergo a transition to the legal state, despite the fact that (even contrary to their own will) they enter into legal relations with each other.

4.6 The Basic Forms of Intersubjectivity in Civic State

According to Kant, the condition of citizenship is a legal status "where public norm-making authority exists" (1910, VI, 255, in the title of the chapter). As Kant notes, it is the civic state, perceived in this way that constitutes the opposition to natural state. Opposition to the *natural state,* therefore, is not the *social state*, as held by Gottfried Achenwall (*vid.* 1910, VI, 306)[9] and criticised in this context by Kant. It is a particular form of legal state in which the unification of arbitrary will (in accordance with a certain norm) shall take place due to a specific purpose; namely, on account of norm determination. Such unified will constitutes the source of *public law*, referred to as "the set of norms which, in order to create legal state, need to be commonly known".[10] *Public law* is not a system of norms designed for a specific, intrinsically unified community, be it by: blood, a common faith, the past, a common

[9] As Kant writes in his notes: "Natural state (*status naturali*) cannot be contrasted with social state (*Sociali*), just like parents cannot be contrasted with children; such distinctions cannot be undertaken. Communities can also exist in *statu naturali*, with the only difference, namely [there] is no public justice, which constitutes the guarantee for everybody of their lawful state [*i.e.* adequate in relation to their entitlements]" [in original version: "Der *status naturalis* kann nicht dem *Sociali e.g.* Eltern und Kinder entgegengesetzt und so die Eintheilung gemacht werden. – Denn *in statu naturali* können auch Gesellschaften seyn nur daß es keine öffentliche Gerechtigkeit giebt die jedem seinen rechtmäßigen Zustand sichert"] (1910, XXIII, 261).

[10] In contrast to them, the norms which in the community such as family or religious community, stipulate the entitlements of particular members of these communities, do not have to be commonly known.

language, living in a common territory, or due to common, substantively specified interests. Public law is (1910, VI, 311):

> [A] system of norms designed for certain people (*Volk*), *i.e.* a certain number of people or for a multitude of peoples who – on account of remaining in mutual interactions – need a legal state to ensure their participation in the legitimate order; namely such legal state in which the sovereignty [over them] shall be exercised by the will uniting them, [*i.e.* they need a] system (*constitutio*).

When the latter state is perceived by us through the prism of the relationship in which individuals remain in relation with one another, this state can be defined as a *civic state* (*status civilis*). In turn, as Kant suggests, the sum of these units, perceived from the perspective of its relations to its own component members, can be referred to as *the state* (*civitas*). On the other hand, when we look at the state through the prism of its form, *i.e.* when we perceive it as a certain whole "unified by common interest of all to be in a state of law", the term that should be given to this whole will be "*das gemeine Wesen* (*res publica latius sic dicta*), namely "common being" or "republic in the broader sense" (1910, VI, 311).

The form of intersubjectivity, which has been characterized following Kantian logic of (re)-constructing these forms, is now the state which is defined as "unification of a certain number of people under legal norms". At the same time, one must bear in mind that legal norms (*Rechtsgesetze*) (in contrast to moral norms – *Moralgesetze*, *moralische Gesetze*) are those in which norm-making is external. For this reason, this form of intersubjectivity in question has a peculiar feature (albeit shared with previous forms of intersubjectivity [re]-constructed by Kant), namely the fact that the participation in this form of intersubjectivity, understood as adherence to legal norm, may even be forced on a person against his arbitrary will. It can be a kind of "consolation" that this coercion stems from reason. At the very least, it should stem from reason and the freedom which was lost because this constraint only turns out to be truly regained in this form of intersubjectivity. We will encounter coercion stemming from reason when these legal norms, under which unification of a number of people takes place, will be "a priori necessary norms, *i.e.* interpreted *per se* from the concepts of external law (but they will not be posited norms [or established by statute])". The state which is in such a way conceived, namely the one in which "*a priori* necessary norms" are prevailing ones, is a state whose form is "a form of state in general, *i.e.* it is the state in the *idea*", or such "as it should be under pure principles of law".[11] In spite of various attempts to depreciate thinking in terms of deontic being, such perceptions of the state as the idea should not be underestimated. As Kant notes, "Such ideas can be treated as guidelines (*norm*) in case of every actual unification [of people] into common being (and accordingly, inside this unification)" (1910, VI, 313).[12]

---

[11] In a translation of W. Hastie: "The Form of the state is thus involved in the *Idea* of the State, viewed as it ought to be according to pure principles of Right" (Kant 1887, 165).

[12] In a translation of W. Hastie: "and this ideal Form furnishes the normal criterion of every real union that constitutes a Commonwealth" (Kant 1887, 165).

This very idea, that some act by which "the people constitute themselves in the form of the state", is known as "original contract" (1910, VI, 315), *contractus originarius*. Only when relying on that original contract it is possible to establish among people "a civil and thus completely lawful system (*Verfassung*) and a commonwealth". Although this is merely the idea of reasoning, and the original contract should not be treated as a certain fact, it is, nevertheless, a concept that has "unquestioned (practical) feasibility: it imposes on every norm-maker – provided the latter wants to be a citizen – the obligation to establish their rights in the way that they may result from the unified will of all the people, and to perceive every subordinate entity – provided he wants to be a citizen – from such perspective as if he, together with others, gave his consent to such will. This is indeed the touchstone of the legitimacy of any public norm" (1910, VIII, 297).[13]

In light of this, we reached the final comment on the first and most crucial of the two phases of improving the forms of intersubjectivity; a phase in which this improvement is realized mainly because of the need: to ensure the best possible conditions for implementing external freedom; and for improving that (perceived) intersubjectivity as intersubjectivity which serves as the best arrangement of intersubjective relations.

The second and, at the same time, latter stage of improving the forms of intersubjectivity is somewhat different. The primary objective of this stage is neither perfecting the possibilities of realizing external freedom, nor improving intersubjectivity for its own sake. Its primary goal is the development of the abovementioned intersubjectivity on account of the intention to improve human beings in the moral sense; or at least, to remove obstacles to man's self-perfection – *i.e.* removal of everything what weakens human willingness to confront evil intentions of wicked principles at hand. Since this factor, which weakens human positive forces is not "rough nature", but the people, "to whom he is related and bound" (1910, VI, 93), what should be therefore changed is the shape of that community; and, more precisely, what is meant here is that similarly like the man has risen *vis-à-vis* legal-civic state, in opposition to the state of nature, man should now ascend from the state which is, from an ethical standpoint, an ethical natural state, to "ethical-civic state", namely start functioning in ethical common existence, that is such which is based on moral laws, or laws of virtue.

This form of common existence, although higher in relation to political form of common existence and dictated by reason, cannot replace the former. This is due to the fact, *inter alia,* that unlike the political form of common existence (in which one is compelled to participate), in the case of ethical common existence the norms of virtue are not supported by coercion. Therefore, coercion is out of question.

[13] And in another translation: "has undoubted practical reality; for it can oblige every legislator to frame his laws in such a way that they could have been produced by the united will of a whole nation [*Volks*], and to regard each subject, in so far as he can claim citizenship, as if he had consented within the general will. This is the test of the rightfulness [*Rechtmäßigkeit*] of every public law" (Kant 2003, 79).

4.7 Conclusion

Two aspects of Kant's doctrine of forms of common existence deserve special emphasis. Thus, so do the levels or stages of constructing the intersubjectivity. Firstly, examples of constitutive character in the forms of intersubjectivity are *a priori* the principle or idea (*i.e.* the aforementioned idea of the source contract). Secondly, strict separation of the political form of common existence from ethical form of common existence is required. On account of the intellectual confusion prevailing in the minds of contemporary politicians (among them also some Polish) and many commentators, the knowledge of Kant's writings would certainly help to cope with the aforementioned turmoil and would aid prioritization of rules and principles over the will of empirical majority. Furthermore, it would undoubtedly dampen the desire to realize the moral purposes by means of political instruments. Familiarity with Kant's view would presumably also allow a determination of the legal-political forms of intersubjectivity from any other forms, which are not indispensable and lack innovation, and which differentiates them from political form, which is necessary and constructed.

References

Kant, I. 1887. *The philosophy of law. An exposition of the fundamental principles of jurisprudence as the science of right.* Trans. W. Hastie. Edinburgh: T. & T. Clark.

Kant, I. 1910. *Kants Gesammelte Schriften herausgegeben von der Königlich Preussischen Akademie der Wissenschaften*. Berlin: Druck und Verlag von Georg Reimer.

Kant, I. 1999. The metaphysics of morals (trans. M. Gregor). In *Practical philosophy*. Cambridge: Cambridge University Press.

Kant, I. 2003. On the common saying: This may be true in theory, but it does not apply in practice. In *Political writings*, ed. H.S. Reiss. Cambridge: Cambridge University Press.

Schütz, L. 2006. *Thomas-Lexikon*. Pamplona: Universität von Navarra. Available at: http://www.corpusthomisticum.org/tlo.html.

Chapter 5
Radbruch's Formula, Conceptual Analysis, and the Rule of Law

Brian H. Bix

5.1 Introduction

Gustav Radbruch (1878–1949) was a prominent German legal theorist, who, in the aftermath of World War II, presented a "Formula" in which he famously argued that a sufficiently unjust rule loses its status as a valid legal norm. This paper will consider the connection between the "Radbruch Formula" and the rule of law, and, in the process, also inquire whether the Formula is best understood as a conceptual claim about law, or rather as ("merely") a prescription for judicial decision-making.

Section 5.2 outlines Radbruch's "Formula," and places it in the context of his overall approach to legal theory, and the way that approach changed over time. Section 5.3 considers the connection between Radbruch's "Formula" and the rule of law. Section 5.4 considers Radbruch's formula critically as a conceptual claim about law, before concluding.

5.2 Radbruch's Formula(s)

In works written right after World War II, Radbruch offered influential ideas about the connection between the moral merits of a purported legal rule and its legal validity.[1] (2006a, b) Radbruch wrote (2006a, 6):

[1] Most commentators consider these post-War writings to be radical changes of view, in relation to Radbruch's pre-War writings (*v.gr.* Hart 1958, 616), but this claim of discontinuity has been contested. (*v.gr.* Paulson 1995, 2006; Leawoods 2000, 501–3) Resolving this dispute about continuity is not important for present purposes.

In focusing on Radbruch's "Formula", and associated post-War writings, I do not mean to slight the significance of his extensive earlier writings, on which, *vid. v.gr.* Pfordten (2008) and Leawoods (2000).

B.H. Bix (✉)
Frederick W. Thomas Professor of Law and Philosophy, University of Minnesota,
229 19th Ave. S., Minneapolis, MN 55455, USA
e-mail: bix@umn.edu

I.B. Flores and K.E. Himma (eds.), *Law, Liberty, and the Rule of Law*,
Ius Gentium: Comparative Perspectives on Law and Justice 18,
DOI 10.1007/978-94-007-4743-2_5, © Springer Science+Business Media Dordrecht 2013

> Positivism is, moreover, in and of itself wholly incapable of establishing the validity of statutes. It claims to have proved the validity of a statute simply by showing that the statute had sufficient power behind it to prevail. But while power may indeed serve as a basis for the 'must' of compulsion, it never serves as a basis for the 'ought' of obligation or for legal validity.

He then goes on to offer two different elaborations of his "Formula" (2006a, 7):

1. The positive law, secured by legislation and power, takes precedence even when its content is unjust and fails to benefit the people, unless the conflict between statute and justice reaches such an intolerable degree that the statute, as 'flawed law', must yield to justice.
2. Where there is not even an attempt at justice, where equality, the core of justice, is deliberately betrayed in the issuance of positive law, then the statute is not merely 'flawed law', it lacks completely the very nature of law. For law, including positive law, cannot be otherwise defined than as a system and an institution whose very meaning is to serve justice.

In the article, the second formula is offered as a clear application of the first formula, but subsequent commentators have, reasonably, treated the two characterizations as separate formulas. And judges have tended to use the first formulation, given the likely problems in trying to apply the second formula, with its focus on legislators' subjective intentions, in actual cases (*v.gr.* Haldemann 2005, 166).

It helps to understand the significance of the "Radbruch Formula", and its place both within European jurisprudential thought and within Radbruch's own work, to compare it with assertions made in Radbruch's pre-War writings. In his early writings, Radbruch argued that there were three elements in "the idea of law": "justice", "expediency or suitability for a purpose", and "legal certainty" (1950, 107–8). In those writings, Radbruch seemed to assert that it was the third element, legal certainty, which was the most important, at least within the idea of law: "It is more important *that* the strife of legal views be ended than that it be determined *justly* and *expediently*. The existence of a legal order is more important than its justice and expediency…." (1950, 108, emphasis in original).[2]

This view then leads Radbruch, in that early work, to say the following about the role and duties of judges in relation to unjust laws (1950, 119):

> [H]owever unjust the law in its content may be, by its very existence, it has been seen, it fulfils one purpose, *viz.*, that of legal certainty. Hence the judge, while subservient to the law without regard to its justice, nevertheless does not subserve mere accidental purposes of arbitrariness. Even when he ceases to be the servant of justice because that is the will of the law, he still remains the servant of legal certainty. We despise the parson who preaches in a sense contrary to his conviction, but we respect the judge who does not permit himself to be diverted from his loyalty to the law by his conflicting sense of the right.

[2] United States Supreme Court Justice Louis Brandeis made a similar observation in relation to precedent: "*Stare decisis* is usually the wise policy, because in most matters it is more important that the applicable rule of law be settled than that it be settled right." *Burnet v. Coronado Oil & Gas Co.*, 285 U.S. 393, 406 (1932) (Brandeis, J., dissenting). Of course, the Brandeis quotation, with its careful limitation of "in most matters", leaves open the argument that the treatment of truly unjust laws should be different.

There seems to be a sharp contrast between Radbruch's recommendation in this earlier work, and what he will prescribe in his later "Formula". One can certainly see a kind of continuity: that Radbruch arguably is still seeing the same factors in the nature of law; he is simply weighing them slightly differently, arguing that certainty, even when combined with "expediency and suitability", is not always predominant, but must give way in those cases where the claims of (in)justice are strong enough.

5.3 The Formula and the Rule of Law

In his pre-War writings, Radbruch spoke of the tension between "the demands of legal certainty", on one hand, and "the demands of justice and expediency", on the other. (1950, 118) While he adds that "[t]he three aspects of the idea of law are of equal value, and in case of conflict there is no decision between them but by the individual conscience", he later offers that "[i]t is the professional duty of the judge to validate the law's claim to validity, to sacrifice his own sense of the right to the authoritative command of the law, to ask only what is legal and not if it is also just." (1950, 118 and 119) As will be discussed at greater length later, this strong – perhaps too-strong – equation of the analysis of the law and prescriptions for judicial behaviour is characteristic of both Radbruch's earlier work and his later writings.

The prescription for judges changed in Radbruch's later works, as can be seen in his "Formula". In another one of his later works, Radbruch writes: "Measured by… higher law, lawlessness remains lawlessness when accomplished through legal forms…" (quoted in Fuller 1954, 484).[3] In such references to "lawlessness" in official actions (see also the title of Radbruch 2006a), we can see a connections being offered between Radbruch's analytical claims and the rule of law.

In Lon Fuller's terms (and, to some extent, reflecting Fuller's particular perspective), Radbruch's "Formula" was a response to (Fuller 1954, 482):

> [T]he dilemma faced by Western Germany and the occupying powers in having, on one hand, to restore lawful procedures and a respect for law, and being forced, on the other, to declare retroactively void some of the more outrageous "laws" of the Nazi regime.

Or, in Fuller's later phrasing: "Germany had to restore both respect for law and respect for justice. Though neither of these could be restored without the other, painful antinomies were encountered in attempting to restore both at once…" (1958, 657).

[3] Fuller cites Gustav Radbruch, "Die Erneuerung des Rechts", in 2 *Die Wandlung* 9 (Fuller 1954, 484fn).

Radbruch's "Formula" had been a focal point in the famous 1958 debate between H.L.A. Hart (1958, 615–21) and Lon Fuller (1958, 648–57). Part of the dispute between Hart and Fuller regarding Radbruch and his "Formula", was about the proper response to evil laws and evil regimes. Hart reads Radbruch as encouraging the courts to treat the evil laws of the Nazi regime as "not law", and therefore no shield for a woman who tried to get her husband killed under the rubric of one such law.[4] Hart, with some hesitation, would support punishing the woman, but would prefer that it be done under frankly "retrospective criminal legislation" (1958, 620). Hart argued for the independent virtue of responding to a moral dilemma with "candour" and "plain speech" (1958, 620 and 621).

Fuller viewed Radbruch's position both as a pragmatic compromise in responding to a change from an evil regime,[5] and as a deep insight into the moral foundations of the nature of law. In particular, Fuller focused on the procedural injustices (the focus of his own "procedural natural law theory) (1958, 1969), like secret and retroactive laws, which, he argued, were contrary to "the very nature of law itself" (1958, 650).

As for the German court cases, and whether the courts made a mistake by treating the unjust Nazi laws as "not law" (and Hart's argument that courts and theorists should separate whether some norm is law from whether it should be applied), Fuller wrote (1958, 655):

> So far as the courts are concerned, matters certainly would not have been helped if, instead of saying, 'This is not law,' they had said, 'This is law but it is so evil we will refuse to apply it.' Surely moral confusion reached its height when a court refuses to apply something it admits to be law.

How all of this fits into debates regarding the rule of law is not self-evident. In part, this is because there are many different notions of the rule of law (Tamanaha 2004; Raz 1994, 354–62; 2009, 210–29).[6] Generally, the arguments about the rule of law focus on certain formal or procedural requirements: that the government is limited by law, that certain forms are followed in the efforts to guide citizen behaviour, and that official discretion in the application of rules is limited ("the rule of law, not men") (Tamanaha 2004, 137–41). A small number of theorists advocate more substantive conceptions of the rule of law; such substantive versions tend to

[4] Apparently, both Hart and Fuller misunderstood the holding of a post-War West German case they were discussing, as it had been misreported in an earlier issue of the *Harvard Law Review* (Pappe 1960, 261–3).

[5] "Intolerable dislocations would have resulted from any… wholesale outlawing of all that had occurred [under the Nazis]. On the other hand, it was equally impossible to carry forward into the new government the effects of every Nazi perversity that had been committed in the name of law…." (Fuller 1958, 648).

[6] One should note that The World Justice Project has created a "Rule of Law Index", which ranks countries based on dozens of factors, based on a view of the rule of law which is primarily procedural. The ranking and information about it can be found at http://worldjusticeproject.org/rule-of-law-index/.

include requirements of democracy and the protection of certain basic human rights (Tamanaha 2004, 102–13).

Whether one sees the "Radbruch Formula" as sharply inconsistent with the rule of law, required by the rule of law, or neither, depends on which conception of the rule of law one accepts. If one's idea of the rule of law is minimal and formal/procedural, then one might even see Radbruch's "Formula" as *contrary to* the rule of law, as the formula seems to require courts to refuse to enforce, on occasion, norms which have been created according to all the procedural requirements of the particular legal system. Julian Rivers (1999) picks up on a detail of the Radbruch Formula, one also emphasized in the Hart-Fuller debate (Hart 1958; Fuller 1958), in his argument that a too-great judicial willingness to override or rewrite unjust laws is contrary to both democracy and the rule of law.[7] Rivers understands that under Radbruch's original formulation, norms only lose their legal status when their injustice reaches "an intolerable level", but he is concerned that courts that apply the "Formula" are likely to be tempted to withhold legal status even from norms that are only moderate in their injustice.

Radbruch's "Formula", and his conception of law, is based on the notion that people may not expect their legal system to be uniformly just and fair, but there *is* an expectation of minimal justice that comes with the notion of "legality". This view could be translated into Robert Alexy's well-known assertion: "Every legal system lays claim to correctness" (2002, 34). And it seems to assert something more than Joseph Raz's conclusion that law necessarily *claims* that it possesses legitimate authority (though, as Raz points out, this claiming need not be well-grounded, and Raz in fact claims that it rarely is) (1994, 199).[8] Though Raz's and Alexy's theoretical positions appear to be similar, there seem to be important differences, reflected in the fact that Raz sees law's claim to authority as consistent with a legal positivist view of law, while Alexy views his "correctness thesis" as central to his critique of legal positivism.

And before one was too quick to connect either of those theories to Radbruch's post-War theory, one should observe that though the Alexy and Raz theories *could* be applied to individuals norms, they are most apt when discussing normative systems as a whole (that is, the question of what it is that makes a normative system as a whole "law"/"legal" or "not law"), while Radbruch's formula is more clearly focused on individual norms (that those that are too unjust are not, or no longer, "law").

In practice, the Radbruch "Formula" is most likely to be applied where there has been some form of transition in the relevant regime, such that a judge from one system or tradition is asked to apply (or not apply) the law of another system or tradition: post-War Germany dealing with its Nazi past; unified German dealing with the East German past; and so on. I am unaware of courts using the Radbruch

[7] Rivers' preference, like that of both Hart and Fuller, is for retroactive legislation (Rivers 1999).

[8] On Raz's view about the obligation to obey the law (*vid.* Raz 1994, 325–38).

"Formula" to refuse enforcement of otherwise valid legal norms enacted by their own regime's legislature[9]; and one assumes that even if there are such instances, they are very rare.

The problem of legal transitions is not often discussed in debates about the rule of law, where the assumption is that we should be focusing on whether officials are sufficiently bound by their own system's rules (not whether the system's rules will continue to bind – and to authorize – even after the society is taken over by a different sovereign). However, as Fuller pointed out long ago, it is during just such transitions where "fidelity to law" and "fidelity to justice" can conflict in ways difficult to respond to well.

In Robert Alexy's defense of the "Radbruch Formula", he characterizes the debate from the beginning as one connected with the rule of law, but the connection is not as evident as he implies. Alexy writes (1999, 15):

> In both cases [the post-World War II cases dealing with Nazi law, and the post-reunification cases dealing with East German law] the following question had to be answered. Should one regard as continuing to be legally valid something which offended against fundamental principles of justice and the rule of law when it was legally valid in terms of the positive law of the legal system which had perished.

Given the focus of this article and this collection, I want to focus on the phrase in Alexy's summary, that the question is about norms which "offend [...] against fundamental principles of justice *and the rule of law*" (emphasis added). As Alexy recognizes, the "Radbruch Formula" is about extreme injustice, with an emphasis on the content of the purportedly legal norm, not its procedural history.[10]

Alexy never makes clear in what way he believes that the norms subject to the Radbruch formula "offend [...] the rule of law", nor, in fact, does he explain what he means by the rule of law. If one takes a conventional view of the rule of law as equivalent with the kind of procedural justice requirements outlined by Lon Fuller's "internal morality of law" (1958, 1969), then extremely unjust laws often are also laws that violated minimal procedural requirements. Fuller himself noted a number of instances among the Nazi rules: secret laws, retroactive laws, and interpretations and applications of law that seemed to differ sharply from the text being applied (1958, 651–5) However, it would be quite another thing to assume (as Alexy's off-hand language appears to assume) that *all* extremely unjust rules, because extremely unjust, violate the rule of law, understood as a requirement of procedure and form

[9] Refusing enforcement on Radbruchian grounds is to be distinguished from more conventional forms of judicial invalidation of otherwise valid norms – *v.gr.* holding the norm invalid because it conflicted with a provision of the regime's own constitution or supra-national constitution or treaty to which the country is a signatory, like the European Convention on Human Rights.

[10] At least in the first formulation of the "Formula". As discussed above, the second formulation refers to the intentions with which legislation was enacted, but that still does not go to the sort of procedural inquiries usually associated with the rule of law.

(Haldemann 2005, 176).[11] There seem to be too many recent counter-examples (from countries like East Germany and pre-Apartheid South Africa)[12] to make that equation.

5.4 The Formula and Conceptual Analysis

Within the Hart-Fuller debate and in Robert Alexy's discussion and adaptation of the work, Radbruch's formula is presented as a central part of an anti-legal positivist theory about the nature of law (Radbruch 2006a; Alexy 1999, 2002; Hart 1958; Fuller 1958; *vid.* also, Sartor 2009). Radbruch himself portrays his "Formula", and his post-World War II writings in general as a turn away from his earlier espousal of legal positivism.[13]

However, it is important to clarify what it might mean to say that the Radbruch Formula is a criticism about legal positivism, as opposed to being a theory in an entirely different debate. Legal positivism is a theory about the nature of law (Bix 2005). The question is to what extent the Radbruch formula should be considered as not directed, or not *primarily* directed, towards debates about the nature of law, but rather directed (primarily) towards questions about how judges should decide cases (a debate at least as controversial, and certainly as important, if not more important, than the debate about the nature of law).

At a surface level, there is no doubt that, whatever else it is, the "Radbruch Formula" does work as instructions to judges as to how to decide cases. Judicial decision-making (by West German courts responding to actions purportedly done under the authorization of Nazi laws) is the context for Radbruch's introduction of his "Formula" in his post-War articles (2006a, 1–6).[14]

Additionally, if Radbruch's "Formula" is a conceptual claim about the nature of law, then it is (by definition) a claim about all existing and all possible legal systems.

---

[11] If one adopts a substantive version of the rule of law, that includes requirements for protecting certain human rights, then laws unjust because they violate those rights will also be (by definition) contrary to the rule of law. However, as discussed above, this is a distinctly minority understanding of the rule of law. Additionally, there are likely to be laws that are unjust without necessarily violating whatever shortlist of human rights a substantive rule of law might include.

[12] Some would argue that there are also plenty of examples of extremely unjust laws (enacted with proper procedures) in the United States and Western Europe, but that is a controversy far beyond the scope of this article.

[13] Though, as earlier noted, *vid. supra* note 1, there are also those who claim a greater continuity and unity in Radbruch's work.

Regarding legal positivism, Radbruch, along with Lon Fuller, asserted that legal positivism played a role in the Nazi's rise to power in Germany (*vid.* Paulson 1994).

[14] And comparable decisions made by the courts in a unified Germany, evaluating actions done purportedly under the authorization of East German law, is the context for some of Alexy's discussion of his version of the Radbruch formula (Alexy 1999, 2002).

That may not be a good description of the "Formula". As regards Radbruch's argument that significantly unjust norms are not valid legal norms, one could certainly understand such a claim made internally to a particular legal system, about the criteria of validity of that legal system. It is far less clear what is meant by a theorist, like Radbruch, making this claim about all (and all possible) legal systems.[15]

The assumption in Radbruch's last works seems to have been: (a) that if a norm is valid in a legal system, then it must be applied to a legal dispute before a court; and (b) if a norm is not a valid norm of a legal system, it should not (or cannot) be applied to a legal dispute before the court. As propositions describing current legal practices,[16] both claims seem to be false.

As to the first claim, that valid legal norms are always applied, it is a common principle in many legal systems that judges have the power to modify or create exceptions in rules (particularly judge-created rules, but also, in some jurisdictions and on some occasions, statutes) when their application would otherwise lead to an absurd or unjust result.[17]

As for the second, that norms that are not valid in the legal system are never applied, there are a number of significant exceptions. There are minor, technical exceptions: as when resolving a dispute requires a court to apply norms from another legal system (*v.gr.* in resolving a contract dispute, when the contract was entered in another country), or norms of a non-public organization (as when the dispute centres on the application of a corporate or club charter), or even the norms of logic or mathematics. There are also well-known general exceptions, when courts are authorized, or perhaps even obligated, to apply extralegal moral or policy norms in the process of elaborating, clarifying, or improving the law. In common-law countries, like the United States and England, judicial development of the law is accepted and frequent, even if not quite as central as it had been in past centuries. When courts change the law, the normative reasons justifying the change (*v.gr.* "justice requires that those who cause harm must compensate for the harm" or "norms should be made as efficient as possible") are almost always norms that are not already valid within the legal system.[18] However, judges see themselves as legally bound, or at

[15] I elaborate this point in the context of a critique of both Alexy and the later Radbruch (*vid.* Bix 2006).

[16] At least of the legal systems with which the author is familiar.

[17] Of course, in most jurisdictions courts also have the authority, and frequently the duty, to refuse to apply a statute when its application would be contrary to the country's constitution or basic law, or contrary to the country's treaty obligations. However, this example is less useful for the purpose of the present discussion, as many commentators would characterize the conflict with the constitution or the treaty as making the statute invalid.

[18] I am putting aside, for the moment, the claim occasionally still heard that most common law reasoning is merely a process of the law "work[ing] itself pure", *Omychund v. Barker* (Ch. 1744), 1 Atk. 21 at 33, 26 ER 15 at 22–3, *i.e.* that such decisions are merely discovering norms that were, in some sense, already part of the law. Few commentators would accept this as universally true of common law decision-making, and there is little evidence of which I am aware that Radbruch supported such a view.

least legally free (and morally bound), to change the law in this way. Given that "valid norm" cannot be equated with "norm that must be applied", the direction to judges "not to apply a norm in particular circumstances" is not helpfully translated into the claim "that norm is not valid".

One can come at the problem from another direction, which clarifies that Radbruch's primary purpose (and the purpose of most of those who support application of his "Formula") is the direction of judicial behaviour, not any analytical claim about the nature of law. Consider this example: How would a believer in Radbruch's "Formula" respond to a judge who applied an extremely unjust norm (without first using Radbruch's test)? One possibility would be for the Radbruch follower to say that what the judge applies, because it is an extremely unjust norm, is simply not a legally valid norm. However, as discussed above, judges apply norms *all the time* that are not valid norms of their legal system (*v.gr.* extralegal moral norms). But that is clearly not what Radbruch was getting at: he wanted judges *not* to apply these unjust norms. To see the debate as strongly analogous to legal realist or Dworkinian debates about whether certain norms or factors are "legal" or "extralegal" and whether judges are obligated to apply them, or can do so at their discretion (*v.gr.* Dworkin 1977, 1–130), would clearly be a misreading. Radbruch's clear point (understood by all interpreters) is that judges should not apply these norms. Thus, the conclusion here offered is that Radbruch is basically offering a prescription for judicial decision-making, not a conceptual (or other theoretical) claim applicable to all (possible) legal systems.

It must be noted that though (as I hope I have shown) one can clearly see the theoretical difference between the distinction between legally valid and invalid norms, on one hand, and whether or not to apply a norm to a legal dispute, on the other hand, the difference may be less evident for the kind of norms on which Radbruch (and his followers) were focusing. Arguably, one would have no trouble finding examples of judges applying norms that are extremely unjust; one can even find numerous such examples for situations where the judge is applying the norm even though the judge considers herself to be doing this as a matter of discretion rather than a matter of duty. What is likely rare are examples of judges applying norms *they* consider to be extremely unjust in circumstances where *they* consider themselves to have discretion whether to apply the norms or not.

While justice may (by most accounts) be an objective matter, it is a matter over which there is pervasive disagreement. When we observe what *we* believe to be the court's application of an extremely unjust law, the judge's perspective will almost always be different. The judge will either not perceive the norm as (extremely) unjust, or will believe that the unjust norm is one that he or she is obligated to apply, despite its injustice.

However, this is a tangent. To return to the basic inquiry: if Radbruch's intention was to direct judges, why did he choose this somewhat indirect route of a theory about the nature of legal validity? Part of the answer may be in the legal and political culture, and indeed the general social expectations, of the time(s) and place(s) in which Radbruch lived. In continental Europe, the strong expectation was that the law was fully present in the civil codes, and the judge's only task was to apply the law.

This was not a universal belief, but the fact that the Free Law Movement (*v.gr.* Gray 1999, 1, 314–8) was considered highly radical for even *suggesting* that judges had and should have discretion, indirectly shows the rigid view of judging in the conventional thought of that day. Against this backdrop, one can see why a theorist would not merely suggest that judges should modify or refuse to enforce otherwise valid law. Such a prescription is easier to make in a common law country (where it is understood that judges develop the law, even if they might claim that they were merely "discovering" it), and to modern legal theorists, who unapologetically discuss judicial discretion and judicial lawmaking. For Radbruch, perhaps the only way to make prescriptions for judicial decision-making palatable to his audience was to coat them in claims about the validity of individual norms.

5.5 Conclusion

Gustav Radbruch's "Formula", indicating that significantly unjust laws should not be enforced, is generally understood (including by its author) as a claim about the nature of law and legal validity. Its connection with rule of law values is uncertain, depending in large parts on whether one accepts a largely formal or procedural conception of the rule of law, or a more substantive one.

There are also questions about whether the "Radbruch Formula" is best or most charitably understood on its own terms, as a claim about the nature of law, rather than more narrowly as a prescription about how judges should decide cases. In most legal systems, courts frequently apply (and see themselves as bound to apply) norms that *are not* valid within their legal system, and the courts also on occasion do not apply (and see themselves as bound not to apply) otherwise applicable norms that *are* valid norms within their legal system. This is part of the complex role of judges, particularly (but not exclusively) within common law legal systems, which includes resolving disputes where the ruling norms come from outside the home legal system (or, from any legal system), and the courts may also have responsibilities to develop the law and to avoid unjust or absurd applications of otherwise valid norms.

It would seem more charitable to read the Radbruch formula as a prescription for judicial decision-making rather than as a descriptive, conceptual or analytical claim about the nature of law. Or, to put the same point a different way, reconstructing Radbruch's "Formula" in this way makes it more sensible and defensible.

The suggested change will not affect the place of the "Radbruch Formula" within debates about the rule of law or the role of courts. The issue remains the same: whether it is consistent with the rule of law not to apply norms otherwise legally valid because they are extremely unjust. Radbruch argued that this is consistent with the general understanding of law and the expectations for law. Other commentators have been concerned that Radbruch's approach undermines the rule of law by giving significant and unpredictable discretion to judges to refuse to apply otherwise valid norms.

References

Alexy, R. 1998. Law and correctness. *Current Legal Problems* 51: 205.

Alexy, R. 1999. A defence of Radbruch's formula. In *Recrafting the rule of law: The limits of legal order*, ed. D. Dyzenhaus. Oxford: Hart Publishing.

Alexy, R. 2002. *The argument from injustice: A reply to legal positivism.* Trans. S.L. Paulson and B. Litschewski-Paulson. Oxford: Clarendon Press.

Bix, B.H. 2005. Legal positivism. In *The Blackwell guide to the philosophy of law and legal theory*, ed. M.P. Golding and W.A. Edmundson. Oxford: Blackwell Publishing.

Bix, B.H. 2006. Robert Alexy, Radbruch's formula, and the nature of legal theory. *Rechtstheorie* 37: 139. Available at: http://papers.ssrn.com/sol3/papers.cfm?abstract_id=892789.

Dworkin, R. 1977. *Taking rights seriously*. Cambridge, Massachusetts: Harvard University Press.

Fuller, L.L. 1954. American legal philosophy at mid-century. *Journal of Legal Education* 6: 457.

Fuller, L.L. 1958. Positivism and fidelity to law – A reply to professor Hart. *Harvard Law Review* 71: 630.

Fuller, L.L. 1969. *The morality of law*, 2nd ed. New Haven: Yale University Press.

Gray, C.B. 1999. *The philosophy of law: An encyclopedia*, II vols. New York: Garland Publishing.

Haldemann, F. 2005. Gustav Radbruch vs. Hans Kelsen: A debate on Nazi law. *Ratio Juris* 18: 162.

Hart, H.L.A. 1958. Positivism and the separation of law and morals. *Harvard Law Review* 71: 593.

Leawoods, H. 2000. Gustav Radbruch: An extraordinary legal philosopher. *Washington University Journal of Law and Policy* 2: 489.

Pappe, H.O. 1960. On the validity of judicial decisions in the Nazi era. *Modern Law Review* 23: 260.

Paulson, S.L. 1994. Lon L. Fuller, Gustav Radbruch, and the 'positivist' theses. *Law and Philosophy* 13: 313.

Paulson, S.L. 1995. Radbruch on unjust laws: Competing earlier and later views? *Oxford Journal of Legal Studies* 15: 489.

Paulson, S.L. 2006. On the background and significance of Gustav Radbruch's post-war papers. *Oxford Journal of Legal Studies* 26: 17.

Pfordten, D. van der. 2008. Radbruch as an affirmative holist: On the question of what ought to be preserved of his philosophy. *Ratio Juris* 21: 287.

Radbruch, G. 1950. Legal philosophy. In *The legal philosophies of Lask, Radbruch, and Dabin*, ed. Patterson, E.W. (trans. Wilk, H.). Cambridge, MA: Harvard University Press.

Radbruch, G. 2006a. Statutory lawlessness and supra-statutory law (trans. Litschewski-Paulson, B. and Paulson, S.L.). *Oxford Journal of Legal Studies* 26: 1.

Radbruch, G. 2006b. Five minutes of legal philosophy (trans. Litschewski-Paulson, B. and Paulson, S.L.). *Oxford Journal of Legal Studies* 26: 13.

Raz, J. 1994. *Ethics in the public domain*. Oxford: Clarendon.

Raz, J. 2009. *The authority of law*, 2nd ed. Oxford: Oxford University Press.

Rivers, J. 1999. The interpretation and invalidity of unjust laws. In *Recrafting the rule of law: The limits of legal order*, ed. D. Dyzenhaus. Oxford: Hart Publishing.

Sartor, G. 2009. Legality policies and theories of legality: From *Bananas* to Radbruch's formula. *Ratio Juris* 22: 218.

Tamanaha, B.Z. 2004. *On the rule of law: History, politics, theory*. Cambridge: Cambridge University Press.

Chapter 6
Law, Liberty and the Rule of Law (in a Constitutional Democracy)

Imer B. Flores

Tse-Kung asked, saying "Is there one word which may serve as a rule of practice for all one's life?"

K'ung-fu-tzu said: "Is not reciprocity (i.e. 'shu') such a word? What you do not want done to yourself, do not do to others."

Confucius (2002, XV, 23, 225–226).

6.1 Introduction

Taking the "rule of law" seriously implies readdressing and reassessing the claims that relate it to law and liberty, in general, and to a constitutional democracy, in particular. My argument is five-fold and has an addendum which intends to bridge the gap between Eastern and Western civilizations, on behalf of both "global harmony and the rule of law" and is dedicated to the memory of Neil MacCormick:

Firstly, we will *a la* Jeremy Waldron, on the one hand, criticize the conceptions, including the *dualist* – or *weak* – and the *monist* – or *strong* – theses explaining the relationship between "law" and "State" that equate the "rule of law" to the formal assertion that the "law rules" and even worse reduce it either to the "rule of precedent" or "adjudicative/judicial rule of law" ("judicialism") or to the "rule of statute" or "legislative rule of law" ("legalism"). Both options fail by presupposing that for a complete apprehension of the "rule of law" it is sufficient to be acquainted with the "law" – by notions such as "precedent" or "statute", as well as "adjudication" or

I.B. Flores (✉)
Law School and Legal Research Institute,
National Autonomous University of Mexico (UNAM), Mexico City, Mexico
e-mail: imer@unam.mx

I.B. Flores and K.E. Himma (eds.), *Law, Liberty, and the Rule of Law*,
Ius Gentium: Comparative Perspectives on Law and Justice 18,
DOI 10.1007/978-94-007-4743-2_6,

"legislation" – to derive mechanically what the "rule of law" is. On the other hand, we will also scrutinize the claim suggesting that instead of presupposing that the comprehension of the "law" will lead us into the knowledge of the "rule of law" it is the other way around: it is necessary to have a better – and more substantial – conception of the "rule of law" to have a better – and more substantial – perception of the "law".

Secondly, in the hunt for a better – and more substantial – awareness of the "law", we intend to revisit the different notions related to the "rule of law". Although it is true that they are neither equivalent nor unequivocal, they might shed some light into our discussion, from the classical distinction between the "government of/under men" ("passion") and the "government of/under laws" ("reason") in Socrates, Plato and Aristotle, and the principles of "equality before/under law" (identified with the Greek word *isonomia*), or "freedom before/under law" in Marcus Tullius Cicero and in Edward Coke to the contemporary distinctions between the "adjudicative/judicial or legislative rule of law" and the "constitutional or institutional rule of law", including the tensions between the *ragione di Stato* (*i.e.* reason of State) and the *Stato della ragione* (*i.e.* State of reason); the *Machtstaat* (*i.e.* State of power/force) and *rechtsstaat* (*i.e.* State of law); *derecho de Estado* (*i.e.* law of State) and *Estado de derecho* (*i.e.* State of law or even State-law); and, *law's empire* – the expression popularized by Ronald Dworkin – or even *empire of law*.

Thirdly, in the pursuit for the embedded principles in a "constitutional rule of law", we pretend to recognize first *a la* Friedrich August Hayek some of the principles of the "rule of law", by revisiting analytically and critically Cicero's thought: the conception of general rules; the conception that we obey the law in order to be and remain free; and the conception that the judge is a law that speaks/with voice and the law is a speechless/voiceless judge. All of which are still in force more or less in those exact terms, except the last one which has been distorted by Charles Louis de Secondat, baron de La Brède et de Montesquieu, into the characterization of the judge as the *bouche du loi*, popularized ever since, and repeated among other by John Marshall. In order to reject this depiction, we will revisit not only Cicero and Coke maxims but also Lon L. Fuller's "implicit laws of lawmaking" or "internal morality of law", which includes eight principles: (1) generality; (2) publicity; (3) irretroactivity – or prospectivity; (4) clarity; (5) non-contradictory; (6) possibility; (7) constancy; and (8) congruity; and Norberto Bobbio's "essential" and "non-essential" attributes of a *bon législateur*. The former are: (1) justice**;** (2) coherence; (3) rationality; and (4) non-redundancy; and the latter: (5) rigorous; (6) systematic; and (7) exhaustive. Also following Bobbio we will revisit the relationship of the *bon législateur* to the *bon juge* – or *juge loyal* – which is committed to an "intelligent" fidelity to law *a la* Fuller, and so must apply the five different types of "legal rationality" that are and must be integrated into a "complex legal rationality" comprising (1) linguistic; (2) legal-formal – or systematic; (3) teleological; (4) pragmatic; and (5) ethical. Above all, we will emphasize that the rule of law functions – contrary to Antonin Scalia conception of "the rule of law" as "the law of rules" – as a limit to both law and rule, and as such it is "the law or rule of principles or reasons" and according to "constitutionalism" of "human rights" and "separation of powers".

Fourthly, we will re-develop the principles related to the "constitutional rule of law" by recalling the existing tensions not only between liberty and other values but also between the two concepts of liberty, *i.e.* "negative" and "positive". In addition, we will reinforce the priority of the former over the latter, by analyzing the relationship between individual liberty and democratic rule, and by critically assessing the problem of the limits of the "majority rule", *i.e.* the so-called "tyranny of the majority". For that purpose, we will revise John Stuart Mill's famous *On Liberty*, which contains the description of such an evil and the prescription of the remedy as well: the priority of individual liberty over all ends of life and the "harm principle" as a justified limitation to liberty. We will also revisit Isaiah Berlin's illustrious "Two Concepts of Liberty" to reinforce the priority of negative liberty over positive one, and hence of individual liberty over democratic rule, identified solely with the majority rule.

Fifthly, since we are critical of the tendency to reduce the "democratic principle" to the "majority principle" and even worse to the "majority rule", *i.e.* to whatever pleases the majority, we will like to confront two competing conceptions of democracy, in the quest for an authentic, pure or true "democracy". For that purpose, we will begin by remembering its etymology, which means "government of the people": neither many nor few, but all the people. And by contrasting two conceptions: on one side, the *majoritarian conception* as the government of the many – and even of the few on behalf of the many; and, on the other, the *partnership conception* as the government of all, both many and few. This distinction can be traced all the way down to Mill's *Considerations on Representative Government* and has been reintroduced recently in Dworkin's *Is Democracy Possible Here? Principles for a New Political Debate*, who by embracing the partnership conception has become the champion of democracy.

Finally, I will like to seize the opportunity to explicit a principle firmly entrenched in the "Eastern" comprehension of the world that is also present in the "Western" one but has remained implicit in our description of the "rule of law". The principle "reciprocity" attributed to Confucius is closely related not only to several of the principles integrated to our conception of the "rule of law", such as "isonomy", "generality", "constancy", "harm principle" – as a justified limitation to liberty – and limits to "majority rule", but also to the classic one contained in the Greek word '*isotimia*' and to the modern "equal concern and respect" advocated among others by Dworkin and Amartya Sen, following John Rawls and his "difference principle".

6.2 "Rule" + "Law" ≠ "Rule of Law"

As stated in introductory section 6.1, the dual aim of this part is: On the one hand, to criticize *a la* Jeremy Waldron (2008) the conceptions, including the *dualist* – or *weak* – and the *monist* – or *strong* – theses explaining the relationship between "law" and "State" that equate the "rule of law" to the formal assertion: "law rules"; and, even worse, that reduce it either to the "rule of precedent" or "adjudicative/judicial rule of law" ("judicialism"), or to the "rule of statute" or "legislative rule of law" ("legalism"). Both options fail by presupposing that for a complete apprehension of the "rule of law" it is sufficient to be acquainted with the "law" – by notions such as "precedent" or "statute", as well as "adjudication" or "legislation" – to derive mechanically what the "rule of law" is. On the other hand, to scrutinize the claim suggesting that instead of presupposing that the comprehension of the "law" will lead us into the knowledge of the "rule of law" it is the other way around: it is necessary to have a better – and more substantial – conception of the "rule of law" to have a better – and more substantial – perception of the "law".

Anyway, let me start by denouncing a common mistake that most jurists or legal theorists formed under the *Staatslehre* and "sovereignty of States" doctrines have and share, whether they hold a weak or a strong theses their mistake is the same. On one side, in the *dualist* or *weak thesis*, "law" and "State" are interconnected to the extent that the announcements "where there is law there must be a State" and "where there is a State there must be law", which lead to the pronouncements "all law has a State form" or "all State has a law form" are redundant and the statements "law of State" and "State of law" are simply tautological (Austin 1832, 9–33; Hart 1961, 49–76, 1994, 50–78; MacCormick 1999, 9–11, 2007, 2).[1] On the other, in the *monist* or *strong thesis*, both "law" and "State" are *unum et idem* to the extent that "law of State" and "State of law" are pleonasms: "all State is a State of law" and "all law is a law of State" (Kelsen 1945, 181–206, 1967, 279–319, 2002, 97–106).

In Hans Kelsen's own voice (1945, xxxviii):

> Austin shares the traditional opinion according to which law and State are two different entities, although he does not go far as most legal theorists who present the State as the creator of the law, as the power and moral authority behind the law, as the god of the world of law. The pure theory of law shows the true meaning of these figurative expressions. It shows that the State as a social order must necessarily be identical with the law or, at least, with a specific, a relatively centralized legal order, that is, the national legal order in contradistinction to the international, highly decentralized, legal order. Just as the pure theory of law eliminates the dualism of law and justice and the dualism of objective and subjective law, so it abolishes the dualism of law and State. By doing so it establishes a theory of the State as an intrinsic part of the theory of law and postulates a unity of national and international law with a legal system comprising all the positive legal orders.

In the words of – one of his critics – Edgar Bodenheimer (1962, 101):

> A term like "government of laws" is considered devoid of meaning by Kelsen. "Every State is a government of laws", he says. To him, "law and the state" are synonymous concepts. The state is nothing but the sum total of norms ordering compulsion, and it is thus coextensive with the law. "The law, the positive law (not justice) is precisely that compulsive order which is the State."

---

[1] *Vid. v.gr.* MacCormick (2007, 2): "Law taken in this sense [*i.e.* as an institutional normative order] is obviously a central important feature of states as such and, in particular, of constitutionalist states or 'law-states'."

Accordingly, if our criticism is right, we can derive two central ideas for this part of the paper: First, it should be clear that "not all State is and must be necessarily of law" and "not all law is and must be necessarily of State". Consider an authoritarian or totalitarian regime of "State" which is by definition antagonistic to "law" or at least to its principles; and the "law" of a primitive community or society, which has not developed, or at least not yet, the characteristics fixed for a "State", as a "municipal legal system" (Hart 1961, 89–90, 1994, 91–2). Second, it is true that even in the case of identity between "law" and "State" there is still difference regarding the expressions "law of State" or "State of law". The latter corresponds to the German *Rechtstaat* (*i.e.* "State of law" or "State-law")[2] and the former to the *Machtstaat* (*i.e.* "State of force/power"); and, correspondingly to the Spanish terms *Estado de derecho* (*i.e.* "State of law" or "State-law") and *derecho de Estado* (*i.e.* law of State) or even *Estado de fuerza/poder* (*i.e.* "State of force/power").

And so, following Waldron, who suggests that the "rule of law" (*RoL*) is different from both "rule" (*R*) and "law" (*L*), and from the aggregation of both ($R+L$), to the extent that it must not be identified and less reduced to them, we consider that the "State of law" (*SoL*) is distinct from both "State" (*S*) and "law" (*L*), and from the conjunction of both ($S+L$), to the extent that it also must not be identified and less reduce to them[3]:

$$RoL \neq R$$

$$RoL \neq L$$

$$RoL \neq R+L$$

Instead, of believing that our knowledge of either *R* and *L* is sufficient for our understanding of *RoL* the result is that it is different to them or at least to the union of both. In a few words, if not all *R* or *L* is identical to *RoL*, then for being consider as such both must have some characteristics beyond merely being *R* and *L*. But which are those characteristics (x) is still an open question looking for answers:

$$R = Rx\,?\,\text{and}\,L = Lx\,?$$

Also, following Waldron, we consider that it is possible to turn the tables in order to invert the implication (→) according to which it is enough to analyze *R* and *L* for our knowledge of what the *RoL* is:

$$R + L \rightarrow RoL$$

[2] *Vid. v.gr.* MacCormick (2007, 3): "This [*i.e.* the distinction between politics and public Law] has much to do with sustaining the character of a state as a law-state. ('Law-state' is here used to refer to a state-under-law, or a constitutionalist state, in which the exercise of power is subjected to effective constitutional constraints and the rule of law obtains, it is equivalent to the German term '*Rechtsstaat*'.)"

[3] Since we consider that *RoL* is equivalent to *SoL*, as we will insist in the following part, hereinafter we will refer explicitly to *RoL*, but *mutatis mutando* it applies implicitly to *SoL*.

On the contrary, we argue that it is the other way around to the extent that the *RoL* is necessary for a better understanding of both *R* and *L*:

$$RoL \rightarrow R + L$$

Therefore, when our comprehension of *RoL* appeared to be subordinated to our knowledge both of *R* and *L* it results that the analysis of *RoL* is essential for understanding both *R* and *L*:

$$RoLx \rightarrow Rx + Lx$$

In other words, instead of deducting what *RoL* is from *R* and *L* it is possible from the characteristics (x) of *RoL* to infer those implanted in *R* and *L* to the extent that it is necessary to have a better – and more substantial – conception of *RoL* to have a better – and more substantial – perception of both *R* and *L*.

6.3 Rule of Law

In this part, in the search for a better – and more substantial – awareness of the "law", we intend to revisit the different notions related to the "rule of law". Although it is true that they are neither equivalent nor unequivocal, they might shed some light into our discussion, from the classical distinction between the "government of/under men" ("passion") and the "government of/under laws" ("reason"), including the principles of "equality before/under law" (*isonomia*) or "freedom before/under law", to the contemporary distinctions between "adjudicative/judicial or legislative rule of law" and "constitutional or institutional rule of law", including the tensions between the *ragione diStato* (*i.e.* reason of State) and the *Stato della ragione* (*i.e.* State of reason); the *Machtstaat* (*i.e.* State of power/force) and *Rechtsstaat* (*i.e.* State of law); *derecho de Estado* (*i.e.* law of State) and *Estado de derecho* (*i.e.* State of law or State-law); and *law's empire* – or the *empire of law*.

It is a common place since ancient classical Greek and Roman times to question: what is better a government of/under men or a government of/under law? On this regard, for instance, Aristotle (1988, 75) begins by "inquiring whether it is more advantageous to be ruled by the best man or by the best laws." Certainly, he prefers the government of the best laws to regulate abstract and general cases with *reason*. But he does not rule out completely the government of the best men to resolve concrete and particular cases with *passion*.[4] In his own voice (Aristotle 1988, 76):

> Hence it is clear that government acting according to written laws is plainly not the best. Yet surely the ruler cannot dispense with the general principle which exists in law; and that is a better ruler which is free from passion than that in which it is innate. Whereas the law is

[4] At the end of the day it seems to be a false dilemma: we must be governed both by the best laws (reason) and by the best human beings (passion). It is in the case of an actual or eventual conflict between them that the laws and reasons ought to prevail over human beings and passion.

passionless, passion must always sway the heart of man. Yes, it may be replied, but then on the other hand an individual will be better able to deliberate in particular cases.

The best man, then, must legislate, and laws must be passed, but these laws will have no authority when they miss the mark, though in all other cases retaining their authority.

Moreover, in the *Nicomachean Ethics*, Aristotle clarifies (1999, 77):

For the just belongs to those who have law in their relations. Law belongs to those among whom injustice is possible; for the judicial process is judgment that distinguishes the just from the unjust. Where there is injustice there is also doing justice, though where there is doing injustice there need not also be injustice. And doing injustice is awarding to oneself too many of the things that, considered without qualification, are good, and too few of the things that, considered without qualification, are bad.

That is why we allow only reason, not a human being, to be ruler. For a human being awards himself too many goods and becomes a tyrant; a ruler, however, is a guardian of the just, and hence of the equal and so must not award himself too many goods.

Likewise, in his *Politics*, he wonders what must happen if law is not enough and it is necessary to be ruled by men, either by one man or by many/all, his answer seems to suggest that the latter is better than the former, because their reason will outmanoeuvre and outsmart his passion (Aristotle 1988, 76):

But when the law cannot determine a point at all, or not well, should the one best man or should all decide? According to our present practice assemblies meet, sit in judgment, deliberate, and decide, and their judgments all relate to individual cases. Now any member of the assembly, taken separately, is certainly inferior to the wise man. But the state is made up of many individuals. And as a feast to which all the guests contribute is better than a banquet furnished by a single man, so a multitude is a better judge of many things than any individual.

Analogously, Cicero – referring to Cato the Elder – insists on the intrinsic advantages of being ruled not by one genius – and his passion – but by many geniuses – and their reason (Cicero 1929, 154–5):

He often said that the form of our government excelled that of all other states because in the latter there had usually been individual law-givers each of whom had given laws and institutions to his own particular commonwealth... Our commonwealth, on the other hand, was the product not of one genius but of many; it was not established within the lifetime of one man but was the work of several men in several generations. For, as Cato said, there had never been a genius great enough to comprehend everything, and all the ability in the world, if concentrated in a single person, could not at one time possess such insight as to anticipate all future needs, without the knowledge conferred by experience and age.

Correspondingly, Sir Edward Coke, Chief Justice of the Court of Common Pleas, first, and of the King's Bench, later, in times of James I, arrives to a similar conclusion ingrained in his notorious conception of law as an "artificial reason". To cut a long story short, in 1607, he objected the absolute sovereignty of the monarch and his decision to exercise the privilege of deciding personally a case at law, because it requires an artificial logic, in which he is not skilled; and, stated the supremacy of the "common law". Ever since, the report on the *Prohibitions del Roy* has become an icon for the modern notions of "rule of law" and an "independent judiciary", by including a portrait of the exchange with James I by Coke himself (1607, 481):

A controversy of Land between parties was heard by the King, and sentence given, which was repealed for this, that it did belong to the Common Law: Then the King said, that he

> thought the Law was founded upon reason, and that he and others had reason, as well as Judges: To which it was answered by me, that true it was, that God had endowed his Majesty with excellent Science, and great endowments of nature; but his Majesty was not learned in the Lawes of his Realm of England, and causes which concern the life, or inheritance, or goods, or fortunes of his Subjects; they are not to be decided by naturall reason but by the artificiall reason and judgment of Law, which Law is an act which requires long study and experience, before that a man can attain to the cognizance of it; And that the Law was the Golden metwand and measure to try the Causes of the Subjects; and which protected his Majesty in safety and peace: With which the King was greatly offended, and said, that then he should be under the Law, which was Treason to affirm, as he said; To which I said, that Bracton saith, *Quod Rex non debet esse sub homine, sed sub Deo et Lege* (*i.e.* The King ought not to be under any man, but under God and the Law).

Actually, one year later, Coke in the *Calvin's Case, or the Case of the* Postnati (*i.e.* those born after the accession of James VI of Scotland to the throne of England as James I) insisted (Coke 1608, 173):

> *Hesterni enim sumus et ignoramus, et vita nostra sicut umbra super terram*: for we are but of yesterday, (and therefore had a need of the wisdom of those that were before us) and had been ignorant (if we had not received light and knowledge from our forefathers) and our daies upon the earth are but as a shadow, in respect of the old ancient days and times past, wherein the Laws have been by the wisdom of the most excellent men, in many successions of ages, by long and continual experience (the trial of right and truth) fined and refined, which no one man (being of so short a time) albeit he had in his head the wisdom of all the men in the world, in any one age could ever have effected or attained unto. And therefore it is *optima regula, qua nulla est verior aut firmior in jure, Neminen oportet esse sapientiorem legibus*: no man ought to take upon him to be wiser than the Laws.

In a few words, the idea of the rule of law as the "government of/under laws" implies that everyone, including the monarch or sovereign, must be under the law. And so, the Elizabethans borrowed from the Greeks the word *isonomia* meaning "equality of laws to all manner of persons": *i.e.* governed and governors, poor and rich (and, nowadays, in a constitutional democracy applicable to... believers and non-believers, foreigners and nationals, heterosexuals and homosexuals, men and women, and so forth). They actually readapted it into the English form "isonomy" to describe a state of "equal laws for all and responsibility of the magistrates" and continued in use during the seventeenth century until "equality before the law", "government of law", and "rule of law" gradually displaced it (Hayek 1960, 164).

In short, the rule of law has been identified with the notion that the law rules – *nomos basileus* for the Greeks and *lex rex* for the Romans – but implies that it must rule not only equally to all who are before/under it, authorities and officials included, but also through reason not passion. Therefore, the ideal of the rule of law accepts the *Stato della ragione* (*i.e.* State of reason) with objective constraints and rejects the *ragione diStato* (*i.e.* reason of State) without such restraints, including the possibility of reconciling both as Carlo V once suggested. In the same way, the rule of law concurs with the principles of a *Rechtsstaat* (*i.e.* State of law) with effective constraints and conflicts with those of a *Machtstaat* (*i.e.* State of power/force) without restraints or not effective. Similarly, although the rule of law includes the *stare decisis* doctrine it cannot be reduced to the "rule of precedent" or "adjudicative/judicial rule of law" ("judicialism"); and, analogously, even though the legislative decisions are binding it neither can be reduced to the "rule of statute" or "legislative rule of law" ("legalism"). Both options fail by presupposing that for a complete apprehension of the "rule of law" it is sufficient to be acquainted with "law" – by notions such as "precedent" or "statute", as well as "adjudication" or "legislation" – to derive mechanically what the "rule of law" is.

Finally, the rule of law as *law's empire* – or *empire of law* – incorporates the notion not of a mere recognition of law by the use of a "precedent" or a "statute" in an "adjudicative/judicial or legislative rule of law" but of a true recognition of law by way of its principles, including "coherence" and "integrity", in what we can label as a "constitutional rule of law" (Dworkin 1986). This model integrates the community's constitutional morality into law by using a constructive-interpretative approach "something like" John Rawls' "reflective equilibrium" (1971, 20–1, 48–51) – or H.L.A. Hart's "critical reflective attitude" (1961, 56, 1994, 57) as pointed out by Wilfrid J. Waluchow, among others (Waluchow 2007; Flores 2002, 155–6, 2008, 285–305, 2009a, 37–74).

6.4 Principles of the Rule of Law

In this part, we intend to recognize *a la* Friedrich A. Hayek some of the principles of the "constitutional rule of law", starting like him by remembering Cicero's conceptions, as well as other principles related to the "rule of law", but which are applicable to all, including the authorities and officials. Since the legislator and the adjudicator must observe these principles which establish limits to their respective activities or functions, we will continue by revisiting Lon L. Fuller's "implicit laws of lawmaking" and Norberto Bobbio's "essential and non-essential attributes of the *bon législateur*", including according to "constitutionalism" the respect for human rights and separation of powers.

It is worth mentioning that Hayek attributes to Cicero the most effective formulations of freedom under the law (1960, 166–7, 462):

1. The conception of general rules – *leges legum*;
2. The conception of obedience to law in order to be and remain free – *omnes legum servi summus ut liberi esse possimus*; and
3. The conception of the judge as a law that speaks/with voice and of the law as a speechless/voiceless judge – *Magistratum legem esse loquentem, legem autem mutum magistratum.*

These three maxims are still in force nowadays, after being received and repeated by many authors, among others, by Montesquieu, in his *De l'espirit des lois*, where he following Cicero not only insisted in the importance of general rules but also redefined liberty and the obedience to civil laws, in the following terms (Hayek 1960, 462):

> Liberty consists principally in not being forced to do a thing where the laws do not oblige: people are in this state only as they are governed by civil laws; and because they live under those civil laws they are free.

Moreover, Montesquieu misinterpreted Cicero's adagio *Magistratum legem esse loquentem, legem autem mutum magistratum* and reduced the judges to the *bouche du loi* (Hayek 1960, 462):

> The national judges are no more that the mouth that pronounces the word of the law, mere passive beings, incapable of moderating either its force or rigor.

Keep in mind that by this time Coke had already sentenced in the *Calvin's Case*: *Judex est lex loquens* (*i.e.* A judge is a law that speaks) (1608, 174). Notwithstanding, John Marshall in *Osborn v. Bank of United States* repeated Montesquieu's characterization of judges as "the mere mouthpieces of the law" and "capable of willing nothing" (1824, 866).

It is clearly not the same to conceive the judges limited to be the *mouth/voice of the law* instead of freed to be the *law with mouth/voice*. The first characterization is reinforced by a very limited understanding of the separation of powers doctrine not only by assuming the existence of an unavoidable conflict between the legislative and the judiciary but also by presuming that such conflict must be solved indefectibly by subordinating the adjudicator to the legislator, due to the arguably democratic, elected and representative nature of the latter and non-democratic, non-elected and non-representative of the former (Flores 2004, 146–54, 2005, 26–52, 2007, 247–66, 2008, 285–305, 2009a, 37–74, 2009b, 91–110). However, the second conception requires a much better understanding of the separation of powers doctrine by promoting collaboration, complementation and coordination between them instead of being necessarily in competition and conflict. Let me bring to mind Waluchow's words (2007, 269–70):

> Seen in this light, judges and legislators need not to be seen to be in *competition* with each other over who has more courage or the better moral vision. On the contrary, they can each been seen to contribute, in their own unique ways, from their own unique perspectives, and within their unique contexts of decision, to the achievement of a morally sensitive and enlightened rule of law... judicial review sets the stage for a "dialogue" between the courts and the legislature... [and] is best viewed not as an imposition that thwarts the democratic will but as one stage in the democratic process.

In addition to the three principles of the rule of law attributed to Cicero, there are several other principles worth noting:

4. The conception of equality before the law, which implies:
    (4a) Isonomy as an equal application to all; and
    (4b) The principle "like cases must be treated alike" as embodied in *ubi eadem ratio ibi eadem iuris disposition* maxim;
5. The conception of a duty to obey the law, including authorities and officials;
6. The conception of legal certainty or security, which recalls principles such as *nulla poena sine lege* and *nullum crimen sine lege*;
7. The conception prohibiting the creation of *ad hoc* tribunals and retroactive legislation or *ex post facto*; and
8. The conception of a due process of law, which includes principles such as *audi alteram partem*, *i.e.* "let no one be a judge in its own cause" and enforcing the

analogous "let no one be a legislator in its own cause", as recognized, for instance, in the XXVII Amendment of the United States Constitution: "No law, varying the compensation for the services of the Senators and Representatives, shall take effect, until an election of Representatives shall have intervened."

Since the principles of the "rule of law" are applicable to all, including the authorities and officials, the legislator and the adjudicator must observe these principles which establish limits to their respective activities or functions. The "rule of law" means that the authorities and officials, including not only adjudicators but also legislators, are subjected to the law and do have limits, as both Fuller and Bobbio had pointed out.

On the one hand, in the 60's, Fuller made explicit the "implicit laws of lawmaking", which he identified with the "internal morality of law", and included among them (1968, 91–110, 1969, 39):

1. *Generality*: laws must be general in their creation and application;
2. *Publicity*: laws must be public in order to be known and observed;
3. *Irretroactivity* – or *prospectivity*: laws must not be retroactive but prospective or at least not abusive of retroactive legislation;
4. *Clarity*: laws must be clear and precise to be understood and followed;
5. *Non-contradictory*: laws must not command at the same time a permission and a prohibition;
6. *Possibility*: laws must not demand something impossible or have a mere symbolic effect;
7. *Constancy*: laws must be applied equally to all cases at hand; and
8. *Congruity*: laws must be enforced according to its purpose as a means to an end.

On the other hand, in the early 70's, Bobbio distinguished not only between essential and non-essential attributes of *bon législateur*, but also between two ideals in opposition (1971, 243–9). On one side, he stipulated that "*essential attributes*" are those necessary prohibitions that the legislator cannot violate, without exceptions (as imperatives); and, "*non-essential attributes*" are those contingent – not necessary – that may under certain conditions institute prohibitions to the legislator with exceptions (as directives). Therefore, he established that the former – essential attributes – included the following:

1. *Justice*: equal treatment to that alike and different treatment to those unlike;
2. *Coherence*: no (logical) contradictions;
3. *Rationality*: in the formal-logical or intrinsic sense of *zweckrationalität – a la* Max Weber; and
4. *Non-redundancy*: no repetition or unnecessary reiteration.

Whereas, the latter – non-essential attributes – comprise the subsequent:

5. *Rigorous:* scrupulous in the process of law-making;
6. *Systematic*: methodical in the order of exposition; and
7. *Exhaustive*: completeness in the determination of specific cases.

As a consequence, he assumes a necessary just, coherent, rational, and non-redundant legislator, and presumes a contingent rigorous, systematic and exhaustive legislator.

On the other, he stated as a general rule the ideal of the *bon législateur* and the *juge loyal*; and, as the exception the ideal of the *bon législateur* complemented by the *bon juge*, in the sense of the well-known *bon juge* Paul Magnaud. The question is whether the ideals of a *juge loyal* and a *bon juge* are compatible or incompatible? In my opinion, a good judge – or adjudicator – is and must be a loyal judge – or adjudicator. Clearly the problem is: loyal to what? (Flores 2004, 149–52, 2005, 38–47.)

On this regard, let me call attention to Fuller's conception of "fidelity to law" and the distinction between "intelligent" and "non-intelligent" fidelities, as he recognized, first, in his celebrated "The Case of the Speluncean Explorers" through an imaginary justice Foster, who embodies his own thought (1999, 1854–9); and, repeated, later, in his renowned "Positivism and Fidelity to Law – A Reply to Professor Hart" (Fuller 1958, 630–72; Hart 1958, 593–629). In most cases a linguistic or literal approach is enough to guarantee the fidelity to law or at least to the words in which law is drafted, but in some cases it will not be sufficient and even non-intelligent, and consequently a different approach is required, *i.e.* a functional one, to have an intelligent fidelity to law, by asking which is the end, interest or purpose of the law itself in the case at hand (Fuller 1999, 1958): "The truth is that the exception… cannot be reconciled with the *words* of the statute, but only with its *purpose*."

We have following critically Manuel Atienza (1989a, 50–1, 1989b, 385–93, 1990, 39–40, 1997, 27–40) advocated elsewhere for a "complex legal rationality", which is the same in adjudication as in legislation and comprises five different types that are and must be integrated into one (Flores 2005, 35–8, 2007, 264–6, 2009b, 108–9):

1. *Linguistic rationality*: laws must be clear and precise to avoid the problems of ambiguity and vagueness (*R1*);
2. *Legal-formal* – or *systematic* – *rationality*: laws must be not only valid – and as such general, abstract, impersonal and permanent – but also coherent, non-redundant, non-contradictory, prospective or non-retroactive, and publicized to avoid problems of antinomies, redundancies and gaps, while promoting the completeness of law as a system (*R2*);
3. *Teleological rationality*: laws must be efficacious in serving as a means to a end and cannot establish something impossible or merely symbolic (*R3*);
4. *Pragmatic rationality*: laws must not only be efficacious, but also socially effective and economically efficient in the case of conflict (*R4*); and
5. *Ethical rationality*: laws must be just or fair and as a result can neither admit an injustice or the violation of basic as a principles and rights (*R5*).[5]

[5] It is worth pointing out that we agree with Atienza that the (good) legislator must begin by using clear and precise language to avoid problems related to ambiguities and vagueness (*R1*) and must carry on by inquiring about the coherency and completeness of the legal system to avoid contradictions and gaps (*R2*). However, we are at variance with him in the order of the pragmatic and teleological rationalities, and hence, have inverted their places. Our explanation is simple: the legislator must continue by drafting at least one end (*R3*) into law, but it may be the case of establishing more than two ends – or sets of interests, purposes or values – (*R4*) and not the other way around. Finally, the legislator must guarantee an overall justified principle embedded into the law or at least not violated by it (*R5*).

Hence, a (good) legislator – and a (good) adjudicator – knows and must know: the intricacies of our language (*R1*); the details of our existing legal system – its past, present and future (*R2*); the minutiae of our scheme of ends, interests, purposes and values (*R3*); the ins and outs of their possible consequences and effects (*R4*); and, the niceties of every single principle of justice (*R5*). And, similarly, integrate these five different types of legal rationality into one "complex legal rationality".

In sum, the targeted conception deeply rooted in "legalism" considers that the adjudicator is and must be loyal to the legislator, who created the general, abstract, impersonal and permanent laws to be applied impartially, and that as an exception becomes a *bon juge* when has to take the place of the *bon législateur* in order to legislate interstitially (Holmes 1917, 221; Hart 1961, 200, 1994, 205). A complete loyalty – and deference – from the adjudicator to the legislator assumes that the latter is just, coherent, rational-reasonable, and non-redundant. It even presumes that it is also rigorous, systematic and exhaustive in its formulations, and specially presupposes that law-making is a sovereign activity completely free or limitless, with the Latin adage *Quod principi placuit vigorem legis habet* ("Whatever pleases the prince has the force of law") as the family motto (Waldron 2002, 10).

On the contrary, the alternative conception embodied in "constitutionalism" considers that the adjudicator is and must be loyal to the legislator, as long as the legislator not only does not violate the prohibitions related to Fuller's "implicit laws of lawmaking" and to Bobbio's "essential and non-essential attributes of the *bon législateur*" but also follows Fuller's "intelligent fidelity to law" by applying a "complex legal rationality" to the problem at hand. Although Justice Antonin Scalia conceives "the *Rule* of law" as "the law of *rules*" (1989, 1187), the "rule of law" is a limit to both law and rule; and as such it is "the law or rule of principles or reasons" and according to "constitutionalism" of human rights and separation of powers (article 16 of the French Declaration of the Rights of Men and Citizen): "*Tout societé dans laquelle la garantie des droits n'est pas assurée, ni la séparation des pouvoirs déterminée, n'a point de constitution.*"

6.5 Constitutional Rule of Law

In this part, we pretend to recall the principles related to the "constitutional rule of law" by recalling the existing tensions not only between liberty and other values but also between the two concepts of liberty, *i.e.* "negative" and "positive". In addition,

By the same token, the (good) adjudicator must begin by asking about the clarity and precision of the language used (*R1*); and, only when the language is neither clear nor precise, must carry on by inquiring about the coherency and completeness of the legal system (*R2*). Analogously, only when the language and legal system appear to be incoherent or incomplete, the adjudicator must go on to request an end (*R3*), as in the case when there are more than two ends – or sets of interests, purposes or values – equally available, by appealing to the better one (*R4*). Finally, only when their consequences and effects are illegitimate, the adjudicator must strive to secure an overall legitimate principle (*R5*).

we will reinforce the priority of the former over the latter, by analyzing the relationship between individual liberty and democratic rule, and by critically assessing the problem of the limits of the "majority rule".

As we have seen the *RoL* can neither be equated with *R* or *L* nor identified with $R + L$ and much less reduced merely to the creation of norms according to adjective-formal procedures by legislators and its "mechanical" or strict application by adjudicators, *i.e.* a "legislative rule of law" or "legalism", as well as its "gastronomical" or soft application by adjudicators to the extent of accepting an interstitial "judicial" legislation, *i.e.* a "adjudicative/judicial rule of law" or "judicialism". On the contrary, the rule of law requires the creation and application of norms to be limited not only by adjective-formal procedures but also by substantive-material principles and a balanced application, *i.e.* a "constitutional rule of law" or "constitutionalism" (Flores 2005, 38–47).

Accordingly, one of the main problems of the rule of law is the tension existing between strict and even rigorous application of the law by evoking the *dura lex, sed lex* adage, and its non-application by invoking the *summum ius, summa injuria* aphorism. In few words, whenever the strict application of the law has – or will have – as a consequence an extreme injustice there are good reasons to question – or at least to doubt – whether such application is really what an intelligent fidelity to law and to the rule of law expects and even requires. So, instead of a literal and an uncritical approach to law and to the rule of law embodied in the Latin adagio *Fiat iustitia, et pereat mundus* (*i.e.* "Let justice be done, though the world perish"), we need a critical attitude.[6]

Actually, in a constitutional rule of law, respect to both human rights and the separation of powers function as a limit to what can be authoritatively consider as law. The rule of law implies the obligation to guarantee such principles and as a result can neither accept the unconstrained abuse of basic rights nor admit the unchecked exercise of powers (*R5*). As John Stuart Mill recalled in the "Introductory Chapter I" to his celebrated *On Liberty* (1989, 6):

> The aim, therefore, of patriots was to set limits to the power which the ruler should be suffered to exercise over the community; and this limitation was what they meant by liberty. It was attempted in two ways. First, by obtaining a recognition of certain immunities, called political liberties or rights, which it was to be regarded as a breach of duty in the ruler to

[6] Although this adage and its twin *Fiat iusticia, ruat cælum* ("Let justice be done, even if heavens falls") have analogous meanings along the lines of "justice must be done at any price or regardless of consequences." Nowadays, the former – popularized by the Emperor Ferdinand I – is used to criticize a legal opinion or practice that wants to preserve maxims in law at any price despite absurd or contradictory consequences, whereas the latter – recognized by William Murray, Lord Mansfield – is used to eulogize the realization of justice despite appearing to be outweighed by a pragmatic or utilitarian consideration: "The constitution does not allow reasons of state to influence our judgments: God forbid it should! We must not regard political consequences; however formidable soever they might be: if rebellion was the certain consequence, we are bound to say '*fiat iustitia, ruat cælum*' (Let justice be done even if the heaven falls)." (Mansfield 1770, 2561–2.)

> infringe, and which, if he did infringe, specific resistance, or general rebellion, was held to be justifiable. A second, and generally a later expedient, was the establishment of constitutional checks, by which the consent of the community, or of a body of some sort, supposed to represent its interests, was made a necessary condition to some of the important acts of the governing power.

Later on, in due time, the rulers became identified with the ruled, by assuming that they were elected by them and are their representatives (Mill 1989, 7): "What was now wanted was, that the rulers should be identified with the people; that their interest and will should be the interest and will of the nation." To the extent that, apparently, there can be no deviation and much less tension between the ruler and the ruled giving rise to the ideals of "self-government" and of "the power of the people over themselves". However, Mill recognized (1989, 7–8):

> The 'people' who exercise the power are not always the same people with those over whom it is exercised; and the 'self government' spoken of is not the government of each by himself, but of each by all the rest. The will of the people, moreover, practically means the will of the most numerous or the most active *part* of the people; the majority, or those who succeed in making themselves accepted as the majority; the people, consequently, *may* desire to oppress a part of their number; and precautions are as much needed against this as against any other abuse of power.

The "tyranny of the majority" – as any other tyrannical form – operates mainly through the actions and laws of the public authorities, but it may be the case that one part of the society oppresses the other. In Mill's voice (1989, 8–9):

> Protection, therefore, against the tyranny of the magistrate is not enough; there needs protection also against the tyranny of the prevailing opinion and feeling; against the tendency of society to impose, by other means than civil penalties, its own ideas and practices as rules of conduct on those who dissent from them; to fetter the development, and, if possible, prevent the formation, of any individuality not in harmony with its ways, and compel all characters to fashion themselves upon the model of its own. There is a limit to the legitimate interference of collective opinion with individual independence: and to find that limit, and maintain it against encroachment, is as indispensable to a good condition of human affairs, as protection against political despotism.

For this reason, it is necessary to check the power not only of formal institutions but also of informal instruments which facilitate the imposition of one conception over the others, by legal and moral means. The majority cannot cancel the possibility of some individuals – a significant minority and even a numerical majority of the society – of freely conceiving and responsibly fulfilling their own plan of life. As Mill clarifies (1989, 13):

> The object of this Essay is to assert one very simple principle, as entitled to govern absolutely the dealings of society with the individual in the way of compulsion and control, whether the means used be physical force in the form of legal penalties, or the moral coercion of public opinion. That principle is, that the sole end for which mankind are warranted, individually or collectively, in interfering with the liberty of action of any of their number, is self-protection. That the only purpose for which power can be rightfully exercised over any member of a civilised community, against his will, is to prevent harm to others.

In consequence the only time in which it is possible to interfere with the realization of someone's plan is to avoid harm to others. The so-called "harm principle" of Mill constitutes a clear limit to the exercise of liberty, since it must always de exercise with responsibility in order not to harm others and less impede someone else from achieving their own ends in life. In Mill's own words (1989, 16):

> No society in which these liberties are not, on the whole, respected, is free, whatever may be its form of government; and none is completely free in which they do not exist absolute and unqualified. The only freedom which deserves the name, is that of pursuing our own good in our own way, so long as we do not attempt to deprive others of theirs, or impede their efforts to obtain it.

At the heart of Mill's doctrine on liberty there is the pursuit of our own plan of life, as long as it does not harm others. Moreover, in a lengthy paragraph, he acknowledges the appropriate region of human liberty and recognizes (1989, 15–6):

> It comprises, first, the inward domain of consciousness; demanding liberty of conscience, in the most comprehensive sense; liberty of thought and feeling; absolute freedom of opinion and sentiment on all subjects, practical or speculative, scientific, moral, or theological. The liberty of expressing and publishing opinions may seem to fall under a different principle, since it belongs to that part of the conduct of an individual which concerns other people; but, being almost of as much importance as the liberty of thought itself, and resting I great part on the same reasons, is practically inseparable from it. Secondly, the principle requires liberty of tastes and pursuits; of framing the plan of our life to suit our own character; of doing as we like, subject to such consequences as may follow: without impediment from our fellow-creatures, so long as what we do does not harm them, even though they should think our conduct foolish, perverse, or wrong. Thirdly, from this liberty of each individual, follows the liberty, within the same limits of combination among individuals; freedom to unite for any purpose not involving harm to others: the persons combining being supposed to be of full age, and not forced or deceived.

In this paragraph Mill not only establishes the "harm principle" as a limit to both individual and collective liberty, but also stipulates two priorities: (1) liberty – and its different kinds – over other ends of life; and, (2) individual liberty over collective liberty. To reinforce these priorities, let me bring to attention that it was Henri Benjamin Constant de Rebeque's distinction amid "liberty of the ancients" and "liberty of the moderns" (1820), which captured, first, the conflict that Isaiah Berlin, the champion of pluralism, later, popularized among the "two concepts of liberty", *i.e.* between "negative" and "positive" liberties (1969, 118–72).

The former is a liberty "from" and entails "absence of interference"; whilst the latter is a liberty "to" and involves "presence in self-government". As a result there are two competing concepts of liberty: one of the ancients or republicans, identified with a liberty to participate in democratic rule, where the collective or political liberty is accentuated and so community and equality are emphasized; and, other of the moderns or liberals, identified with a liberty from interference, where the individual or civil liberty is highlighted and so individuality and liberty are stressed.

Although the two concepts are in competition nothing precludes the possibility of their collaboration. As Berlin acknowledges (1969, 130): "Self-government may, on the whole, provide a better guarantee of the preservation of civil liberties than other régimes, and has been defended as such by libertarians. But there is no necessary connection between individual liberty and democratic rule." Actually, if democratic rule can suppress individual liberty, as Berlin points out, for a society to be truly free it is necessary to be governed by two interrelated principles (1969, 165):

> [F]irst, that no power, but only rights, can be regarded as absolute, so that all men, whatever power governs them, have an absolute right to refuse to behave inhumanly; and, second, that there are frontiers, not artificially drawn, within which men should be inviolable, these frontiers being defined in terms of rules so long and widely accepted that their observance has entered into the very conception of what it is to be a normal human being, and, therefore, also of what it is to act inhumanly or insanely; rules of which it would be absurd to say, for example, that they could be abrogated by some formal procedure on the part of some court or sovereign body.

Both principles reinforce the primacy of a right – negative liberty – over a power – positive liberty – not only to the degree that certain rules cannot be abrogated by formal procedures but also to the extent that certain minimum area of individual liberty must not be violated by democratic rule (1969, 124):

> Consequently, it is assumed… that the area of men's free action must be limited by law. But equally it is assumed… that there ought to exist a certain minimum area of personal freedom which must on no account be violated; for it is over-stepped, the individual will find himself in an area too narrow for even the minimum development of his natural faculties which alone makes it possible to pursue, and even to conceive, the various ends which men hold good or right or sacred. It follows that a frontier must be drawn between the area of private life and that of public authority.

Additionally, Berlin's suggestion is summarized in a well-known paragraph (1969, 171):

> Pluralism, with the measure of 'negative' liberty that it entails seems to me a truer and more humane ideal than the goals of those who seek in the great disciplined, authoritarian structures the ideal of 'positive' self-mastery by classes, or peoples, or the whole of mankind. It is truer, because it does, at least recognize the fact that human goals are many, not all of them commensurable, and in perpetual rivalry with one another.

Thus, to reinforce the priority of the negative over the positive liberty, in the remainder of this part we will revisit the relationship between individual liberty and democratic rule, by critically assessing the problem of "majority rule". Since the "unanimity" is virtually impossible, the "majority principle" has been adopted as a device that enables the government to rule by facilitating, on one side, the election of our rulers, including our representatives, and the (national) representation as such, and, on the other, the decision-making process, and the governance. However, the "majority principle" does not imply that any election or decision is justified *per se*. As we have already pointed out, it is not enough to comply with adjective-formal procedures but to abide by substantive-material principles. All in all, the problem is that the "majority rule" is not identical to a "democratic rule". In a democracy it does not suffice to be concerned with the legitimate interests of the majorities since the minorities must also be respected in order for the legislative decisions to represent the common general interest and be truly general in both their creation and application.

Even though it is true that the majority is legitimated to rule it is also true that it represents – and must represent – the minorities, by respecting their legitimate interests. The problem is that the majority principle tends to degenerate into majority rule by creating winners that take it all without sharing the corresponding part with the losers that end up with nothing at all. In a nutshell, the majority rule, in which the winner takes it all, makes politics a zero sum game of win-lose (them or us), instead of a win-win situation for all (them and us).

The justification of the majority principle relies on the notion of "virtual representation", *i.e.* the winners represent all, both those who voted for and against them, and two principles of reciprocity: (1) the majorities are fluid and not fixed beforehand; and (2) the minorities are capable of becoming part of the governing coalition or majority in the future. Moreover, when the majority consistently and constantly excludes the minority and/or systematically and thoroughly rejects its demands, to the extent not only of ignoring their legitimate interests but also of destroying the virtual representation and the principles of reciprocity, by transforming the legitimate "majority principle" into is antithesis: "majority rule" – also known as the "tyranny of the majority" (Guinier 1994, 102–5). In Mill's words (1989, 8): "in political speculations 'the tyranny of the majority' is now generally included among the evils against which society requires to be in guard." In addition, a couple of years later, in 1861, he added in his *Considerations on Representative Government* (1958, 104):

> The injustice and violation of principle are not less flagrant because those who suffer by them are a minority; for there is not equal suffrage where every single individual does not count for as much as any other single individual in the community. But it is not only a minority who suffer. Democracy, thus constituted, does not even attain its ostensible object, that of giving the powers of government in all cases to the numerical majority. It does something very different: it gives them to a majority of the majority, who may be, and often are, but a minority of the whole.

The problem is that, despite the virtual representation and the principles of reciprocity, the majority neither recognizes nor represents the interests of the minority, as Tocqueville emphasized (1969, 253–4):

> The majority, being in absolute command both of lawmaking and of the execution of the laws, and equally controlling both rulers and ruled, regards public functionaries as its passive agents and is glad to leave them the trouble of carrying out its plans.

Notwithstanding, when the majority possess all the power and exercises it beyond any proportion it may lose all its legitimacy, as Madison pointed out one of the objectives of establishing a government is to avoid the dominance of any group with particular interests by recognizing (1961, 323): "It is of great importance in a republic not only to guard the society against the oppression of its rulers but to guard one part of the society against the injustice of the other part." And, reiterating (1961, 324):

> In a society under the forms of which the stronger faction can readily unite and oppress the weaker, anarchy may as truly be said to reign as in the state of nature, where the weaker individual is not secured against the violence of the stronger…

Actually, Tocqueville insisted that the will of the majority is the essence of the democratic rule (1969, 247):

> The moral authority of the majority is partly based on the notion that there is more enlightenment and wisdom in a numerous assembly than in a single man, and the number of the legislators is more important than how they are chosen…

> The moral authority of the majority is also founded on the principle that the interest of the greater number should be preferred to that of those who are the fewer.

However, he warns that the germ of the tyranny is found precisely in the "omnipotence of the majority". On this regard, he affirms (1969, 251): "I will never grant to several that power to do everything which I refuse to a single man." The majority will must be moderated to control the possibilities of becoming a tyranny. Moreover, the use of power is not necessarily good (1969, 256): "This irresistible power is a continuous fact and its good use only an accident."

In a democracy, the "majority rule" is justified *prima facie* as long as the majority does not exercise all the power and oppress the minority, by not protecting their interests and rights. It is incontestable that the majority is entitled to a majority of seats but not all since some of them belong to the minority and much less to be unconstrained. The legislative body ought to be a micro-cosmos of the constituency, where both majorities and minorities are represented according to their true representativeness without either adulterations or dilutions of any type. The majority principle means that it is not sufficient to represent the majority but all the people, including the minority.

Likewise, Hamilton warned (1985, 101): "Give all the power to the many, they will oppress the few. Give all the power to the few they will oppress the many. Both therefore ought to have power, that each may defend itself against the other." In other words, democracy is more than the government of the majority. In a pure or true democracy the power is neither in the majority nor in the minority but in all the people. As Mill emphasized (1958, 102–3):

> The pure idea of democracy, according to its definition, is the government of the whole people by the whole people, equally represented. Democracy as commonly conceived and hitherto practice is the government of the whole people by a mere majority of the people, exclusively represented. The former synonymous with the equality of all citizens; the latter, strangely confounded with it, is a government of privilege, in favor of the numerical majority, who alone posses practically any voice in the State. This is the inevitable consequence of the manner in which the votes are now taken, to the complete disfranchisement of minorities.

6.6 Constitutional Democracy and the Rule of Law

In this part, since we have been critical of the tendency to reduce the democratic principle to the majority rule, *i.e.* to whatever pleases the majority, we will like to confront two competing conceptions of democracy. For that purpose, we will begin by remembering its etymology, which means "the government of the people": neither many nor few, but all. And by contrasting two conceptions: the majoritarian conception as the government of the many – and even of the few on behalf of the many; and, the partnership conception as the government of all, both many and few.

According to its etymology – *demos* (people) and *kratos* (government, power or rule) – "democracy" means "government, power or rule of the people". It is *prima facie* a form of government in contraposition to other forms of government. The classical typology includes not only three "pure" forms: (1) "autocracy" (better known as "monarchy") as government of *one* – *i.e.* the monarch; (2) "aristocracy" as government of *few* – *i.e.* the better ones; and (3) "democracy" as government of *all* – *i.e.* the people. But also three "impure" or "corrupt" forms: (1) "tyranny" as government of *one* – *i.e.* the tyrant; (2) "oligarchy" as government of *few* – *i.e.* the rich; and (3) "demagogy" as government of *many* (on behalf of all) – *i.e.* the poor (or the mob).

It is worth to mention that Aristotle considered "democracy" pejoratively, an equivalent to the term "demagogy", as one vicious extreme in contraposition to "oligarchy" as the other vicious extreme, whereas his *politeia* was the virtuous middle term by comprising the government of both the poor and the rich. Let me explain that dislike him I will reserve "demagogy" for the "impure" or "corrupt" form and "democracy" for the "pure" or "true" one. But I will assume like him that the latter is the government of *all* the people: not only of both the poor and the rich but also of both the many and the few (or alternatively of both the majority and the minority).

The problem is that for some authors "democracy" seems to be reduced to the government of the *many* or of the *majority* in detriment of the *few* or of the *minority*, a so-called majoritarian or populist democracy. On the contrary, an authentic or true "democracy" and democratic government must be neither of poor or rich, nor of many or few (nor of majority or minority), but of all: both of poor and rich, both of many and few (both of majority and minority).

So far the notion of "democracy" as a form of government and the typology has served to emphasize the ownership (or partnership) "of" the political or sovereign power, depending on whether it corresponds to one, few, many, or all. Nevertheless, the exercise of this political or sovereign power not only must be done directly and indirectly "by" its owners (or partners) and their – legitimate – representatives, but also must be done "for" them and their benefit, not in their detriment. The three ideas already sketched can be put together into an integral definition, such as the one contained in Abraham Lincoln's maxim (1990, 308) and in the Fifth French Republic's motto: "government *of* the people, *by* the people, *for* the people".

Thus, a pure or true "democracy" must be the government of, by and for all the people: both poor and rich, many and few, men and women, heterosexuals and homosexuals, believers and non-believers… and so on. Hence, "democracy" is "government *of* all the people, *by* all the people – directly on their own ("direct democracy") or indirectly through their representatives ("representative democracy") – and *for* all the people".

However, as stated a couple of paragraphs above, the problem is that there are two competing conceptions of democracy (Dworkin 2006, 2011; Flores 2010). As far as I know the distinction can be traced all the way back to Mill, who almost 150 years ago, in his *Considerations on Representative Government*, under the epigraph "Of True and False Democracy: Representation of All, and Representation of the Majority Only", indicated that the two different ideas were usually confounded under the name "democracy". On one side, the true idea was the "government of the whole people by the whole people equally represented"; and, on the other, the false "the government of the whole people by a mere majority of the people, exclusively represented" (Mill 1958, 102–3).

Nowadays, as Dworkin pointed out the two competing conceptions of democracy not only coexist but also are still in conflict (2006, 131):

> The two views of democracy that are in contest are these. According to the *majoritarian* view, democracy is government by majority will, that is, in accordance with the will of the greatest number of people, expressed in elections with universal or near universal suffrage. There is no guarantee that a majority will decide fairly; its decisions may be unfair to minorities whose interests the majority systematically ignores. If so, then the democracy is unjust but no less democratic for that reason. According to the rival *partnership* view of democracy, however, democracy means that the people govern themselves each as a full partner in a collective political enterprise so that a majority's decisions are democratic only when certain further conditions are met that protect the status and interests of each citizen as a full partner in that enterprise. On the partnership view, a community that steadily ignores the interests of some minority or other group is just for that reason not democratic even though it elects officials impeccably by majoritarian means. This is only a very sketchy account of the partnership conception, however. If we find the more familiar majoritarian conception unsatisfactory, we shall have to develop the partnership view in more detail.

Actually, as he acknowledges, the United States of America is neither a pure example of the majoritarian conception of democracy nor of the non-majoritarian (or partnership) one. Although the bipartisan system and the majority rule reinforced the former, since the founding fathers limited the power of the majorities in various forms, by including anti-majoritarian devices, such as the filibuster and the judicial review of the constitutionality of the acts of the other (elected) branches of government, it can be said that they also supported the latter (Dworkin 2006, 137 and 135).[7]

On one side, a minority of either 34 or 41 (out of the 100 senators) can block the majority of bringing a decision to a final vote, depending on whether it is a substantive or procedural issue. And, on the other, the power of the political majorities is limited by the recognition of individual constitutional rights that the legislative majorities cannot infringe and much less step over.

Aside Dworkin alerts that the degraded state of the public debate endangers the partnership conception of democracy and strengthens the majoritarian one, including viewing the other as an enemy and politics as a war (2006, 132–3):

> If we aim to be a partnership democracy… the degraded state of our political argument does count as a serious defect in our democracy because mutual attention and respect are the essence of partnership. We do not treat someone with whom we disagree as a partner – we treat him as an enemy or at best as an obstacle – when we make no effort either to understand the force of his contrary views or to develop our own opinions in a way that makes them responsive to his. The partnership model so described seems unattainable now because it is difficult to see how Americans on rival sides of the supposed culture wars could come to treat each other with that mutual respect and attention.

---

[7] In fact, the existence of the Senate was designed to divide the most dangerous branch of government and to give stability to the government by protecting the minorities against a speedy and unreflected legislative majority in the House of Representatives.

6.7 Conclusion

To conclude let me explicit one more principle that intends to bridge the gap between East–West but has remained implicit in our description of the "rule of law". The principle known as "shu", *i.e.* "reciprocity" is attributed to K'ung-fu-tzu-Westernized as Confucius– and is closely related not only to several of the principles already integrated in our conception of the "rule of law", such as "isonomy", "generality", "constancy", "harm principle" – as a justified limitation to liberty – and limits to "majority rule", but also to the classic one contained in the Greek word '*isotimia*' and to the modern "equal concern and respect" – that any society must have and show to its individual members and partners, especially those less advantaged – advocated among others by Dworkin (1978, 223–39, 1985, 181–204, 1986, 297–301, 1996, 26–9, 2000, 120–34) and Amartya Sen (1992, 12–30), following John Rawls and his "difference principle" (1971, 75–83).

As you know Confucius had an apparent simple set of moral and political principles, including: (1) to love others; (2) to honor one's parents; (3) to do what is right instead of what is of advantage; (4) to practice "reciprocity", *i.e.* "don't do to others what you would not want yourself"; (5) to rule by moral example instead of by force and violence; and so forth.

These are very humane principles developed arguably without a hint of the ideals of individual liberty that are the basis of the modern liberal society, but "reciprocity" as a golden rule is compatible not only with the liberal "harm principle" but also with the egalitarian "difference principle". As Rawls claims (1971, 102–3):

> [T]he difference principle expresses a conception of reciprocity. It is a principle of mutual benefit. We have seen that, at least when chain connection holds, each representative man can accept the basic structure as designed to advance his interests. The social order can be justified to everyone, and in particular to those who are least favoured; and in that sense it is egalitarian.

Additionally, he contends (Rawls 1971, 105–6):

> A further merit of the difference principle is that it provides an interpretation of the principle of fraternity. In comparison with liberty and equality, the idea of fraternity has had a lesser place in democratic theory. It is thought to be less specifically a political concept, not in itself defining any of the democratic rights but conveying instead certain attitudes of mind and forms of conduct without which we would lose sight of the values expressed by these rights… It does seem that the institutions and policies which we most confidently think to be just satisfy its demands, at least in the sense that the inequalities permitted by them contribute to the well-being of the less favoured.

And, finally, concludes (Rawls 1971, 106):

> On this interpretation, then, the principle of fraternity is a perfectly feasible standard. Once we accept it we can associate the traditional ideas of liberty, equality, and fraternity with the democratic interpretation of the two principles of justice as follows: liberty corresponds to the first principle, equality to the idea of equality in the first principle together with equality of fair opportunity, and fraternity to the difference principle. In this way we have found a

place for the conception of fraternity in the democratic interpretation of the two principles, and we see that it imposes a definite requirement on the basic structure of society. The other aspects of fraternity should not be forgotten, but the difference principle expresses its fundamental meaning from the standpoint of social justice.

Anyway, "reciprocity" – in the form not only of "fraternity" but also of "community" or "solidarity" – complements both liberty and equality. Actually, the *Declaration of the Rights of Man and of the Citizen* of 1789 defined liberty in article 4 as follow: "Liberty consists of being able to do anything that does not harm others: thus, the exercise of the natural rights of every man or woman has no bounds other than those that guarantee other members of society the enjoyment of these same rights." Thus, in the quest for "global harmony and the rule of law", the French revolution slogan must be readapted into "Liberty, equality and reciprocity".

References

Aristotle. 1988. *Politics*. Cambridge: Cambridge University Press.

Aristotle. 1999. *Nicomachean ethics*. Trans. T. Irwin, Indianapolis: Hackett.

Atienza, M. 1989a. Sociología jurídica y ciencia de la legislación. In *El derecho y sus realidades. Investigación y enseñanza de la sociología jurídica*, ed. R. Bergalli. Barcelona: PPU.

Atienza, M. 1989b. Contribución a la teoría de la legislación. *Doxa* 6: 385.

Atienza, M. 1990. Para una teoría de la argumentación jurídica. *Doxa* 8: 39.

Atienza, M. 1997. *Contribución a la teoría de la legislación*. Madrid: Tecnos.

Austin, J. 1832. *The province of jurisprudence determined and the uses of the study of jurisprudence*, ed. J. Austin Indianapolis: Hackett.

Berlin, I. 1969. *Four essays on liberty*, ed. I. Berlin Oxford: Oxford University Press.

Bobbio, N. 1971. Le bon législateur. In *Le raisonnment juridique/Legal reasoning/Die jurisdiche argumentation*, ed. H. Hubien. Bruxelles: Établissements Émile Bruylant.

Bodenheimer, E. 1962. *Jurisprudence. The philosophy and method of the law*. Cambridge, MA: Harvard University Press.

Cicero, M.T. 1929. *On the commonwealth*. Trans. G.H. Sabine and S.B. Smith. Columbus: The Ohio State University Press.

Coke, E. 1607. Prohibitions del Roy. In *The selected writings of Sir Edward Coke*, vol. I, ed. S. Sheppard. Indianapolis: Liberty Fund.

Coke, E. 1608. Calvin's case, or the case of the *postnati*. In *The selected writings of Sir Edward Coke*, vol. I, ed. S. Sheppard. Indianapolis: Liberty Fund.

Confucius (2002), *Analects*. Trans. James Legge. Available at Project Gutenberg Etext, The Chinese Classics (Confucian Analects).

Constant, B. 1820. *Collection complète des ouvrages*. París: Béchet Libraire.

Dworkin, R. 1978. *Taking rights seriously*, 2nd ed. Cambridge, MA: Harvard University Press.

Dworkin, R. 1985. *A matter of principle*. Cambridge, MA: Harvard University Press.

Dworkin, R. 1986. *Law's empire*. Cambridge, MA: Harvard University Press.

Dworkin, Ronald. 1996. *Freedom's law. The moral reading of the American constitution*. Cambridge, MA: Harvard University Press.

Dworkin, Ronald. 2000. *Sovereign virtue. The theory and practice of equality*. Cambridge, MA: Harvard University Press.

Dworkin, R. 2006. *Is democracy possible here? Principles for a new political debate*. Princeton: Princeton University Press.

Dworkin, R. 2011. *Justice for hedgehogs*. Cambridge, MA: Harvard University Press.

Flores, I.B. 2002. In the dark side of the conventionality thesis? In *Studies in social, political and legal philosophy. Philosophy of law and of politics*, ed. E. Villanueva. Amsterdam: Rodopi.
Flores, I.B. 2004. Assessing democracy and rule of law: Access to justice. In *Proceedings of the 21st IVR world congress, Lund (Sweden), 12–17 August, 2003, Part I: Justice*, ed. A. Peczenik. Stuttgart: Franz Steiner Verlag.
Flores, I.B. 2005. The quest for legisprudence: Constitutionalism *v*. Legalism. In *The theory and practice of legislation: Essays on legisprudence*, ed. L.J. Wintgens. Aldershot: Ashgate.
Flores, I.B. 2007. Legisprudence: The forms and limits of legislation. *Problema. Anuario de Filosofía y Teoría del Derecho* 1: 247.
Flores, I.B. 2008. The living tree: Fixity and flexibility. A general theory of (judicial review in a) constitutional democracy? *Problema. Anuario de Filosofía y Teoría del Derecho* 2: 285.
Flores, I.B. 2009a. The living tree constitutionalism: Fixity and flexibility. *Problema. Anuario de Filosofía y Teoría del Derecho* 3: 37.
Flores, I.B. 2009b. Legisprudence: The role and rationality of legislators – vis-à-vis judges – towards the realization of justice. *Mexican Law Review* 1(2): 91.
Flores, I.B. 2010. Ronald Dworkin's *Justice for hedgehogs* and partnership conception of democracy (with a comment to Jeremy Waldron's "A majority in the lifeboat"). *Problema. Anuario de Filosofía y Teoría del Derecho* 4: 65.
Fuller, L.L. 1958. Positivism and fidelity to law –A reply to professor Hart. *Harvard Law Review* 71: 630.
Fuller, L.L. 1968. *The anatomy of law*. New York: Frederick A. Praeger.
Fuller, L.L. 1969. *The morality of law*, 2nd ed. New Haven: Yale University Press.
Fuller, L.L. 1999. The case of the speluncean explorers. *Harvard Law Review* 112: 1851.
Guinier, L. 1994. *The tyranny of the majority. Fundamental fairness in representative democracy*. New York: The Free Press.
Hamilton, A. 1985. Speech, June 18, 1787. In *Selected writings and speeches of Alexander Hamilton*, ed. M.J. Frisch. Washington, DC: American Enterprise Institute.
Hart, H.L.A. 1958. Positivism and the separation of law and morals. *Harvard Law Review* 71: 593.
Hart, H.L.A. 1961. *The concept of law*. Oxford: Oxford University Press.
Hart, H.L.A. 1994. *The concept of law*, 2nd ed. Oxford: Oxford University Press.
Hayek, F.A. 1960. *The constitution of liberty*. Chicago: The University of Chicago Press.
Holmes, O.W. 1917. *Southern Pacific* v. *Jensen*, 244 U.S. 205.
Kelsen, H. 1945. *General theory of law and state*. Cambridge, MA: Harvard University Press.
Kelsen, H. 1967. *Pure theory of law*, 2nd ed. Trans. M. Knight, Berkeley: University of California Press.
Kelsen, H. 2002. *Introduction to the problems of legal theory*. Trans. B. Litschewski-Paulson and S.L. Paulson. Oxford: Oxford University Press.
Lincoln, A. 1990. New birth of freedom. The Gettysburg address, November 19, 1863. In *Lincoln on democracy*, ed. M.M. Cuomo and H. Holzer. New York: Harper Collins.
MacCormick, N. 1999. *Questioning sovereignty: Law, state and nation in the European commonwealth*. Oxford: Oxford University Press.
MacCormick, N. 2007. *Institutions of law. An essay in legal theory*. Oxford: Oxford University Press.
Madison, J. 1961. No. 51. In *The federalist papers*, ed. C. Rossiter. New York: Mentor.
Mansfield, W.M. 1770. *R* v. *Wilkes*, 4 Burr 2527 [98 ER 327].
Marshall, J. 1824. *Osborn* v. *Bank of United States*, 22 U.S. 738.
Mill, J.S. 1958. *Considerations on representative government*. Indianapolis: Liberal Arts Press.
Mill, J.S. 1989. On liberty. In *On liberty and other writings*, ed. S. Collini. Cambridge: Cambridge University Press.
Rawls, J. 1971. *A theory of justice*. Cambridge, MA: Harvard University Press.
Scalia, A. 1989. The rule of law as a law of rules. *University of Chicago Law Review* 56: 1187.
Sen, A. 1992. *Inequality reexamined*. Cambridge, MA: Harvard University Press.

Tocqueville, A. 1969. *Democracy in America*. New York: Anchor Books.
Waldron, J. 2002. Large legislatures. In *Legal and political philosophy. Philosophy of law and of politics*, ed. E. Villanueva. Amsterdam: Rodopi.
Waldron, J. 2008. The concept and the rule of law. *Georgia Law Review* 43: 1.
Waluchow, W.J. 2007. *A common law theory of judicial review. The living tree*. Cambridge: Cambridge University Press.

Chapter 7
The Rule of Law: Is the Line Between the Formal and the Moral Blurred?

Gülriz Uygur

7.1 Introduction

Jeremy Waldron states that "some things are green, some are blue; but on the borderlines there are blue/green cases of uncertainty" (2002, 149). Waldron rightly states that we can encounter some cases that are sort of green and sort of blue (2002, 161). Similarly, the principles of the rule of law may be regarded on the line between formal and moral and one may claim that this line is blurred. To explain this point, we may move from Waldron's ideas about competing conceptions of the law. Waldron states that there are "arguments of reason that maintain competing contentions about what exactly the law is. Inevitably, the line between characterization and normativity in these arguments will be blurred. One party will argue that a particular proposition cannot be inferred from the law as it is; the other party will respond that it can be inferred if we just credit the law with more coherence than people have in the past. Our account of what the law is, then, is not readily separable from our account of how the law aspires to present itself. Our response to the pressure for coherence may well alter our sense of what the law already contains." (2008, 49)

Similarly, regarding the principles of the rule of law, one party will argue that a particular proposition cannot be inferred from these principles; the other will argue that the inference is possible. If we have an account of the rule of law connected with the inner morality of law, we may claim that our formal account of the rule of law is not separable from the political ideal of it.

In this paper, I will argue, in Sect. 7.2 that the rule of law has features that lead to claims that it is on the line between the formal and the moral, and I will explain why this line is blurred. Secondly, in Sect. 7.3, I will try to show that our formal account of the rule of law is not separable from the political ideal of it.

G. Uygur (✉)
Law Faculty, Ankara University, Ankara, Turkey
e-mail: guygur@law.ankara.edu.tr

I.B. Flores and K.E. Himma (eds.), *Law, Liberty, and the Rule of Law*,
Ius Gentium: Comparative Perspectives on Law and Justice 18,
DOI 10.1007/978-94-007-4743-2_7,

7.2 The Rule of Law on the Borderline[1]

What are the reasons that lead to the claim that the rule of law is on the line between the formal and the moral?

1. There are requirements associated with the rule of law that lead to regard it as being on the borderline.

The rule of law has multiple requirements. We may explain these within a single conception of the rule of law. However, there are also different such conceptions. It is difficult to classify these conceptions because some of them are not completely different from each other. They are "different but compatible conceptions of the rule of law" (Barber 2004, 475).

On the other hand, some are competing conceptions of a single concept. An example of these competing conceptions concerns the instrumental version and the substantial version of the rule of law. While the instrumental version is connected with an efficacious legal system, the substantial version is the basis of political morality (Radin 1989, 783). Their main questions about the requirements of the rule of law are different. The instrumental version focuses on the requirements of the rule of law for an efficacious legal system. These requirements are related to the formal aspect of the rule of law and are usually explained according to Lon Fuller's version of the rule of law.[2] On the other hand, the substantive version stresses the values furthered by such as fairness, freedom, autonomy. It is also possible to explain this aspect of the rule of law according to its formal features or Fuller's version of it. Then, we may say that there are formal aspects of the rule of law that lead some theorists to regard it as an inherently moral ideal but some others to regard it not as a moral-political ideal. To explain how this is possible, we should move from the formal aspects of the rule of law.

Generally, one may say that the formal aspects of the rule of law are connected with the formal constraints on lawmaking, law-application, and law-enforcement (MacDonald 2001, 98). Robert S. Summers classified these constraints as methodological, procedural, accommodative and authorizational. Some of the principles of the rule of law, such as clarity and prospectivity, are methodologically formal, *i.e.* they are connected with the creation of the law, "with how that very law itself is to take shape, and with what that shape is" (1999, 1701). Some of the principles of the rule of law, such as due process, are procedurally formal and they apply to law-making and law-applying processes. In relation to accommodatively formal, all of the principles of the rule of law have extensive generality of scope (1999, 1701). Furthermore, some of the principles of the rule of law are authorizationally formal. "That is, they confer or limit authority and so pertain to validity" (1999,

[1] In this part of the article, I am indebted to David Luban for valuable suggestions on both content and style.

[2] Fuller's eight principles are publicity, retroactivity, clarity, constancy, feasibility, prospectivity, generality, congruence (Fuller 1978, 65).

1702). Summers collected these four senses of the formal under the title of affirmatively formal "in that each signifies a positive feature or features actually present, as distinguished from merely lacking or failing to express an opposite attribute" (1999, 1702).

In addition to the affirmatively formal, we might use the term formal to contrast the rule of law with something else – for example, substantive principles such as human rights (Summers 1999, 1702). The second meaning of the contrastively formal is connected with the governance by law, not men (1999, 1703). In fact, the rule of law is generally regarded as opposed to the governance by people.

Focusing on the supposed contrast between governance by law and governance by people, Joseph Raz rightly stated that we must be governed by human beings. Legal actors such as legislators and judges are human beings (2001, 290). In this regard, we may say that governance by law is impossible without human beings. If so, can we say that there is no difference between governance by law and governance by people? Is there "no rule, acting as a metaphorical wall separating the law from politics, or law from men"? (West 2003, 24)

If not, what is the meaning of the governance by law?

We may say that it includes constraints on arbitrariness. In connection with this arbitrariness, there can be two views in the literature. One of them derives from the political theory, the other from the analysis of the concept of law. The former is related to the restriction of the arbitrary use of public power. For this, government in all its actions is bound by rules fixed and announced in advance. According to the latter, the rule of law is related to certain features that the law should possess to be able to guide human conduct. In this regard, the ideal of the rule of law reduces the arbitrariness that is connected with the law itself (Dyzenhaus 2009, 12–3).

There are grounds supporting both views. To evaluate them, we should examine the relationship between the rule of law and the legal system.

2. There is a relationship between the rule of law and the legal system: anything purporting to be a legal system must satisfy the rule of law criteria to at least some extent if the system is to be recognizable as a legal system at all.[3]

Legal systems must meet most of the formal requirements of the rule of law, at least to some degree. In fact, the rule of law and the legal system are intrinsically connected concepts. Legal rules guide human conduct, and to regulate conduct these rules must have certain characteristics that are associated with the formal requirements of the rule of law. As John Rawls rightly stated, these requirements are "implicit in the notion of regulating behaviour by public rules" (1991, 238). From this definition we may derive the claim that every legal system by its nature needs procedural rules. In this manner the rule of law and the legal system are intrinsically connected: "A legal system can be in better or worse shape, but after a point it can be in such bad shape that it does not satisfy the criteria for being a legal system at all" (Waldron 2008, 45).

[3] I am indebted to David Luban for pointing out the need to make this point explicit.

3. If the rule of law and the legal system are intrinsically connected, we may say that a legal system should embody the ideal of the rule of law. But is this ideal a moral-political one, or not, or is the line between the formal and the moral blurred? I argue that the line is blurred.

With regard to the connection between the rule of law and the legal system, it is possible to see it as a better vehicle and also a moral ideal. As a better vehicle, the rule of law is understood as "a prerequisite for any efficacious legal order" (Radin 1989, 783). It is necessary for the efficacy of the legal system. As a moral ideal it serves moral values. In this regard, we may say that the rule of law is not only a moral ideal to which the law should aspire, but also it is a criterion that enables the evaluation of legal systems (as better or worse). This claim is connected with the procedural aspects of the rule of law. According to a generally accepted view, the formal understanding of the rule of law does not require, at least directly, anything substantive. For example, Fuller's account of the rule of law requires that "the state should do whatever it wants to do in an orderly predictable way, giving us plenty of advance notice by publicizing the general norms on which its actions will be based, and that it should then stick to those norms and not arbitrarily depart from them even if it seems politically advantageous to do so" (Waldron 2008, 8). David Luban observes, however, that one of Fuller's aims in bringing his eight canons is "not simply conditions of efficacy of a legal system, but moral requirements".[4] Specifically, "Fuller in fact emphasizes the practical efficacy of governance through rules. But Fuller also believes that the canons push the law away from a certain kind of moral badness" (Luban 2010, 39), namely a despotism that operates by creating uncertainty about what the rules are that people must follow.

At this point, we may claim that the line between the formal and the moral is blurred in respect of the rule of law. But one may oppose to this view. For example, Matthew H. Kramer considers it a divided phenomenon: "As the set of conditions that obtain whenever any legal system exists and operates, the rule of law is *per se* a morally neutral state of affairs. Especially in any sizeable society, the rule of law is indispensable for the preservation of public power and the coordination of people's activities and the securing of individuals' liberties; but it is likewise indispensable for a government's effective perpetration of large-scale projects of evil over lengthy periods… It therefore lacks any intrinsic moral standing. All the same, when the rule of law is operative within a benign regime, its moral value goes beyond lending itself to worthy uses. It does indeed promote the attainment of worthy ends by enabling governmental officials and private citizens to pursue and realize such ends, but, within a benign regime, it also does more. Instead of merely being instrumentally valuable, it furthermore becomes expressive of the very ideals which it helps to foster. Its basic features take on the moral estimableness of those ideals, for the sustainment of the rule of law in such circumstances is a deliberate manifestation of a society's adherence to liberal-democratic values" (Kramer 2007, 102).

[4] Luban states with regard to Fuller's other aim: "he announced that the canons are conditions that make law possible – in other words, that enactments which deviate too much from the canons are not bad law, but rather no law at all" (*vid.* Luban 2010, 31).

In this regard, Kramer defines two principal incarnations of the rule of law: "Firstly, as a general juristic phenomenon, it amounts to nothing more and nothing less than the fundamental conditions that have to be satisfied for the existence of any legal system. Secondly, whenever that juristic phenomenon obtains specifically in liberal-democratic societies – which exhibit rich diversity among themselves in their detailed institutions and practices – it is a morally charitable expression of commitments to the dignity and equality of individuals. Yet, because the rule of law is a morally precious desideratum in some settings and not in others, any attribution of invariance to its key features is prone to mislead" (2007, 102).

Kramer says that his conception of the rule of law belongs to the domain of legal philosophy, not of political philosophy. He claims that the jurisprudential conception of the rule of law implies sufficient conditions for the existence of the legal system. This conception of the rule of law is itself morally neutral. On the other hand, Kramer states that the moral-political conception of the rule of law belongs to the domain of moral-political theory. In this respect, formal principles of the law are not to be regarded as "necessary and jointly sufficient conditions for the existence of the legal system, but as precepts of political morality". Though they are compatible with each other, the moral-political conception of the rule of law is larger than the jurisprudential conception of it (Kramer 2007, 143). Kramer explains this divided phenomenon by referring to Fuller's eight principles.

In respect of morality, Fuller's eight principles are closely linked to the law regimes that are liberal-democratic in substance. In this regard, one may claim that in liberal-democratic societies the matters of form can become matters of substance.

7.3 The Moral Non-neutrality of the Rule of Law

"Our formal account of the rule of law is not separable from the political ideal of it" or the rule of law is not a morally-neutral concept.[5]

To explain this, first, I move from the relationship between the legal system and the rule of law and following Waldron I claim that there are two aspects of this relationship.

1. The relationship between the legal system and the rule of law has two aspects.

According to Waldron legal systems need to fulfil certain elementary requirements. These are the existence of functioning courts, general public norms, positivity, orientation to the public good, and systematicity. Waldron states that among these requirements, three "are intimately connected with Rule-of-Law requirements: (A) systematicity is associated with the Rule-of-Law requirement of consistency or integrity; (B) the existence of general norms is associated with the Rule-of-Law requirements of generality, publicity, and stability; and (C) the existence of the distinctive institutions we call courts is associated with the Rule-of-Law requirement of procedural due process" (2008, 44).

[5] I was inspired in this point by Waldron (2008, 49).

One of these aspects is connected with the "a conceptual account of the rule of law… that emphasizes rules and a Rule of Law ideal that concentrates on their characteristics like their generality, determinacy, etc." (Waldron 2008, 58). While this aspect of the rule of law is about general rules, the second aspect of the rule of law is connected with the impartial administration of such rules. The procedural aspect of the rule of law is connected with the procedural aspects of the courts (their distinctive procedures and practices-like legal argumentation) and the features of natural justice (2008, 55). The first and second aspects of the rule of law, Waldron states, "are intimately connected with one another" (2008, 59), since a legal system requires more than rules and this system and the rule of law are bound together (2008, 58):

> There is a natural correlation between a conceptual account of the rule of law… that emphasizes rules and a Rule of Law ideal that concentrates on their characteristics like their generality, determinacy, etc. Additionally, there is a natural correlation between a conceptual account of law that focuses not just on the general norms established in a society but on the distinctive procedural features of the institutions that administer them, and an account of the rule of law that is less fixated on predictability and more insistent on the opportunities for argumentation and responsiveness to argument that legal institutions provide.

Furthermore to provide determinacy or predictability or to make a clear rule we need the second aspect, *i.e.* impartial administration of justice. But impartial administration is not enough to provide determinacy or predictability, because our aims are not determinate and our words have open texture, particularly in vague or general rules. For this reason, for example, a judge cannot decide according to pre-existing rules or two judges, both aiming at impartial interpretation, might arrive at different answers to the same interpretive question.[6] Accordingly, we may claim that to provide predictability to the law, it is necessary to regard legal practices and especially legal argumentation. In this regard judges should be aware of the true grounds of the rule of law, namely substantive aspects of it (West 2003, 23): "Courts, hearings, and arguments are aspects of law which are not optional extras; They are integral parts of how law works and they are indispensable to the package of law's respect for human agency. To say that we should value aspects of governance that promote the clarity and determinacy of rules for the sake of individual freedom, …, is to truncate what the rule of law rests upon: respect for the freedom and the dignity of each person as an active center of intelligence" (Waldron 2008, 60).

Inspiring Fuller's lawyers as lawgivers and law-appliers, we may regard the second aspect not only from the standpoint of judges but also of other law-appliers, for example lawyers, prosecutors.[7]

To explain the first aspect in the context of the moral-political ideal of the rule of law I move from Kramer's claim about the relationship between liberal democratic-society and the rule of law. Then, I explain that the second aspect of the relationship between the legal system and the rule of law needs substantive accounts.

---

[6] Here I elaborate an idea of David Luban's stated in his comments.

[7] I was inspired at this point by David Luban (2007, 104)

2. In connection with the first aspect of this relationship, it is true that in a liberal-democratic society the rule of law can become a deliberate manifestation of a society's adherence to liberal-democratic values.

If we accept this statement, we should also accept that the rule of law has a minimum of moral content.

However, Kramer claims that the rule of law is an instrument and can be used for good or bad purposes. For example, according to Kramer, "the rule of law, as the realization of the necessary existence of the necessary and sufficient conditions for the existence of a legal system, is itself morally neutral. It is indispensably serviceable for the pursuit of benevolent ends on a large scale over a sustained period, but is also indispensably serviceable for the pursuit of wicked ends on such a scale over such a period" (2007, 143). In other words, like coordinating people on the one hand and pursuing of government's effective projects of evil on the other, it serves opposite aims. Kramer also states that "it is neutral on all moral and political questions, for example, concerning the uses to which law should be put, the appropriate limits on legal regulation of individuals' lives, the legitimacy or illegitimacy of various patterns of differentiation among people under the terms of legal norms, the conditions under which a regime of law is a just regime" (2007, 143).

In fact, formal principles of law, at least directly, do not limit the content of the rules. It is true that the formal principles of the rule of law have form-prescriptive content, they prescribe formal features of the precepts, institutions. Almost all of them are connected with the procedures in which law is created and implemented. Some of them are connected with the judicial procedures and structural institutions (Summers 2006, 337). In this regard they do not specify the policy or other substantive content of value. For example in connection with clarity, Hart says that "there is no (…) special incompatibility between clear laws and evil. Clearer laws are (…) ethically neutral though they are not equally compatible with vague and well-defined aims" (Soper 2007, 62; Hart 1965, 1287).

There is always a possibility that a well-designed norm may be combined with a bad policy (Soper 2007, 63). This does not imply, however, that the rule of law has not any moral value.

The state may use it for good or bad policies. "But the qualified serviceability of legal practices for self-interested goals does not undermine the claim of those practices to embody moral standards; nor does it suggest that the practices are morally neutral" (Simmonds 2005, 63). The rule of law does not justify bad policies. It is an essential precondition for the attainment of certain good states of affairs.[8] If the legal system is recognizable despite its bad shape, we may demand from it other requirements of the rule of law. In this regard to say that it is a legal system does not mean that "we rest satisfied with these minimum credible degrees. There is always room for improvement, and there is also danger of deterioration" (Waldron 2008, 46). In this respect, it is an essential precondition for the attainment of certain

[8] I was inspired in this point by Nigel Simmonds (2005, 62).

good states of affairs. That is, "adherence to principles of the rule of law tends to beget good content in the law being made" (Summers 2006, 343). However, we should notice that the formal principles of the rule of law guarantee the impartial and regular administration of rules. These principles "impose rather weak constraints in the basic structure, but ones that are not by any means negligible" (Rawls 1991, 236).

There are many ways to explain why these principles impose weak constraints or include a moral minimum, or why in the liberal-democratic society the rule of law can become a deliberate manifestation of a society's adherence to liberal-democratic values. For example, like Rawls, one may state the relationship between the formal conception of the rule of law and substantive values. Rawlsian principles of the rule of law are different from Fuller's and his principles may be easily connected to substantive values.[9] Rawls states that these principles provide a more secure basis for liberty: "It is clear that, other things equal, the dangers to liberty are less when the law is impartially and regularly administered in accordance with the principle of legality… One who complies with the announced rules need never fear an infringement of his liberty." (1991, 241) A second way is to regard these principles as constitutive of the same values: "Consider, for example, procedural fairness, as served by principles of the rule of law requiring fair notice of a criminal charge or of an adverse claim, and requiring fair opportunity to respond in court. The form-prescriptive contents of these principles go far to define the very nature of such fairness. Here form is constitutive and not merely instrumental" (Summers 2006, 343). In this regard fair procedures have values intrinsic to them, "for example, a procedure having the value of impartiality by giving all an equal chance to present their case" (Rawls 1996, 422). A third way to derive morality from the principles of the rule of law is not to begin with those principles but with the political ideal that the rule of law aims to realize.

A fourth way is to follow Fuller's idea that the eight canons of the rule of law contain the moral minimum. In this way, we can move from features of these canons and explain how it is possible to say that governance by law implies morality. This way provides an argument against Kramer's views. In this regard, I will follow Luban's views about Fuller's eight canons.

Unlike the positivists who deny the necessary relations between legal rules and morality, Luban states that Fuller insists that lawmaking is itself a moral enterprise. Luban says that "Fuller's arguments about the morality of law are meant to show that lawmaking has its own distinctive virtues (conformity to eight canons) and its own distinctive moral outlook (respect for the self-determining agency of the governed), both of which follow from the nature of the lawmaking enterprise and not directly from general morality" (2007, 118).

---

[9] Rawls, in the list of the first principle of justice, also gives a place to the rights and liberties covered by the rule of law beside other rights and liberties (Rawls 2003, 44). For example, "freedom from arbitrary arrest and seizure as defined by the concept of the rule of law". In this respect his rule of law conception provides a more secure basis for the liberties.

This view is different from Kramer's. Kramer says that "we can… benefit from Fuller's reflections in two ways, which correspond to the two versions of the rule of law" (2007, 103). As we stated before, according to Kramer, the two versions of the rule of law are the jurisprudential conception of the rule of law and the moral-political conception.

Luban's views about Fuller's idea reflect a different understanding of the rule of law.[10] Far from the concept of the rule of law as a divided phenomenon, the rule of law has its own moral "properties that designers may never have intended or even thought about, and that are connected only indirectly to general morality. Identifying the morality of institutions, the virtues and vices of participating in them, is a matter of discovery, not invention – a matter of reason rather than fiat" (Luban 2007, 118).

Luban stresses that Fuller's eight canons have substantive features, since they constrain legal content (Luban 2010, 32). He claims that "there is nothing procedural about them. To say that laws cannot be vague, or logically inconsistent with each other, are content-based conditions. So too the requirement that the behaviour laws demand is feasible for people to perform. And so too the canon of prospectivity: forbidding, as it does, laws that penalize behaviour retroactively, the canon builds a content-based dating requirement into the law" (2010, 34).

Luban's claim about these canons' substantive features does not mean that they constrain legal content according to requirements of morality or public policy choices (2010, 35):

> Rather, they are substantive in a more literal way: they constrain what laws can say, what requirements can say, what requirements can or cannot be included in the corpus juris. A law cannot demand something inconsistent with an existing law that remains in force, or require the impossible, for example that subjects change their behaviour retroactively. To be sure, these requirements place quite minimum constraints on the content of law. But they are nevertheless constraints on law's content, and – equally important – they have nothing to do with the procedures through which laws are enacted.

Luban does not ignore that "obviously, very harsh laws can be promulgated clearly, publicly, prospectively, and so on. But the rule of law does deprive governments of some of their favourite devices of intimidation, namely vague laws, secret laws, retroactive laws, confusing and inconsistent laws, all of which are used to keep citizens cautious and fearful… The point is not that the rule of law is logically incompatible with despotic government or harsh laws. Rather, the point is that the rule of law robs despotism of some of its most characteristic devices, and in this way it is practically incompatible with despotism" (2010, 40).

If the rule of law is practically incompatible with despotism, we cannot claim that a despotic regime is best protected by the rule of law. If so, we may say that there is no relationship between a despotic regime and the rule of law like the relationship

---

[10] In this respect, we should notice three perspectives regarding the rule of law in this text. Two of them are Kramer's two conceptions of the rule of law. The third one, which occurs as the basic problem of this text, explains it in connection with moral theory (I am indebted to Brian Bix for the distinction among three perspectives regarding the rule of law in this text).

between a liberal regime and the rule of law. Thus, we cannot say that in a despotic regime, the rule of law can become a deliberate manifestation of a society's adherence to the despotic regime. If we cannot claim this, we should accept that the rule of law contains a minimum morality.

As stated before, Fuller does not ignore that his eight canons are connected to the efficacy of the legal system. As Luban rightly observes, however, "while Fuller agrees that the principles of legality are instrumentally necessary to make governance by law effective, he thinks that governing by law rather than managerial direction represents a sacrifice of expediency in the name of principle. The ultimate justification of the principles of legality is therefore moral, not instrumental" (2007, 112). Regarding this, Luban stresses Fuller's distinction between governance by law and managerial direction. Fuller states that the canons of clarity, consistency, feasibility, constancy through time, and publicity are in a different context in the managerial direction from the governance by law. While these canons concern only efficacy in the managerial direction, in the governance by law they reflect morality. "There, they are professional virtues of the lawgiver, part and parcel of the mutual respect that Fuller believes is at the heart of the relationship between a lawmaker and those whom she governs" (Luban 2007, 115).

In the relationship between governor and governed, Luban states these eight canons as virtues of law-making. The canons of generality and congruence between rules and their enforcement which are specific for the governance by rule, require the commitment to bind the governed only through general rules and that the commitment that "also binds the lawmaker establishes the moral relationship of reciprocity between governors and governed. These two canons are moral commitments that define the enterprise as lawgiving rather than something else" (2007, 116).

In accordance with this minimum morality, following Luban, we may claim that Fuller's eight canons of the rule of law enhance human dignity. As Luban rightly states, the reason for this is "not that procedural requirements can generate substantive requirements, but rather that surprisingly minimal substantive requirements can unexpectedly implicate far-reaching choices about freedom and dignity" (2010, 35). Luban says that "Fuller believes that the rule of law enhances human dignity" (2010, 40) for two reasons. One of them is that the rule of law is practically incompatible with a despotic regime. To explain this point, Luban invokes his human dignity conception. According to Fuller, human dignity is thought to be connected with respectful relationships. While respectful relationships honour human dignity, humiliating relationships violate it (2010, 40). For this reason "lawmaking that violates Fuller's canons offends against human dignity by subjecting people to an especially humiliating condition: that of perpetual uncertainty and fearfulness because one's fate lies in the hands of official whim, which can choose at will to stigmatize conduct as criminal" (Luban 2010, 41).

The other reason connected with the human dignity concerns the connection between general rules and autonomy. In the framework of these rules, people can plan their life and make decisions (Luban 2010, 41). "Rule of law regimes count on citizens to understand and interpret their requirements in particular cases"

(Luban 2010, 42). In other words, the generality of rules provides a framework within which citizens behave like an autonomous agency.[11]

In short, Fuller's eight canons are related to respect for human agency[12]: "To embark on the enterprise of subjecting human conduct to the governance of rules involves… a commitment to the view that man is, or can become, a responsible agent, capable of understanding and following rules, and answerable for his defaults" (Waldron 2008, 27–28). In this manner, we may claim that the morality of the rule of law has primacy over the efficiency.[13]

3. We cannot avoid relying on substantive content.

As stated before, according to Waldron, there are two aspects of the rule of law. Regarding the first aspect which insists on rules and their characteristics like their generality, determinacy, *et cetera*, I moved from Kramer's claim, but unlike him I tried to show that the rule of law contains a minimum morality. While I was doing this, I based on Luban's ideas and tried to explain law's minimum morality regarding the enterprise of lawmaking. Concerning the second aspect of law, I will start with a paragraph from Rawls and try to explain how this aspect is related to morality (1999, 495–6):

> The rule of law means the regulative role of certain institutions and their associated legal and judicial practices. It may mean, among other thing, that all officers of the government, including the executive, are under the law and that their acts are subject to judicial scrutiny, that the judiciary is suitably independent, in that civilian authority is supreme over the military. Moreover, it may mean that judges' decisions rest on interpreting existing law and relevant precedents, that judges must justify their verdicts by reference thereto and adhere to a consistent reading from case to case, or else find a reasonable basis for distinguishing them, and so on. Similar constraints do not bind legislators; while they may not defy basic law and can try to politically to change it only in ways the constitution permits, they need not explain or justify their vote, though their constituents may call them to account. The rule of law exists so long as such legal institutions and their associated practices (variously specified) are conducted in a reasonable way in accordance with the political values that apply to them: impartiality and consistency, adherence to law and respect for precedent, all in the light of a coherent understanding of recognized constitutional norms as viewed as controlling the conduct of all government officers.

---

[11] On the other hand, whether legal autonomy enhances human dignity is a different problem. In fact, this conception of autonomy, David Luban rightly states, does not suffice to guarantee human dignity: "Private oppression, domestic violence, workplace exploitation, and radical inequality are evils that legal autonomy will not cure. Indeed, legal autonomy may contribute to them by insulating private power from the state" (2010, 43).

[12] In this respect, Luban rightly states that this is also connected with what is wrong in Fuller's theory: "those whose self-determining agency law aims to further need not include the entire population subject to the law, because the rules may really be addressed only to a numerical or power majority … That is, it may well be that the legal edifice of patriarchy aims to enhance the self-determining agency of men. But it does so at the expense of women, who are subject to the tyranny… of their husbands and fathers. Justice for guys coexists with injustice for women" (2007, 126).

[13] Meanwhile, these canons are also considered in the context of the law's action-guiding function. But, Waldron rightly states, positivists, although they accept this function of the law, may not accept that it is connected with a dignitarian value. In this respect, it seems important to insist on distinctiveness of "an action-guiding rather than a purely behaviour-eliciting model of social control" (2008, 28).

It is possible to deduce three points from this paragraph:

(A) Following Rawls, first, it is important to state that there are legal institutions and their practices in the legal system and the rule of law is a regulative model for these institutions. In this regard, it is also important to regard Fuller's eight canons as governing not only lawgivers, but also law-appliers. Rawls considers judges as law appliers. However, he uses general terms such as legal institutions and their practices. Then, we may claim that this includes other law-appliers.

One of the means of the rule of law as a regulative model for legal institutions is its requirement that independent courts act and control the conduct of all government officers. It is also possible to explain the relationship among the rule of law, natural justice, and the courts according to Waldron and Fuller.

According to Waldron, the courts constitute one of the necessary elements of the legal system. To explain this he moves from Hart's distinction between primary and secondary rules. Among the institutions connected with the rules of adjudication regarding secondary rules are the courts (2008, 21). Waldron also mentions Raz's ideas about courts as norm-applying institutions. According to Raz, courts are a key to understanding a legal system (Waldron 2008, 22).

According to Waldron, the relationship between the rule of law and the courts is connected to the procedural aspects of the courts and the features of natural justice. Waldron says that "when people say, for example, that the Rule of Law is threatened on the streets of Islamabad or in the cages at Guantanamo, it is the procedural elements they have in mind, much more than the traditional virtues of clarity, prospectivity, determinacy, and knowing where you stand. They are worried about the independence of Pakistani courts and about due process rights of detainees in the war on the terror" (Waldron 2008, 9). Waldron is right to stress this aspect. In Turkey, for example, the rule of law is discussed in the context of these two requirements. In connection with the independence of the courts, we have serious problems regarding political power, especially with the executive branch. When people claim that the rule of law is threatened, they intend to explain this point. We also have problems with the rights of detainees.

Fuller also sees that courts are necessary for the legal system and states that one of the most important conditions of the rule of law is judicial independence. Furthermore, with regard to his canon of congruence, procedural devices such as elements of procedural due process rights are also important.[14]

(B) Secondly, according to Rawls, as stated above, it is not enough for the rule of law that the judiciary is independent, but also that the judges' decisions are consistent

[14] While Fuller stresses the importance of the courts, for him it is not enough to insist solely on these institutions. Fuller says that "in this country it is chiefly to the judiciary that is entrusted the task of preventing a discrepancy between the law as declared and as actually administered. … there are, however, serious disadvantages in any system that looks solely to the courts as a bulwark against the lawless administration of the law. It makes the correction of abuses dependent upon the willingness and financial ability of the affected party to take his case to litigation" (1978, 81).

and reasonable in the light of a coherent understanding of recognized constitutional norms. The independence of the judiciary is not by itself adequate for the rule of law.[15] Namely, "the problem of judicial constraint is not that simple, and the strategies that are adequate to advance the predictability and uniformity of the law defy easy summary. The rule of law requires sound practical judgement by judges of integrity" (Solum 2002, 23).

We may also explain this requirement according to Fuller's canon of congruence which requires congruence between the law in books and the law in action. According to Fuller, the reality of law is in human action and not in mere words and the existence of the law depends on both (1968, 11). He says that "though much of the law today is statutory, this law is not actually applied to human affairs by the legislature which enacts it. That is the task of the courts. It is in the courtroom, then, that life and law intersect. Here it is that the Word becomes the Deed and in the process acquires a meaning that is identical with its projection into human affairs." (1968, 12).

Fuller accepts that fidelity to law does not make the role of the judges passive and that judges inescapably have a creative role (1978, 87). In this regard, their task is not only to articulate the law, but also to reconstruct it. Kenneth Winston states that "the judge's task of applying the law involves the elaboration of authoritative standards in previously unanticipated directions, under the guidance of common aims and ideals. In this sense, it is an inescapably interpretive and normative task" (1994, 409). However, this creative role does not imply judicial arbitrariness.

Fuller says that in respect of maintaining congruence between law and official action, the matter of interpretation is important. "Legality requires that judges and other officials apply statutory law, not according to their fancy or with crabbed literalness, but in accordance with principles of interpretation that are appropriate to their position in the whole legal order" (1978, 82). Fuller states a great variety of ways by which this congruence may be destroyed: "mistaken interpretation, inaccessibility of the law, lack of insight into what is required to maintain the integrity of a legal system, bribery, prejudice, indifference, stupidity, and drive toward personal power" (1978, 81). Then, "they may give the law a meaning in action quite different from that properly to be found in its words. When this occurs, the gap separating the Word from the Deed is reopened" (1968, 12).

Fuller gives to interpretation a central position in the internal morality of the law (1978, 91). It is connected with the interpretive agent's ethics. Fuller says that "the human element can of course fail, and it can fail not simply because of corruption or sloth, but for lack of a sense of institutional role and a failure to perceive the true nature of the problems involved in constructing and administering a legal system" (1968, 39–40).

In connection with Fuller, we may claim that judges have an important role in realizing and securing his eight canons. Since there are gaps or indeterminacy in law,

[15] For example, in Turkey, there is a serious problem connected with the discretionary power of the courts, especially in political and gender-related cases. It is possible to see easily that the determinants of law are prejudices, ideologies or the judges' beliefs in many cases.

judges are not only law-applying persons, but also law-makers. When they act as law-makers, they are subject to eight canons[16] and should also justify their decisions. Regarding this and interpretation, however, there should be some methods, argumentation and reason for realizing the inner morality of law.

At this point, it is possible to claim that law enhances human dignity in respect of the decisions of courts. Court decisions affect the basic rights and duties of citizens and "men have to rely on the decisions of courts and shape their affairs by them" (Fuller 1968, 14). If so, judges far from deciding arbitrary should reach a decision according to the requirements of congruence. Fuller says that "to act on rules confidently, men must not only have a chance to learn what the rules are, but must also be assured that in case of a dispute about their meaning there is available some method for resolving the dispute" (1978, 57). In this regard, it is important to emphasize the argumentative aspect of law.

Regarding this point, it is also possible to claim that judges' decisions should meet the expectations of citizens. This is connected with predictability. According to Aleksander Peczenick, to satisfy people's expectations in modern society legal decisions should be not only highly predictable but also highly acceptable from the moral point of view. He says that "Ceteris paribus, the higher degree of such predictability, the higher the chance of an individual to efficiently plan his life. And, ceteris paribus, the higher the degree of moral acceptability of legal decisions, the higher the chance of one to make the life thus planned satisfactory" (2008, 25–6). Then, if the law respects the human being as an autonomous agent, it is necessary to apply argument and reason.

Furthermore, Waldron clearly states that this aspect of the rule of law is "indispensable to the law's respect for human agency. To say that we should value aspects of governance that promote the clarity and determinacy of rules for the sake of individual freedom, but not the opportunities for argumentation that a free and self-possessed individual is likely to demand, is to truncate what the rule of law rests upon: respect for the freedom and dignity of each person as an active center of intelligence" (2008, 60).

(C) Thirdly, Rawlsian rule of law also emphasizes the role of justification. As stated before, Rawls says that "the rule of law exists so long as such legal institutions and their associated practices (variously specified) are conducted in a reasonable way in accordance with the political values that apply to them: impartiality and consistency, adherence to law and respect for precedent, all in the light of a coherent understanding of recognized constitutional norms as viewed as controlling the conduct of all government officers". Following this statement, it is possible to say that sound practical judgement requires adherence to law and respect for precedent, accordance with political values and all of these should be made in the framework of coherent understanding of the constitution which is viewed as controlling the conduct of all government officers.

---

[16] I was inspired at this point by Luban (2010, 44).

One may easily see that Rawls incorporates descriptive and normative elements in sound practical judgement. These elements are important for legal reasoning. Peczenick states that legal reasoning consists of two components: one is connected with the sources of law, and the other is "a continual creation of value judgements that tell one whether to follow or not these sources, evaluations and norms" (2008, 36). Rawls states sources of law as statutes and precedents, which are evaluated not only from the political values of the rule of law but also from the political ideal of it.

This definition reflects not only the formal requirements of the rule of law, but also the substantive requirements of it, since it includes political ideal. Then we may say that the second aspect of requirement of the law implies its political ideal.[17]

In fact, not only from Rawls's conception, but also from moving the issue of interpretation of the constitution, it is possible to reach the same result, since this is generally seen as a moral issue. Namely, not only the Rawlsian Constitution, but also most constitutions have moral content, since they regulate the area of human rights and civil liberties and draw the limits of political authorities. If so, we may say that coherent understanding of recognized constitutional norms should include moral and political considerations. This understanding is important for finding a solution to the problems of indeterminacy and moral issues. Ronald Dworkin also states this point (2003, 5):

> In the decades after World War II, more and more of these democracies gave judges new and – except in the United States – unprecedented powers to review the acts of administrative agencies and officials under broad doctrines of reasonableness, natural justice and proportionality, and then even more surprising powers to review the enactments of legislatures to determine whether the legislatures had violated rights of individual citizens laid down in international treaties and domestic constitutions. The impact of moral pronouncement on judicial argument thus became much more evident and pronounced. In recent years international courts of different kinds, including international 'constitutional' courts like the European Court of Human Rights, have become progressively more important, and the role and powers of judges have therefore acquired yet a further dimension.

Dworkin explains the judge's new role in three ways which are connected with each other. Judges confront moral issues. "First, the need for judges to confront moral issues is more pervasive in general administrative regulation, and much more pervasive in constitutional and international adjudication, than it is either ordinary statutory interpretation or common law development". Since standards connected with the judge's role are in moral language, moral judgement is more effective in administrative regulation (2003, 5). Likely, in constitutional and international adjudications there are moral standards. In these adjudications, cases that are connected with moral standards are difficult cases. Dworkin accepts that to a certain degree the judge's moral reflection is shaped by practice and precedent. But how and in what degree it is shaped by them is a difficult question of political morality. Dworkin

[17] At this point, one may claim that arbitrariness in law is connected with the arbitrariness in political theory, since to reduce arbitrariness in law is appealed to political morality.

states secondly that moral issues in constitutional regulation are the most divisive and controversial in the community (2003, 6). Dworkin gives examples from the United States. Some of them are problems of minority groups in relation to discrimination. Thirdly, Dworkin says that the issues for judges in constitutional cases and administrative adjudication are "largely matters of political morality rather than individual ethics" (2003, 7).

Then, we may say that moral consideration is indispensable for justification. If so, regarding the rule of law, we should put emphasis on its political ideal.

7.4 Conclusion

In this paper, I tried to show that the rule of law has a moral minimum and, that legal institutions and practices should be governed in the light of this minimum on the borderline of the formal and the moral. As stated above, this minimum requires the application of its political ideal.

To explain this, I started from the meaning of governance by law, which includes constraints on arbitrariness. In connection with this arbitrariness, there can be found two views in the literature. One of view concerns political theory and is related to the restriction of the arbitrary use of public power. The other concerns the concept of law and claims that the rule of law is related to certain features that the law should possess to be able to guide human conduct. In this regard, the ideal of the rule of law reduces the arbitrariness that is connected with the law itself. These views do not separate each other. When I say that "our formal account of the rule of law is not separable from the political ideal of it", I want to state this point. That is, if the ideal of the rule of law reduces the arbitrariness that is connected with the law itself, it needs its political idea or political morality.

To explain this point, I started from the last view and tried to reach from the internal point of view to the external point of view. For this, I used two important keys. One of them is the relationship between the rule of law and the legal system; the other consists of the rule of law that lead to regard it as being on the borderline of the formal and the moral.

In fact, these two keys are connected to each other, since the requirements of the rule of law which are generally the same as, or close to, Fuller's eight principles, are in a central place in the relationship between the rule of law and the legal system. One can easily see this in the relationship between the rule of law and the legal system. Following Waldron, we may state that there are two aspects of this relationship that are inherently connected with each other.

One of these aspects is connected with the features of rules. In connection with the rules, the formal principles of the rule of law or Fuller's eight canons are evaluated in terms of the efficiency of the legal system and the rule of law is considered a better instrument. From this point of view, if the rule of law is considered a better instrument or it is true that in the liberal-democratic society the rule of law can become a deliberate manifestation of a society's adherence to liberal-democratic values, formal principles of the rule law or Fuller's eight canons include a minimum morality. Following Luban and Waldron, it is possible to explain this morality according to the relationship between the rule of law and human dignity.

On the other hand, this relationship is connected with the internal morality of law. It does not necessarily imply political morality. For this, we need the second aspect of the rule of law.

The second aspect of the rule of law concerns legal institutions and their practices. Among others, it emphasizes argument, procedure and reason. For legal practice, this aspect is also connected with human dignity. It secures that citizens are treated "with respect as active centers of intelligence" (Waldron 2008, 59). That is, it secures the inner morality of law. At this point, the inner morality of law should be completed by the political ideal of the rule of law, since this aspect requires sound judgements that are justified by political values and the political ideal of the rule of law.

This result may be thought of as the blurred point of both the external and the internal morality of law. If so, the question is not whether the rule of law is on the borderline of the formal and the moral, but whether the rule of law is on the borderline of both the external and the internal morality of law.

Acknowledgements The author is thankful to Brian Bix and David Luban for constructive comments and helpful suggestions on earlier drafts; and to David Luban, Ioanna Kuçuradi and Sahir Özdemir for the English editing.

References

Barber, N.W. 2004. Must legalistic conceptions of the rule of law have a social dimension? *Ratio Juris* 17: 474–488.
Dworkin, R. 2003. The Judge's new role: Should personal convictions count? *Journal of International Criminal Justice* 1: 4.
Dyzenhaus, D. 2009. The legitimacy of the rule of law. In *A simple common lawyer: Essays in honour of Michael Taggart*, ed. D. Dyzenhaus et al. Oxford: Hart Publishing.
Fuller, L.L. 1968. *Anatomy of the law*. New York: Frederick A. Praeger.
Fuller, L.L. 1978. *The morality of law*. New Haven: Yale University Press.
Hart, H.L.A. 1965. Book review of the morality of law. *Harvard Law Review* 78: 1281.
Kramer, M.H. 2007. *Objectivity and the rule of law*. Cambridge: Cambridge University Press.
Luban, D. 2007. *Legal ethics and human dignity*. Cambridge: Cambridge University Press.
Luban, D. 2010. The rule of law and human dignity: Re-examining Fuller's canons. *Hague Journal on the Rule of Law* 2: 29.
MacDonald, L. 2001. Positivism and the formal rule of law: Questioning the connection. *Australian Journal of Legal Philosophy* 26: 93.
Peczenick, A. 2008. *On law and reason*. Dordrecht: Springer.
Radin, M.J. 1989. Reconsidering the rule of law. *Boston University Law Review* 69: 781.
Rawls, J. 1991. *A theory of justice*. Cambridge, MA: Harvard University Press.
Rawls, J. 1996. *Political liberalism*. New York: Columbia University Press.
Rawls, J. 1999. *Collected papers*. Cambridge, MA: Harvard University Press.
Rawls, J. 2003. *Justice as fairness: A restatement*. Cambridge, MA: Harvard University Press.
Raz, J. 2001. The rule of law and its virtue. In *Law and morality: Readings in legal philosophy*, ed. D. Dyzenhaus and A. Ripstein. Toronto: University of Toronto Press.

Simmonds, N. 2005. Law as a moral idea. *University of Toronto Law Journal* 55: 61.
Solum, L. 2002. A law of rules: A critique and reconstruction of justice Scalia's view of the rule of law. Available at: http://papers.ssrn.com/sol3/papers.cfm?abstract_id=303575.
Soper, P. 2007. On the relation between form and substance in law. *Ratio Juris* 20: 56.
Summers, R.S. 1999. The principles of the rule of law. *Notre Dame Law Review* 74: 1691.
Summers, R.S. 2006. *Form and function in a legal system. A general study*. Cambridge: Cambridge University Press.
Waldron, J. 2002. Is the rule of law an essentially contested concept? *Law and Philosophy* 21(2): 137.
Waldron, J. 2008. The concept and the rule of law. *Georgia Law Review* 43: 1.
West, R. 2003. *Re-imagining justice: Progressive interpretations of formal equality, rights and the rule of law*. Aldershot: Ashgate.
Winston, K.I. 1994. Legislators and liberty. *Law and Philosophy* 13: 389.

Chapter 8
Political Deliberation and Constitutional Review

Conrado Hübner Mendes

8.1 Introduction

Prominent advocates of judicial review have claimed that constitutional courts are deliberative forums of a distinctive kind.[1] Surprisingly enough, however, they have not entirely come to grips with the sorts of requirements that should be met if courts want to live up to that promise. Important questions remain unanswered while others endure unasked. Constitutional talk is thus deprived of a set of qualitative standards that guides us in assessing how different courts, for better or worse, may do and are actually doing in terms of that presupposed and esteemed decisional virtue.

This under-elaborated assumption needs to be fleshed out. This article briefly describes how a constitutional court has been conceived in that light, diagnoses the incompleteness of that approach and points to additional elements that are necessary for that theoretical path.

The first topic shows how the ideal of political deliberation has been tied, though yet insufficiently, to constitutional courts and what further steps would be relevant for a comprehensive account.

[1] Despite the crucial differences between "constitutional courts" and "supreme courts", I will use the former expression as encompassing the latter one. For the purposes of this paper, what matters is their basic commonality: the power to overrule legislation on the basis of the constitution. This commonplace will be diagnosed and thoroughly described later in the paper.

C.H. Mendes (✉)
Humboldt Foundation Post-Doctoral Fellow at Wissenschaftszentrum Berlin (WZB) and at Humboldt University
e-mail: conrado@hubner.org.br

I.B. Flores and K.E. Himma (eds.), *Law, Liberty, and the Rule of Law*,
Ius Gentium: Comparative Perspectives on Law and Justice 18,
DOI 10.1007/978-94-007-4743-2_8,

8.2 Constitutional Courts as "Custodians" of Public Deliberation

Political frictions between parliaments and courts were not born in North-American soil with the advent of judicial review of legislation in the beginning of the nineteenth century. The chronicles of the modern rule of law show that their origins can be traced further back. Neither have these quarrels been always formulated in the perspective of the democratic legitimacy of an unelected body with the legal competence to overrule the acts of an elected one.

Nevertheless, the emergence of judicial review, and specially its gradual enhancement over time, has significantly dramatized that historical tension. It resonated in constitutional theory and triggered new sorts of questions then inspired, indeed, by the democratic ideal. What was originally a US feature became, later in the twentieth century, through the burgeoning of constitutional courts and the accompanying judicialization of politics in Western democracies, a multinational one.

The dispute upon the democratic legitimacy of the existence of judicial review, and upon the valid scope of its practice, has been fervent throughout the twentieth century. It was first Thayer and then, decades later, Bickel, who ventilated this concern in the most notorious way. The fear of "democratic debilitation" (Thayer 1893), to the former, and the nuisance brought by the "counter-majoritarian difficulty" (Bickel 1961, 16–8), to the latter, just furnished catchier slogans to the ingrained Jacksonian conception of democracy that persevere in part of the American political mind.

This populist take on democracy was not entirely embraced by later cycles of constitutional fertility in Western democracies. The constitutional courts created by the post-war, post-fascist or post-communist constitutional regimes were not seen as "deviant institutions".[2] Neither has the "counter-majoritarian difficulty" automatically travelled together with them. One cannot assume, however, that the general theoretical justification of constitutional courts is settled, or that these courts do not face resembling challenges in their everyday operation. The argument, indeed, is far from over.

Advocates for judicial review of legislation often conceive it as a reconciliatory device of (liberal) constitutionalism and (representative) democracy. It would be an institutional compromise that recognizes the priority of the right over the good (Rawls 1971, 31), or the co-originality of individual rights and popular sovereignty (Habermas 1996). It institutionalizes the irreducible tension between procedures and outcomes in the concept of political legitimacy, and recognizes that the electoral pedigree is not enough reason, all of the time, for decisional supremacy in a democracy.

Variations of this simple idea abound. But there is nothing, so far, that connects constitutional courts with deliberation. As a matter of fact, deliberativists are, more often than not, suspicious, if not forthrightly unsympathetic, of the deliberative prospects of courts. Deliberative democrats resist putting too much weight on courts not only due to their elitist character. They do so because of the supposedly restrictive code that shapes the argumentative abilities of this forum.

---

[2] Another expression of Bickel (1961, 18).

Courts would be straitjacketed by the apparently stringent vectors of legal language. Nothing could be more at odds with the openness of the deliberative ideal than this. Waldron, Glendon, Zurn and others have expressed doubts about the possibilities of legal argumentation to encompass deeper moral considerations (Waldron 2009; Glendon 1993; Zurn 2007). Judicial discourse would be legalistic and myopic, a distraction from the nub of the matter. Their patterns of reasoning would impede judges to see what is genuinely at stake. Their professional duty to take legal materials into account would harm straightforward deliberation. The operation of law would simply not comport with the transformative claims to which deliberative politics should be permeable. This concern is a serious one, but cannot be too quickly generalized as an inevitable or universal feature of constitutional courts.[3] Moreover, it is little comparatively informed and typically based on the reasoning habits of US Supreme Court.

This caveat does not entail that no deliberativist accommodates constitutional review within a deliberative democracy. Many actually do. However hesitant and refusing to accept any deliberative eminence of the constitutional review process, it may have a room to occupy in the background. Habermas, for example, calls on the court to assure the "deliberative self-determination" of lawmaking and to assess whether the legislative process was undertaken under decent deliberative circumstances (1996). The court, in his account, needs to mediate between the republican ideal and the degenerate practices of real politics. It is a tutor that guarantees the adequate procedural channels for rational collective decisions rather than a paternalistic regent that defines the content of those choices. It does not substitute for the moral judgments made by the legislator, but investigates the procedural milieu under which these judgments were formed. Zurn largely reproduces this justification. Within his "proceduralist version of deliberative democratic constitutionalism", he carves a space for constitutional review. He accepts an external agency to enforce procedures but, like Habermas, refuses to accord it substantive moral choices. The court would not second-guess parliament, but just make sure it is in good working order (Zurn 2007). Their notion of "procedure", though, is a robust one and the extent to which it is successfully severed from substance remains an open question.

Both Nino and Sunstein play in unison with the logic of this account. Nino does not doubt that a constitutional court is an aristocratic body and that the assumption of any judicial superiority to deal with rights evokes "epistemic elitism" (Nino 1996, 188). However, he accepts that the belief on the value of democracy presupposes certain conditions. The exceptions to the default preference for majoritarian processes constitute the mandate of courts, and they are of three kinds: first, the court needs to draw the line between *a priori* and *a posteriori* rights and to protect the former if genuine democratic deliberation is to ensue; second, in the name of personal autonomy, the court needs to quash perfectionist legislation that oversteps the domain of intersubjective morality and establishes an ideal of human excellence; finally, the court

[3] Kumm, for example, rejects this generalization by showing how the "rational human rights paradigm", employed by several European courts, avoids this legalistic trap (2007).

needs to preserve the constitution as a stabilized social practice against abrupt breaks (Nino 1996, 199–205).

Sunstein also defends that the Supreme Court has a role to play in the maintenance of the "republic of reasons" to which, for him, the American constitution committed itself. His advice for "leaving things undecided" through a minimalist strategy to kindle broader deliberation by the citizenry is the best-known part of his account. The less-known portion is its complement: when "pre-conditions for democratic self-government" are at stake, a maximalist take is, according to him, the pertinent one.[4] In some enumerated circumstances, rather than crafting "incompletely theorized agreements", the court should look for complete ones (1995). Nonetheless, he supposes, the cost of maximalism is the consequent impoverishment of deliberation in the public sphere with respect to these judicially bared issues.

Despite defending constitutional review, the deliberative concern of these authors lies actually elsewhere. Such function, for them, is justified only to the extent that it unlocks, safeguards and nurtures deliberation in other arenas. The court is just the warden of democratic deliberative processes, not the forum of deliberation itself. This is not the angle I want to illuminate.

8.3 Constitutional Courts as "Public Reasoners" and "Interlocutors"

There are three more robust ways to couple constitutional courts with deliberation. Rather than a mere custodian of democratic deliberative processes, the court may be a more intrusive participant of societal deliberation either as a "public reasoner", as an "interlocutor" or yet as a "deliberator" itself. The public reasoner and the interlocutor supply public reasons to the external audience. Both images ignore, however, how judges internally behave and disregard whether they have simply bargained or aggregated individual positions to reach common ground. The qualifying difference is that an interlocutor, unlike a public reasoner, is attentive to the arguments voiced by the other branches and dialogically responds to them. Finally, the court as a deliberator, apart from being an inter-institutional interlocutor, is also characterized by the internal deliberation among judges. When courts are referred to as "deliberative institutions", it is not always clear which of these three specific senses is under reference. I will briefly sketch these three images so that their occasional weaknesses become clearer.

"Public reasoner" is an evocative umbrella-term that encompasses a prolific dissemination of derivative images. They all share a very similar insight. Rawls and Dworkin are probably the leading figures on that account. Their proposal of a court

[4] This is not his only hypothesis for allowing maximalism to supplant minimalism (Sunstein 2001, 57).

as an "exemplar of public reason" or as a "forum of principle" is not only a description of the American Supreme Court, but also a prescription of how this function should be incorporated into a democracy. Two other creative accounts fit in this category too. Alexy thinks of a constitutional court as a "venue for argumentative representation" and Kumm, in turn, conceives it as an "arena of Socratic contestation". I proceed to condense each one.

Rawls is largely enthusiastic about constitutional review. He asserts that, "in a constitutional regime, public reason is the reason of its supreme court" (1997a, 108). He even assumes that "in a well-ordered society the two more or less overlap" (1997a, 10fn). Or, yet, in his most confident passage, he suggests a litmus test for knowing whether we are following public reason: "how would our argument strike us presented in the form of a supreme court opinion?" (1997a, 124) For him, the constraint of public reason applies to all institutions, but in an exceptionally burdensome way to constitutional review: "the court's special role makes it the exemplar of public reason" (1997b, 768). In other moments, he moderates his terms and remarks that the court "may serve as its exemplar", as well as the other branches (1997a, 114). The comparative advantage of courts, however, is to use public reason as its sole idiom. The court would be "the only branch of government that is visibly on its face the creature of that reason and of that reason alone" (1997a, 111).

In such account, the court is a key device for the regime to comply with the liberal demand of legitimacy: a politics of reasonableness and justifiability deserved by each and every citizen as equal and free members of the political community. Coercion is admissible to individuals only if based on reasons that all "may reasonably be expected to endorse" (Rawls 1997a, 95). Public reason is thus the linchpin of such machinery. The readiness and willingness to listen and to explain collective actions in terms that could be accepted by others is the pivotal democratic virtue, labelled by him as "duty of civility" or as a manifestation of "civic friendship". Not all reasons, therefore, are public reasons, but only those which refuse to engage in a comprehensive doctrine of the good, and keep within the bounds of a strictly political conception of justice. Such discipline, moreover, does not apply to any issue, but only to constitutional essentials and matters of basic justice. The role of the court is to ascribe public reasons "vividness and vitality in the public forum", to force public debate to be imbued by principle. There would reside its educative quality too.

Dworkin adopts a similar approach. The distinction between principles and policies is at the core of his theory. Principles ground decisions based on the moral rights of each individual, whereas policies inform decisions concerning the general welfare and collective good. Both co-exist in a democracy. They embody two different types of legitimation, one based on reasons, the other based on numbers. The catch is that, when in conflict, the former trumps the latter. Neither law as integrity, nor democracy as partnership (which, in Dworkin's "hedgehog approach" to values, are interdependent), can be exhausted by arguments of policy. They cannot be squared with this purely quantitative perspective.

For Dworkin, judicial review is democracy's reserve of principled discourse, its "forum of principle". Only a community governed by principles manages to promote the moral affiliation of each individual. Political authority becomes worth to be respected thanks to its ability of voicing arguments and displaying "equal concern and respect", not to its techniques of counting heads. The institutions of such a regime need to foster communal representation, apart from a statistic one. Judges, on that account, do not represent constituents in particular, but a supra-individual entity – the political community as a whole. An elected branch cannot be sufficiently trusted as the "forum of principle" because of the counter incentives it faces.

To remove questions of principle from the ordinary political struggle is the court's mission. Other types of argument may obfuscate the centrality of principle. There is no legitimacy pitfall on that arrangement because democracy, correctly understood, is a procedurally incomplete form of government – there is no right procedure to attest whether its pre-conditions are fulfilled. The promotion of pre-conditions can emerge anywhere. When it comes to principles, the legitimacy test is a consequentialist one. We measure it *ex post*, by assessing whether a decision is correct, or at least attempting to provide the best possible justification. Procedural inputs do not matter for that purpose. The court is not infallible, but the attempt to institutionalize an exclusive place for the promotion of principle cannot be illegitimate because of its inevitable fallibility (Dworkin 1985, 34, 1986, 1990, 1995, 1996, 1998). Lesser fallibility, if plausible, is enough. The legitimacy of the court depends, then, on its independence from ordinary politics.

Alexy keeps the same tune. Judicial review is reconcilable with democracy if understood as a mechanism for the representation of the people. It is representation, though, of a peculiar kind: rather than votes and election, it works by arguments (2007, 578–9). A regime that does not represent except through electoral organs would instantiate a "purely decisional model of democracy". Alexy, however, believes that democracy should contain arguments in addition to decisions, which would "make democracy deliberative". Elected parliaments, to the extent that they also argue, may embody both kinds of representation – "volitional or decisional as well as argumentative or discursive" – whereas the representation expressed by a constitutional court is an exclusively argumentative one. The two conditions for argumentative representation to obtain are the existence of, on the one hand, "sound and correct arguments", and, on the other, rational persons, "who are able and willing to accept sound or correct arguments for the reason that they are sound or correct". The ideal of discursive constitutionalism, for him, intends to institutionalize reason and correctness. Constitutional review is a welcome device if it is able to do that (2007, 581).

For Kumm, at last, judicial review is valuable because it institutionalizes a practice of Socratic contestation. This practice engages authorities "in order to assess whether the claims they make are based on good reasons" (2007, 3). Liberal democratic constitutionalism, he contends, has two complementary commitments: for one, elections promote the equal right to vote; for the other, Socratic contestation guarantees that individuals have the right to call public acts into question and receive a reasoned justification for them. Parliaments and constitutional courts are the respective "archetypal expressions" of both commitments. If legitimacy, on that liberal frame, depends on the quality of reasons that ground collective decisions, judicial review is a checkpoint that impedes this demand to dwindle over time. The Socratic habit of subjecting every cognitive statement to rigorous doubt helps democracy to highlight and test the quality of substantive outcomes, instead of passively resting merely on fair procedures. Constitutional courts, through this "editorial function", hold parliaments accountable for the reasons upon which they decide. They probe collective decisions and, by doing that, have the epistemic premium of casting aside, at least, legislative decisions that are unreasonable (2007, 31).

The cursory description above does not do justice to the complexity of each author. It shows, still, the similar logic of their arguments. All equally tackle a monotonic picture of democracy that relentlessly pervades objections against counter-parliamentary institutions like constitutional review. Their chorus intones: "democracy is not only that". Democracy is rather shaped by a duality. However this less intuitive component is called (public reasons, principles, rational arguments, contestation), there would be no genuine democracy without it. The court does not have a monopoly of such code, but has the virtue of operating exclusively on that basis. It is a monoglot. There lies its institutional asset. It avoids the danger of political polyglotism, the cacophony of reasons that may lead to harmful trade-offs and prostrate this cherished yet permanently endangered dimension of the complex ideal of collective self-government.

I am not discussing whether their arguments on the legitimacy of judicial review are sound. Neither am I interested in thematizing whether elected parliaments or other institutions could play that function as much as courts. The description of the expectations they place on courts, however, enables us to grasp some implications later.

Courts as "public reasoners", therefore, entail more than what was prescribed by Habermas and other deliberativists. Courts as "interlocutors" too. This image springs from "theories of dialogue", which echo an old insight of Bickel, for whom the court should prudently engage in a continuing "Socratic colloquy" with other branches and society (Bickel 1961, 70). These theories have developed through many sophisticated stripes since the 1980's (Mendes 2009). Some of their statements underline what other aforementioned authors also claimed: the court can catalyse deliberation outside it. For these theories, though, the court is not an empty ignition of external deliberation, but rather an argumentative participant. And unlike ivory-tower reason-givers, as the previous image suggested, "interlocutors" join the interaction in a more modest and horizontal fashion. They do not claim supremacy in defining the constitutional meaning. Dialogical courts know that, in the long run, last words are provisional and get blurred in the sequence of legislative decisions that keep challenging the judicial decisions irrespective of the court's formal supremacy.

8.4 Constitutional Courts as "Deliberators"

Constitutional courts have been so far seen as deliberation-enhancing, but still not, necessarily, as deliberative themselves. Those accounts, I submit, are unsatisfactory. They fail to open the black-box of collegiate courts and to grasp whether those taxing expectations are plausible, or under what conditions they are achievable, and to what degree. They rely on an optimistic presumption: since judges are not elected, their superior aptitude to deal with public reasons eventuates. This inference conceals several mediating steps. There is a lot to be done between the premise and this putative effect. It is intriguing how that presumption could overlook the internal dynamics of this conflictive multi-member institution.

This is not a prolifically discussed question in constitutional theory. Apart from some thoughtful testimonies from famous constitutional judges (Sachs 2009, 270; Barak 2006, 209), the specific value of collegial deliberation for constitutional courts has not been fully explored yet. Do the roles of "public reasoner" or "interlocutor" require some sort of good internal deliberation? Are they compatible with non-deliberative aggregation? If the practice of Socratic contestation between branches is likely to improve the outcomes of the political process, is it not plausible to argue that deliberative engagement among judges is likely to improve, in turn, the quality of Socratic contestation? Would it be acceptable to replace a collegiate court by a wise monocratic judge that produces well-reasoned decisions? Michelman hints why this may not be the case (1986, 76):

> Hercules, Dworkin's mythic judge, is a loner. He is much too heroic. His narrative constructions are monologues. He converses with no one, except through books. He has no encounters. He has no otherness. Nothing shakes him up. No interlocutor violates his inevitable insularity of his experience and outlook… Dworkin has produced an apotheosis of appellate judging without attention to what seems the most universal and striking institutional characteristic of the appellate bench, its plurality. We ought to consider what that plurality is for. My suggestion is that it is for dialogue, in support of judicial practical reason, as an aspect of judicial self-government, in the interest of our freedom.

"Plurality" and "dialogue", in the light of "judicial practical reason" and for the sake of "judicial self-government" resound some deliberative virtues. We ignore how courts deliberate at our own theoretical peril. We may be missing something potentially valuable and immunizing judges from critical challenge when they decide to turn a deaf ear to the arguments of their peers and opt to act as soloists or strategic dealmakers. We remain deprived from any critical template.

The superficial yet widely accepted assumption that courts are special deliberative forums calls for refinement. Not much is said about what a deliberative forum entails. That contention simply stems from the institutional fact that courts are not tied to electoral behavioural dynamics, hence their impartiality and so their better conditions to deliberate. We should certainly not underestimate that courts occupy an interesting institutional position for deliberation. It is still not clear, though, whether courts are being as deliberative as that presumption believed, or why they should deliberate in the first place. In contemporary regimes, we will find all sorts of constitutional courts, some better than others in the deliberative exercise, some absolutely null.

Rawls and Dworkin conceived the deliberative ability of courts merely as reason-givers. They do neither elaborate on how courts may oscillate when pursuing that function nor, indeed, on how we may discern that oscillation. They would probably accept that some courts are better reason-givers than others but, to assess that variable quality, they do not offer much analytical resource apart from a liberal theory of justice. For them, we would have to confront the substantive controversy on its face: whether the outcomes are right or wrong, better or worse. Alexy and Kumm, in turn, offer the structure of proportionality reasoning. Though less substantive, it still does not tell much about what surrounds the decision.

The court as an interlocutor gains a subtle attribute in relation to the reason-giver: it is more cautious in modulating the decisional tone and in demonstrating that all arguments are given due regard. It displays that, apart from being a good arguer, the court is also a good listener and digests the reasons from the outside. Both images catch, in any event, a still defective picture of a constitutional court's potential as a deliberative institution. Courts can be and, to various extents, actually are, deliberative in a more fecund sense. Its institutional context and procedural equipment create peculiar conditions to do so. To grasp only the reason-giving aspect is to miss a broader phenomenon. We need to measure these variances and to see whether they have any implication for the legitimacy of constitutional review.

Ferejohn and Pasquino pushed that debate to a richer stage. They agree that courts face a tighter regulation with respect to the delivery of reasons. For them, the separation of powers encompasses various kinds of accountability, each of which occupying distinct spots of a "chain of justification". The longer the thread of delegation, or the more distant an authority is from election, the greater will be its duty of reason-giving "in return". On one extreme, a weightier deliberative burden compensates for the electoral deficit. On the other, the deliberative deficit is counterbalanced by the closeness to the people. These varying charges are "inversely correlated with democratic pedigree" (Ferejohn 2008, 206).

Thus, they share with Rawls the claim that courts are "exemplary deliberative institutions". They note, though, that there is not just one way to be deliberative. Deliberation can be internal or external and has a distinct target in each case: "to get the group to decide on some common course of action", in the former, and "to affect actions taken outside the group", in the latter. One "involves giving and listening to reasons from others within the group", whereas the other "involves the group, or its members, giving and listening to reasons coming from outside the group" (Ferejohn and Pasquino 2004, 1692).

This distinction is a useful one and sheds light on separate functions and settings. The recognition of the court as an actual "deliberator" becomes more evident. Judges deliberate internally while striving to reach a single settlement, and externally while exposing their decision to the public. The authors then compare the features of a set of courts through these lenses. From what they managed to see, two main patterns are inferred: the US Supreme Court, which represents a model that centres on external deliberation, with little face-to-face engagement among judges and a liberality to express themselves in multiple individual voices; and the Kelsenian courts, which would value clarity and hence tend to communicate, after struggling in secret deliberation, through a single voice in most cases (Ferejohn and Pasquino 2002, 35). One archetype is outward-looking whereas the other prioritizes the inside. Despite all the dissimilarities between the courts under inspection,[5] the authors observe that

---

[5] They are considering the US Supreme Court, and the German, Italian and Spanish constitutional courts. They also examine the French Constitutional Council, but it does not fit these patterns because a system of parliamentary sovereignty brings variables that impede such stable categorization.

all, in their own ways, "retained the exemplary deliberative character" proclaimed by Rawls (Ferejohn and Pasquino 2002, 22).

This description is then followed by some intriguing explanatory hypotheses. The Kelsenian model, where the authority of review is concentrated exclusively in a special court, would require more unity "if ordinary courts are to be able to apply" the constitutional court's decisions (Ferejohn and Pasquino 2002, 33). The US model, characterized by a diffused authority to declare unconstitutionality across the judiciary, would require greater coordination between the Supreme Court and inferior judges. Hence the multiple individual voices, which allow the other actors of the legal system to anticipate the court's actions (Ferejohn and Pasquino 2002, 35).

Each deliberative pattern would be contingent on the political situatedness of the court. This independent variable would determine how deliberation looks like in each context. Both the internal and external aspects are always present, but "partly in conflict": "If the individual Justices see themselves as involved in a large discussion in the public sphere, they may be less inclined to seek to compromise their own views with others on the Court" (Ferejohn and Pasquino 2004, 1697–8). In that light, the US Supreme Court would be much more "externalist" than its European counterparts.

Once the two patterns are elucidated, Ferejohn and Pasquino culminate in a critical assessment of the US court and in a normative appeal for denser internal deliberation, *a la* European courts. American justices "ought to commit themselves to try hard to find an opinion that everyone on their court can endorse" (2004, 1673). Reforms would be necessary to galvanize justices to "spend less time and effort as individuals trying to influence external publics" and to focus on finding common ground, like genuinely deliberative bodies would do (2004, 1700). Despite the positive aspects that multiple opinions might have in some circumstances, they believe the US Supreme Court to have gone too far. The advisable step back, for them, comprises the two fronts of political behaviour: first, the authors recommend an institutional reform to make the court less partisan, namely, a new mode of appointment and tenure; second, they urge the legal community to demand from judges the compliance with deliberative norms oriented towards the pursuit of consensus and an ethics of compromise and self-restraint with regards to the public exhibition of personal idiosyncrasies.

Their series of articles, without doubt, made significant progress toward a broader understanding of how courts might or should be deliberative. The conceptualization of two sorts of deliberation and the call for reforms that confront both design and ethical issues are clear achievements. Their concern is fair: the liberality for multiple voices, and the absence of any constraint, ethical or otherwise, against such practice, harms the capacity of the US Supreme Court to play a deeper deliberative role. However, they have not gone far enough in fleshing out what that role is. In addition, the way they suggest a conflict between internal and external is sometimes misleading.

To start with, their definition of "external" is unstable. One can capture, in their writings, at least three senses of external deliberation: as reason-giving in public *tout court*, which is a common trait of any court; as multiple reason-giving in public, through individual opinions; or as an individualist attitude towards the public by the disclosure of non-deliberated disagreement.[6] Sometimes, therefore, the authors seem to imply that external corresponds to the soloist US style, which permits individual justices to publicize their own statements regardless of internal dialogue. In other passages, they adopt a more flexible notion and accept that there are different manners to be externally deliberative, even through single opinions.[7]

The relation between external deliberation and the formal style of decision publicly delivered is, therefore, ambiguous: if it means simply the use of reason with the purpose of prompting and affecting the public debate, either single or multiple-voice decision could potentially do; if it means exposing the court's internal disagreement, then, indeed, multiple-voice would be the only way to go.

The connection between internal and external is also problematic. They suggest two unconvincing or, at best, under-demonstrated causalities. First, a bond between, on the one hand, a *per curiam* decision and the prevalence of internal deliberation at the expense of external; second, between a *seriatim* decision and external deliberation, which would overpower the internal. Even if the descriptive portrait is accurate, the inference of an inevitable causal link between the way judges interact among themselves and the way the decision is presented to the public remains strained and little illuminating.

Such formal criterion does not convey much about the substantive quality of reasoning and its ability to shape citizenry discussion. It does not matter whether the court manifests itself through *seriatim*, *per curiam* or something in the middle. As long as it is not oracular or hermetic, any decision may spark external deliberation.[8] A court could arguably struggle internally, but still manifest itself *seriatim*,[9] or be internally non-deliberative and speak *per curiam*. The degree of external deliberativeness, therefore, does not derive exclusively from the form, but more likely from the content and other circumstances. Comparative constitutionalism has several examples of *per curiam* decisions that electrified external argumentative engagement.

Again, from the descriptive accuracy of both patterns, it does not follow that there are inevitable trade-offs between the two, or that the maximization of one precipitates the respective minimization of the other. It is yet to be demonstrated that a court could not excel on both. One might certainly claim that the more the court deliberates internally, the greater chances it would have to reach a consensus

---

[6] Some extracts give an idea of the variety of definitions of external deliberation: "The Court rarely tries to speak with one voice, apparently preferring to let conflict and disagreement ferment." (Ferejohn and Pasquino 2002, 36); "part of the wider public process of deciding what the Constitution requires of us as citizens and potential political actors." Or later: "It may lead citizens and politicians to take or to refrain from actions of various sorts, or perhaps to respect the Court and its decisions. There is, however, no singular focus on a particular course of action that politicians or citizens must take." Finally: "to engage in open external dialogue about constitutional norms with outside actors." (Ferejohn and Pasquino 2004, 1697–8) "Its aim is to convince those who are not in the room." (Ferejohn 2008, 209)

[7] "There are various ways in which a court may play a role in external deliberation." (Ferejohn and Pasquino 2004, 1698)

[8] Even narrowly reasoned decisions may stir deliberation up. This is, for example, Sunstein's defence of minimalism (1995, 2001).

[9] One classic example is the House of Lords (Paterson 1982).

and manifest itself through a single opinion. This would not, however, discourage external deliberation. Otherwise, the mostly consensual European courts could not be said to motivate external deliberation.

Unless the court simply refuses to offer reasons to ground its decisions, external deliberation cannot be seen as a choice. The outside audience will be able to argue with those reasons regardless of the particular form through which they are communicated – *per curiam* or *seriatim*. But two fertile dilemmas still remain. First, the court needs to ponder whether to have internal deliberation, which, unlike the external, is indeed a choice. Second, the judges should contemplate, in the light of many other considerations, whether to express themselves individually or collectively. European courts certainly diverge from the US Supreme Court. This is not due, nevertheless, to their lack of capacity or willingness to spark external deliberation, but due to a cultural factor: a thicker "aim at unanimity" animates their internal processes (Ferejohn and Pasquino 2004, 169). The American practice, consolidated in the last decades, notoriously strays from that.

In overall, Ferejohn and Pasquino have raised important empirical and normative questions, but have not entirely answered them. Their endeavour to relate constitutional review to deliberation remains, if not too hasty, surely unfinished. There are at least six aspects to be further explored. First, the notion of external deliberation, if excessively tied to one of the forms of public display (the *seriatim*, in their case), fails to capture how the substance of the decision, be it *seriatim* or *per curiam*, may be important from both the empirical and normative prisms. There are ways of reasoning that, even if communicated in the *per curiam* mode, sensibly incorporate disagreements and respectfully engages with them. A cryptic *seriatim* would obviously obtain a lower score in that respect and would simply prevent the faintest external discussion.

Second, their notion of external deliberation still overlooks two different stages and practices in this public setting: the pre-decisional phase, where the court may competently inflame public debate and administer various techniques for receiving argumentative inputs, and the post-decisional, where the court delivers its product until a next round of deliberation on the same issue ensues. The task at each moment and the respective virtues that are necessary to carry them out are not coincidental. The distinction, thus, is not trivial.

Third, Ferejohn and Pasquino, despite defending internal deliberation, do not give a sufficiently comprehensive account of why it may be desirable, except for the values of uniformity, predictability and coordination. In other words, deliberation would be valuable only for the sake of these conventional formal principles of the rule of law. There might be more benefits in deliberation than intelligible and uniform reason-giving though.[10] The willingness to persuade and to be persuaded in an ambient

[10] Shapiro points to the distinction: "Some commentators try to capture this aspect of deliberation by reference to reason-giving, as when courts are said to be more deliberative institutions than legislatures on the grounds that they supply published reasons for their decisions. But significant though reason-giving is to legitimacy (particularly in the unelected institutions in a democracy), it does not capture the essence of deliberation." (2002, 197)

of reciprocity, as deliberation is usually defined, may not lead to consensus, but is no less important when dissensus withstands.

Fourth, when considering institutional design, they call for a qualified legislative quorum in the appointment process and for a fixed term of tenure. For them, this reform would approximate the US Supreme Court to the European ones, because its composition would be less driven by partisan behaviour. Despite crucial, this device still does not exhaust the set of incentives that may push the court to be more deliberative. It remains too reductive and narrow.

Fifth, they rightly add to their suggestion of institutional design a call for deliberative norms, that is, for an ethics that acknowledges the importance of deliberation. However, they do not flesh that out. Behind the abstract exhortation to engage in the process of persuasion, there are minute virtues that can turn such a task more discernible.

Finally, assuming that the legitimacy of constitutional courts is somehow connected to their deliberative quality, as many submit, and since deliberation is a fluctuating phenomenon, a theory must be able to measure different degrees of attainment of the ideal. Put differently, it needs to conceive of measures of deliberative performance. Therefore, if a constitutional court is to become a plausible deliberator, and not only a reason-giver or an interlocutor, these additional questions have to be tackled.

8.5 Conclusion

In a constitutional democracy, there are a variety of more-or-less deliberative institutions. They stand on some point between lawmaking and law-application, between broader or narrower discretionary compasses. Trivial though this may be, judicial tribunals, by a conventional definition, stand closer to the latter end of the spectrum. Closer, at least, than legislatures, most of the time. Constitutional courts, however, turn this convention more complicated. They are situated at a unique position of the political architecture. The distinctions between legislation and adjudication, on the one hand, and between politics and law, on the other, become much less stark than in ordinary instances. There is hardly a sharp criterion to draw that line. This is not due, as it is generally contended, to the open-ended phraseology of the constitutional text, but rather to the underlying quality of constitutional scrutiny: it frames, in a conflictive partnership with the legislator, the boundaries of the political domain.

Constitutional courts have no exclusivity over constitutional scrutiny. It is a fact, though, that they participate in such enterprise. This peculiarity has naturally charged courts with a heavy justificatory burden. The apprehension of a constitutional court through the lenses of its allegedly special deliberative circumstances and capacities may be a significant component of such a justification. That basis, though, remains fragile so far. If deliberation enhances the existential condition of constitutional courts, such courts need to be more than "exemplars of public reason" or "forums of principle", more than reason-givers or interlocutors. These expressions, and the respective expectations that they convey, are in need of deeper elaboration.

References

Alexy, R. 2007. Thirteen replies. In *Law, rights and discourse*, ed. G. Pavlakos. Oxford: Hart Publishing.

Barak, A. 2006. *The judge in a democracy*. Princeton: Princeton University Press.

Bickel, A. 1961. Foreword: The passive virtues. *Harvard Law Review* 75: 40.

Dworkin, R. 1985. *A matter of principle*. Cambridge: Harvard University Press.

Dworkin, R. 1986. *Law's empire*. Cambridge: Harvard University Press.

Dworkin, R. 1990. Equality, democracy and constitution: We the people in court. *Alberta Law Review* 28: 2.

Dworkin, R. 1995. Constitutionalism and democracy. *European Journal of Philosophy* 3(1): 2.

Dworkin, R. 1996. *Freedom's law. A moral reading of the American constitution*. Cambridge, MA: Harvard University Press.

Dworkin, R. 1998. The partnership conception of democracy. *California Law Review* 86: 453.

Ferejohn, J. 2008. The Citizen's assembly model. In *Designing deliberative democracy: The British Columbia Citizens' assembly*, ed. M. Warren and H. Pearse. Cambridge: Cambridge University Press.

Ferejohn, J., and P. Pasquino. 2002. Constitutional courts as deliberative institutions: Towards an institutional theory of constitutional justice. In *Constitutional justice, east and west*, ed. W. Sadurski. The Hague: Kluwer Law International.

Ferejohn, J., and P. Pasquino. 2004. Constitutional adjudication: Lessons from Europe. *Texas Law Review* 82: 1671.

Glendon, M.A. 1993. *Rights talk: The impoverishment of political discourse*. New York: Free Press.

Habermas, J. 1996. *Between facts and norms: Contributions to a discourse theory of law and democracy*. Trans. W. Rehg. Cambridge, MA: MIT Press.

Kumm, M. 2007. Institutionalising Socratic contestation: The rationalist human rights paradigm, legitimate authority and the point of review. *European Journal of Legal Studies* 1(2): 1.

Mendes, C.H. 2009. Not the last word, but dialogue: Deliberative separation of powers II. *Legisprudence* 3(2): 191.

Michelman, F. 1986. Foreword: Traces of self-government. *Harvard Law Review* 100: 4.

Nino, C.S. 1996. *The constitution of deliberative democracy*. New Haven: Yale University Press.

Paterson, A. 1982. *The law lords*. London: Macmillan Press.

Rawls, J. 1971. *A theory of justice*. Cambridge: Harvard University Press.

Rawls, J. 1997a. The idea of public reason. In *Deliberative democracy: Essays on reason and politics*, ed. J. Bohman and W. Rehg. Cambridge, MA: MIT Press.

Rawls, J. 1997b. The idea of public reason revisited. *The University of Chicago Law Review* 64: 765.

Sachs, A. 2009. *The strange alchemy of life and law*. Oxford: Oxford University Press.

Shapiro, I. 2002. Optimal deliberation? *The Journal of Political Philosophy* 10(2): 196.

Sunstein, C. 1995. Incompletely theorized agreements. *Harvard Law Review* 108: 1733.

Sunstein, C. 2001. *One case at a time: Judicial minimalism on the Supreme Court*. Cambridge, MA: Harvard University Press.

Thayer, J.B. 1893. The origin and scope of the American doctrine of constitutional law. *Harvard Law Review* 7(3): 129.

Waldron, J. 2009. Judges as moral reasoners. *International Journal of Constitutional Law* 7: 1.

Zurn, C. 2007. *Deliberative democracy and the institutions of judicial review*. Cambridge: Cambridge University Press.

Chapter 9
The Rule of Law and Human Rights Judicial Review: Controversies and Alternatives

Tom Campbell

9.1 Introduction

This contribution presents an overview of some of the core considerations relating to the institutional compatibility and practical efficacy of combining electoral democracy and human rights-based judicial review. Its distinctive emphases are on the relevance of competing notions of the rule of law to this debate and the suggestion that the compatibility and efficacy problems can be addressed by having a bill of rights that serves the purpose of legislative rather then judicial review (Campbell 2006, 332–7). These themes are developed principally in the context of the UK and Australian constitutional systems.

The American model for "constitutional democracy", which includes a constitutionally entrenched Bill of Rights with "strong" judicial review (that is, following *Marbury v. Madison* 1 Cr. 137 (1803), courts having the power to override legislation that they deem to be in conflict with the Bill of Rights), has become something of a benchmark for the constitutional arrangements of contemporary liberal democracies (Thayer 1893; Dworkin 1996; Tushnet 2007). In the United Kingdom, under the Human Rights Act 1998, there is a rather weaker, and constitutionally unentrenched, version of this model in which it is technically possible for Parliament to reject a finding of the courts that an act of Parliament is "incompatible" with the European Convention on Human Rights (Gearty 2004; Kavanagh 2009). A rather stronger, entrenched, version exists in Canada where a court decision that legislation is in conflict with the Canadian Charter of Rights and Freedoms, can, in theory,

T. Campbell (✉)
Centre for Applied Philosophy and Public Ethics (CAPPE), Charles Sturt University,
Locked Bag 119, Kingston, ACT 2604, Australia

School of Law, King's College, London, UK
e-mail: tcampbell@csu.edu.au

I.B. Flores and K.E. Himma (eds.), *Law, Liberty, and the Rule of Law*,
Ius Gentium: Comparative Perspectives on Law and Justice 18,
DOI 10.1007/978-94-007-4743-2_9, © Springer Science+Business Media Dordrecht 2013

be nullified only by further legislation that is passed 'notwithstanding' its incompatibility with the Charter (Hogg and Bushell 1997). However, Australia, a country whose representatives were closely involved in drafting the United Nations' Universal Declaration of Human Rights, is an almost solitary exception to this constitutional trend (Galligan 1995).

As a result of Australian "exceptionalism" over bills of rights, which is, perhaps, more an historical accident than anything else, bills of rights are a controversial topic in that country, despite attempts over the past few decades to introduce such a bill at the federal level. There is little likelihood that this will succeed in the foreseeable future (Galligan and Morton 2006) although there are Human Rights Acts on the UK model in the state of Victoria (Williams 2006) and in the Australian Capital Territory (ACT) (Charlesworth 2006), and in 2009 there was a government initiated consultation process which received more than 35,000 submissions, concluded that "An Australian Human Rights Act that is broadly consistent with the Victorian and ACT legislation could provide a resilient thread in the federal quilt of human rights protection" (Commonwealth of Australia 2009, 377). However, there is a persistent if fluctuating campaign for doing something about what some human rights advocates see as a human rights stain on the Australian polity, which keeps the controversy over bills of rights going (Byrnes et al. 2009).

Australian exceptionalism over bills of rights is important. It provides an experimental control against which to test comparative claims that human rights judicial review makes a significant difference to human rights outcomes. It also provides an opportunity to consider novel approaches to human rights institutionalisation in the light of persistent critiques of human rights judicial review. In other jurisdictions, it is the question of how to implement their bills of rights rather than the question of whether to have one that is hotly debated. Thus, in the United States, while it is almost unheard of to recommend the abolition of strong human rights-based judicial review, there is considerable controversy over how the US Supreme Court should exercise its powers with respect to its bill of rights. Some experts see the purpose of strong judicial review as upholding the original intention of the framers of the constitution (Scalia 1997). There are those who commend interpretation which protect democratic process (Ely 1980). Others look to the courts to use the bill of rights to intervene on behalf of oppressed minorities (Dworkin 1996). While others urge the Supreme Court should to use the Bill of Rights to promote controversial moral and political causes in relation to such matters as abortion, or capital punishment, or campaign finances. These controversies persist mainly because of the great difficulty that there is in reconciling strong judicial review with basic democratic principles, a challenging issue with a long history and a vast literature (for instance: Thayer 1893; Waldron 1993; Sadurski 2002; Bellamy 2006), some of which emphasises the role of political institutions in promoting human rights (Tushnet 1999).

In this context, the essay revisits, through the perspective of the rule of law, two closely related and relatively neglected critiques of human rights judicial review that may be classified under the general criticism that court-based human rights judicial review of legislation is in conflict with the fundamental principle of democracy that law-makers should be accountable to their people. Section 9.2, "Human Rights

Judicial Review: the Controversies", presents these two critiques: (1) a (formal) rule of law objection, that the bills of rights on which human rights judicial review is based are contrary to the principle that rules of law which courts are called upon to apply should be specific and clear as to what they require and permit, thereby reducing the accountability of elected governments, and (2) a practical objection: that human rights judicial review is largely ineffective in promoting human rights goals. Both objections involve the controversial nature of the decisions that courts are called upon to make when "interpreting" the abstract moral principles which make up the characteristic content of bills of rights.

Section 9.3, "Bills of Rights: Alternatives Approaches", goes on to argue (1) that the weaker "Dialogue" or "Commonwealth" versions of court-based human rights judicial review do not successfully evade either the rule of law or the efficacy critiques, and (2) that a better alternative is to institutionalise bills of rights as part of political constitutions involving mechanisms such as legislative review of existing and prospective legislation in order to promote and protect human rights in ways which are politically more effective and more in accordance with the twin democratic doctrines of the rule of law and the separation of legislative and judicial powers.

9.2 Human Rights Judicial Review: The Controversies

The prime and perennial objection to judicial review of legislation and government action in general on the basis of the constitutionalised requirements of a bill or charter of rights is the inherent contradiction of enshrining the right to political equality through a process that substantially restricts the citizens' right to have an equal say with respect to all the most fundamental political issues which arise within their society. Here, this democratic deficit is approached, first through the idea of the rule of law, in order to demonstrate how conflicting conceptions of the rule of law affect the debate, second in terms of the inefficacy of human rights judicial review in a democratic political culture.

9.2.1 The Rule of Law Objection

The rule of law case against bills of rights is based on the assumption that the rule of law is a necessary although not a sufficient basis for effective democratic control of government (Campbell 1996, 32–36; 2000). However, most arguments in favour of the rule of law present it as a way of limiting the power of government, in both its political and judicial forms, so as to protect the individual. It is said that the rule of law achieves this in two very different ways, the first of which deploys a formal conception of the rule of law, and the second of which deploys a substantive conception of the rule of law (Raz 1977; Craig 1997). Formal rule of law criteria relate solely to properties which can be stated independently of the content of the law, such as generality, specificity, and prospectivity. Substantive rule of law criteria relate to what it is that the law requires, permits or prohibits (Schauer 1988).

The first way in which the rule of law is said to protect the individual is by requiring governments to rule through the medium of general rules (rather than particular commands) that are couched in sufficiently specific and objective language to make it clear to the subject what is required, prohibited or permitted. In this way the formal conception of the rule of law restricts arbitrariness and brings a degree of clarity and certainty to the exercise of government power. This, it is contended, promotes efficiency, through making the legal rights and obligations of citizens clear, practicable and enforceable. At the same time it provides an element of fairness by giving citizens advance warning of their enforceable obligations and making it more difficult for governments to target particular individuals (Fuller 1969).

The second way in which the rule of law is said to protect individuals is by identifying those things which governments must or must not do for or to its citizens, even through the enactment of general and specific rules, thus restricting the scope of legitimate government power. This second function involves a substantive conception of the rule of law which is dependent on it meeting certain basis moral requirements, usually expressed in terms of fundamental human rights (Craig 1997; J. Allan 2001; T.R.S. Allan 2001; Christiano 2008, 172–6).

Both of these conceptions (the formal and the substantive versions of the rule of law) can, in theory, operate within societies which are non-democratic in the sense that that they do not have electoral accountability along with freedom of the press and freedom of association. However, in democratic polities, the rule of law has the further function of serving as a tangible focus for the assessment of the performance of government. This may be seen in the way in which legislative programs feature in political manifestos during election periods and the focus of political debate in general on the legislative achievements and commitments of competing political actors and organisations. Here the function of the rule of law is to serve as a basis for promoting democratic accountability through the popular critique of and ultimate electoral control over the enactment of the laws that are applied to members of the polity.

To serve this democratic function legislative manifestos and enacted laws must have clarity and precision that makes them amenable to rational criticism and endorsement. According to this rule of law function within democratic institutions, it is not enough that electorates can choose governments, they must also be able to exercise significant control over these governments, and this can be achieved in part through their being assessable in terms of their legislative programs and their predicted and actual outcomes. This democratic function of the rule of law requires a particular view of the separation of powers according to which elected legislatures should make laws, and judges should apply them. The aspect of separation of powers enables the government to be held accountable as the officials responsible for the outcomes of their laws, something that only makes sense if these laws are being accurately implemented. In this way, accountable government requires an operative political constitution in which elected governments makes the ordinary laws of the jurisdiction while judges are confined to applying those laws in the light of their findings of fact in particular cases (Barendt 1995). Here the generality requirement of the rule of law, which promotes efficiency and fairness, overlaps with the democratic requirement that accountable government must operate be via the medium of law, in that all these goals necessitate a model of laws as rules that are clear rather than obscure, specific not vague, and prospective not retrospective.

On the other hand, there is a conflict between the substantive version of the rule of law, which requires that legitimate laws have a particular content, and the formal conception which excludes reference to content. It is the latter, not the former, conception of the rule of law that features in the democratic function ascribed to the rule of law. This ambiguity renders unanalysed propositions about the rule of law which do not distinguish between its formal and its substantive versions inherently obscure, not only with respect to the role of law in promoting democratic accountability, but also with respect to its compatibility with human rights judicial review. Thus, on the American model of strong judicial review, human rights are seen as part of a substantive conception of the rule of law which renders unconstitutional legislation whose content is incompatible with the content of the bill of rights in force. Moreover, bills of rights are characteristically expressed in terms which are so vague and imprecise as to violate the formal conception of the rule of law which requires precision and clarity as standards of good law independently of its content.

The choice between conflicting conceptions of the rule of law and their associated conceptions of law and legality cannot be based on common usage or any one established tradition. Conceptual analysis reveals that there is no single idea of law that commands general agreement, as the history of legal philosophy amply illustrates (Raz 1977). In these circumstances, the important thing is to make it clear which conception of the rule of law is being utilised and what bearing this has on any argument for or against human rights judicial review. As presented here, the competing conceptions of the rule of law point to very different moral considerations representing two different moral views as to the significance of law in human affairs. The moral outlook associated with the formal conception of the rule of law is graphically presented in Lon Fuller, *The Morality of Law* (1969), where Fuller identifies eight formal requirements for good law-making and legal adjudication that produce effective, fair and liberating government. However, it should be noted that Fuller goes on to suggest, erroneously in my view, that formally good law, leads to a measure of substantively good law, and that he does not include in his analysis the democratic function of formally good law outlined above or consider its incompatibility with human rights judicial review.

Historically, the emphasis on formally good law derives from the work of Jeremy Bentham, the founder, albeit in the tradition of Thomas Hobbes, of legal positivism. Bentham's legal positivism does not rest simply on the fact that we can distinguish between law as it is and law as it ought to be, the so-called "separability thesis" (Hart 1961, 185–6), but is a form of legal positivism that sets out a blue-print for what law ought to be like, not in its content, but in its form. This may be called "ethical legal positivism", or "prescriptive legal positivism" (Campbell 1996; 2004), to emphasise that it is a legal theory that rests on moral foundations and requires an ethical commitment to the rule of positive law on the part of judicial officials. In the context of the bill of rights debate, it may also be called 'democratic positivism', since from Bentham's approach to democratic accountability we can derive the thesis that government ought to be conducted via authoritative rules than can be understood, followed and applied without recourse to controversial moral or other speculative judgments. Thus, Fuller's arguments from efficiency and fairness, can be supplemented by the further consideration, which can also be traced to Bentham, that formally good positivist laws empower citizens to achieve greater control over their elected governments, The particular point made here is that, if the people or their representatives make rules that are unclear and have to be made specific by those who interpret and enforce them, then the rules which are actually applied are not those made by the elected government. To the extent that this is the case, the polity in question is less like a democracy and more like a juristocracy, *i.e.* a government by judges (Hirschl 2004). We may call such a system a "constitutional democracy" but it is, in extreme cases, no more a democracy than a UK style "constitutional monarchy" is a monarchy.

Lawyers and other caught up in the study and implementation of law, rightly point out that actual laws are inevitably vague to some extent and in some respects, and frequently unclear in unexpected ways that require the attention of courts. When this happens, the moral opinions and political assumptions of judges inevitably seep into the content of the judicial reasoning that is said to be only a matter of 'interpretation'. Nevertheless, it is evident that, within a particular culture considerable measure of consensual public meaning can be attained. In such societies there are palpable differences between formally good and formally bad law, and, given an attainable measure of formally good legislation, judiciaries are in practice able to understand the laws they are meant to apply in terms of the manifest intentions of the law-makers and the precedents available to them. Inevitably, rule by means of formally good positive law is an ideal which cannot be fully realised, but that does not mean that political systems cannot approximate to it most of the time and should not strive to do what they can to implement the formal conception of the rule of law. One context in which this is evident is in the relative formal inadequacies of most of the content of typical bills of rights which have the form and content of moral principles that cannot be turned in to concrete legal decisions without the exercise of considerable, and usually controversial, moral judgments. This, Ronald Dworkin, the most distinguished contemporary advocate of the rights-based judicial review, concedes, and indeed welcomes, in his "moral reading" of the American constitution (1996).

It is evident from the rule of law objection that these difficulties with strong judicial review on the basis of bills of rights do not apply equally to all bills of rights, some parts of which can be quite precise, intelligible and clear. For instance, instead of a prohibition of "cruel and unusual punishments" or of "inhumane treatment", which are unacceptably vague and dependent on the moral beliefs of their interpreters, there may be a constitutional prohibition on capital punishment, which is reasonably precise and empirically applicable. There are, of course, other democratic objections to such entrenched provisions, particularly where constitutions are very difficult to amend, but by and large, and whether good or bad in content, they are acceptable as formally good positive law.

Despite these exceptions, the process of the rendering precise the vague moral ideals expressed in the standard bills of rights, such as the free speech, freedom of contract, or the sanctity of life itself, so as to arrive at rules which are clear and specific enough to decide issues of defamation (in the case of free speech), duress and misleading advertising (in the case of freedom of contract), or abortion and euthanasia (in the case of life), is ultimately a matter of moral rather than legal reasoning. Such judgments raise competing moral intuitions and involve complex social and economic factors for which courts are empirically ill equipped and lack moral and political authority. Moreover, in this process, the lines between politics and law become blurred and the separation of powers between law-making and law-application breaks down, so that the advantages of the rule of law, namely the limitation of government power by the requirement that it be exercised through and under the law, are seriously diminished.

These considerations are not lost on courts when they are involved in human rights judicial review. Indeed, it is because courts are acutely aware of the democratic deficit of human rights judicial review and the danger that its use will bring courts into disrepute by exposing the controversial political nature of their judgments in such cases, that they are in general reluctant to override the law-making powers of elected governments. What then, it may be asked, is all the fuss about? If courts are reluctant to be "activist" by revising or negating the laws enacted by democratic governments then no great harm is done through human rights judicial review. One response to this is to say that the democratic deficit of judicial review must be constantly brought to our attention to ensure that judicial deference to legislatures continues to be the norm. That apart, the routine deference of courts to political authority is a central factor in the second objection to human rights judicial review: namely its ineffectiveness in terms of realising substantive human rights values.

9.2.2 *The Ineffectiveness of Human Rights Judicial Review*

Those, in Australia, who argue for a Federal bill of rights, try to, but cannot, make much of a case in terms of Australia's human rights record on the basis of comparable social realities, a fact which should give pause to those who think that human rights based judicial review is a vital part of a successful human rights regime. Australia is far from perfect in human rights terms (Charlesworth 2002; Williams 2007). It has disadvantaged minorities, particularly with respect to its indigenous population. There is a degree of racial prejudice, there is some corruption in its police forces, and a clear advantage to the wealthy in legal disputes and political campaigning. Currently, there is a renewed harsh regime for dealing with asylum seekers and illegal migrants, and Australia is marginally involved in an arguably illegal war. Nevertheless, in general Australia come out near the top of comparative tables which attempt to quantifying human rights outcomes, and its citizens do not believe that their human rights are under threat (Commonwealth of Australia 2009, 384–91). Often, it is argued that not having an entrenched bill of rights is in itself a human rights deficit, but this rather begs the question as to whether bills of rights promote or retard conformity with human rights goals. Nevertheless, it is argued that all this is at risk because the human rights of Australians are not explicitly guaranteed in human rights language and through judicial review mechanisms. Parliament, it is said, can take these rights away at any time. So, even if Australia does have reasonably fair trials, habeas corpus, freedom of speech; and considerable welfare provisions, without a bill of rights these, it is argued, are at considerable risk (Charlesworth 2002).

Is this really the case? Does the security of human rights depend on giving courts the power to override or reinterpret legislation in accordance with statements of fundamental values? Clear examples are hard to find. In fact, over the long term, the norm is for courts to reflect rather than ignore majority opinion (Tushnet 1999; Waldron 1999; Bellamy 2006, 40–1). One contemporary test case is the world-wide development of anti-terrorist measures which diminish civil liberties. We can compare the extent of the restrictions on traditional civil liberties that have been introduced in so many jurisdictions as a response to terrorist incidents. In liberal democracies throughout the world there are new provisions, introduced in response to terrorist incidents which have occurred in places that were hitherto thought to be exempt from such outrages, provisions that make significant inroads into civil liberties relating to such matters as preventive detentions, and burdens of proof, secrecy and availability of evidence to the defence in criminal trials. As elsewhere, there are in Australia provisions for preventive detention, intrusive surveillance, closed tribunals without due process and further limitations on free speech. Such rights have been reduced or removed from the citizens of very many countries, but this has happened whether or not they are 'protected' by bills of civil rights and powers of strong judicial review (Williams 2006; Tomkins 2011).

Now, of course, it is arguable that such limitations of civil and political rights are justified in such emergency situations, and are not therefore violations of human rights at all, a point which illustrates just how variable the implications of vaguely worded constitutional rights may be. Nevertheless, the fact that there is no significant difference between jurisdictions with or without bills of rights, in situations which are precisely those that minority populations need protection from panicking majorities, is an example of how courts in times of crisis have not taken a strong line in favour of civil rights. If these are the rights we value and the aim of a bill of rights is to protect minorities in times of stress, then, quite simply, they do not work. Indeed it is arguable that some of the most extreme violations of human rights arising from recent terrorist incidents have occurred in the home of strong judicial review, the United States of America.

A better case for bills of rights with strong judicial review is that they can be a source of progressive decisions in constitutional cases deriving from bills of rights. These do not relate to the protection of universally applauded fundamental freedoms, but advance the cause of progressive social movements which promote social change relating to cutting edge issues of considerable controversy, like abortion, euthanasia, capital punishment, and same sex marriages. These may or may not be admirable in content, but they are certainly not in the category of protecting existing rights from untrustworthy governments. However, the incidence of this type of reform Australia is not markedly different from jurisdictions with justiciable bills of rights.

There are, of course, many justifying objectives that can be associated with bills of rights that are deployed through judicial review. One of these objectives is the introduction of controversial social policies which democratic politicians find too risky. This can take give appropriately greater weight to the convictions of intense minorities than to the views of less zealous majorities. Another justifying objective is to provide a basis for political cohesion in federal structures with weak central governments, as in the European Union. A third is simply to provide human rights with a higher profile. Certainly, one way to make governments take human rights seriously is to institutionalise a mechanism for overturning their decisions. These rationales can provide support for human rights judicial review in particular political circumstances, although the outcomes in terms of distinctively human rights values is normally very limited. Even if these objectives are to some extent achieved in certain places at certain times, we still have to weight up to the long-term damage done to the democratic process and to public support for human rights generally when significant matters of great moral concern are removed from the political domain on the dubious grounds that they are better served through legal rather than political mechanisms and movements. Further, there is the particular danger that governments can use the endorsement of courts for legislation which is highly questionable from a human rights point of view to head off criticism from human rights activists and organisations.

Overall, for whatever reasons that are given to justify human rights judicial review, there is little evidence that it is in fact an effective protection against government abuses of civil and political rights, and even less evidence that it has a significant impact on social and economic rights (Hirschl 2004). If anything, such constitutional provisions provide an unfortunate de facto legitimation of systematic human rights failures (Waldron 1999, 288; Bellamy 2006, 34). In these circumstances it makes sense consider alternative ways of giving effect to bills of rights as vehicles for the realisation of human rights.

9.3 Bills of Rights: Alternative Approaches

In response to the sort of democratic and rule of law arguments outlined above, there have emerged alterative models for human rights protection and promotion (Hirschl 2004; Hiebert 2006, 7–8). This section, first considers some of the weaker forms of human rights judicial review which are put forward as responses to the alleged democratic deficit critique of human rights judicial review, concluding that weak forms of human rights judicial review do not avoid either the rule of law or the ineffectiveness objections. After that, a more radical alternative is introduced which replaces judicial with legislative human rights review, and it is suggested that this is likely to be more compatible with democratic institutions and more productive of human rights outcomes.

9.3.1 The "Dialogue" Model

The democratic critique of human rights strong judicial review has been responded to in a number of ways. Thus, it is sometimes argued that any system is democratically legitimate if it has been adopted by a democratic process or has the support of the majority of the relevant population. This contention comes immediately up against the difficulty that a decision to abandon or weaken democracy, whether or not it is the outcome of as democratic process, does have the outcome of abandoning or weakening democracy, just as people who choose to become slaves become slaves even when their choice is of their own making. A second, more persuasive, argument, is that bills of rights are primarily for the purpose of maintaining democratic institutions, and the political equality that underpinnings, so that it cannot be perceived as being in conflict with democratic ideals. This may be countered either by pointing out that actual bills of rights go far beyond seeking to guarantee certain political processes, or by asking to whom the those exercising the powers of judicial review are accountable with respect to the actual outcome rather than the justifying intentions of the constitutional mechanism in place.

Another more historically favoured approach is to suggest a weaker, compromise model of human rights judicial review which has democratic safeguards built in. The suggestion is that there is a type of human rights judicial review that meets the democratic objection head on by subsuming the mechanism itself under the banner of democratic process. Thus a democratic version of human rights judicial review may be present it as a deliberative process within the normal confines of democracy in which the final authority remains with the populace as exercised through its elected representatives (Hiebert 2006, 9; Gardbaum 2001).

Although the dialogue label was used first in relation to the Canadian human rights regime, the UK Human Rights Act 1998 is the paradigm of the dialogue model of human rights protection that has been adopted in one of the eight states and one of the two territories within Australia, and a version of which is favoured by the recent, Australian, *National Human Rights Consultation* (Commonwealth of Australia 2009, 241). The core provisions of the UK Human Rights Act are that courts are required to interpret legislation so as, if possible, to make it in accordance with the European Convention on Human Rights, and, if this is not possible, they may issue a 'declaration of incompatibility' which does not invalidate the legislation but enables the government to initiate a fast-track process to amend the legislation in order to make it compatible with the courts understanding of the European Convention on Human Rights. The dialogue model, in its UK version, is distinguished by the fact that the elected legislature has the power to override the courts when the courts give what they regard as a human rights interpretation of a legislative provision and may ignore the findings of courts which declare that a piece of legislation is incompatible with its understanding of the bill or convention of rights in question. The Australian state and territory versions of these sections of the UK Act vary the formulations but retain the general import of the provisions, neither of which are thought to negate the "sovereignty of Parliament" as the ultimate law-making authority and both of which are held to counter the tendency of elected legislatures to ignore the interests of minorities as they seek to gain the support of the majority of voters (Byrnes et al. 2009, 59–60; Williams 2006, 93; Gardbaum 2001, 748).

The chief advantage claimed for this apparently rather neat compromise is the added political prominence which such Human Rights Acts give to human rights considerations and the public acknowledgement of the need to be mindful of the tendency of elected governments to undervalue human rights in the pursuit of electoral advantage. However, 10 years on from the UK Human Rights Act, there is considerable dissatisfaction with it on the part of both its supporters and its detractors. Critics point out that dialogue between courts, legislatures and executive government has not been the outcome. In the first place, when courts use the interpretive power they do not simply to resolve ambiguities but change the evident meaning of the legislation in question (Campbell 2001; J. Allan 2001; T.R.S. Allan 2001; Debeljak 2007, 38–9). This is not done after discussion with government, nor is it something for which governments have a fast-track mechanism for correcting or countering. Indeed the process of amending the law to counter radical re-interpretations of legislation which negate their view of the intention of Parliament is rarely a practical option, so that the apparently innocuous power of interpretation becomes a de facto legislative power (Allan 2006, 914; Hiebert 2006, 18). Given these practicalities, it turns out that the use of the interpretive powers given to courts by the Human Rights Act 1998 places the courts in a position that is comparable to that enjoyed by courts in systems of strong judicial review. Consequently the formal rule of law objection and the associated problems over the separation of powers, applies equally to both systems.

Further, UK governments have responded to requirements of the Human Rights Act by bringing forward legislation that has been "Convention-proofed" by drawing on legal advice is designed to anticipate possible declarations of incompatibility by courts. This is an unwelcome complexity for governments intent on implementing legal changes and is considered to generate bad publicity for government policies and to be avoided on this account. The result is that governments adopt a largely legalistic approach to basically moral questions as to what is and what is not in conflict with the moral ideals set out in the European Convention on Human Rights (JCHR 2006; Bellamy 2006, 37). This is not a political dialogue on fundamental issues but a process of second-guessing the courts' responses to legislation on the basis of legal precedent and prediction.

All this, of course, can be presented as being precisely what the UK Human Rights Act 1998 was intended to achieve, namely to oriented legislation more towards respecting the human rights which they have a tendency to neglect. However, quite apart from the fact that it is always debateable whether the altered outcomes do in fact better protect human rights as they are understood from a moral rather than a legal perspective; the process is far removed from any exchange of views or invitation for governments to reconsider the matters in question on their moral and political merits. Government reluctance to enter into what would in fact be a dispute with the courts is based on the understandably widespread idea that the central objective of the Human Rights Act is undermined if governments and parliaments do not defer to the interpretations and declarations of courts on matters of human rights. This reflects the political reality that giving courts more say in what the law should be has brought about a transfer of political power in a way that undermines both the democratic and the efficiency benefits of that version of the rule of law which involves the separation of law-making and law-enforcing powers (Tushnet 2003, 834).

Much of this can be expressed in terms of the rule of law objection. In this context this objection points to the fact that incorporating a document such as the European Convention on Human Rights into a legal system is to introduce a considerable indeterminacy into the law which runs counter to the formal conception of the rule of law. The very idea that courts and parliaments should exchange their thoughts in a dialogue on what the listed rights might mean reveals that they are not seen as engaging in a discussion of what the law is, but about what it ought to be. Evading this by both parties to the dialogue relying on prior legal decisions, originating largely from other jurisdictions, introduces more precision but at the expense of a necessary de facto acceptance that, in the human rights sphere, the courts are the law-makers. To that extent, the separation of powers and the sovereignty of Parliament are diminished.

This analysis may be faulted on the grounds that it is expressed in terms of a dialogue or conflict between courts and government, whereas the model in question is focussed on courts and Parliament. On this theme, an important consequence of the Human Rights Act has been the creation of a Joint Parliamentary Committee on Human Rights, drawn from both Houses of Parliament, with the role of scrutinising draft legislation as it comes before Parliament, drawing the attention of Members of Parliament to relevant human rights issues, and requiring the executive to provide evidence in favour of the legislation in question. This is an important development which is considered further in the next section of this contribution. However, the short answers to the criticism that my analysis misses the mark, is that, in parliamentary systems, governments almost always control parliaments rather than vice versa. Moreover, it is clear that the Joint Committee on Human Rights has largely followed to same processes of Convention-proofing as takes place when the Ministers responsible for a bill assert, as the Human Rights Act requires them to do, whether the bill they are presenting to Parliament is in their view compatible with the European Convention on Human Rights (JCHR 2006).

If weak forms of human rights judicial review are really not so very different in practice from strong forms this may explain why British courts are largely inactive in promoting their understanding of the European Convention. While it is difficult to provide an objective account of the extent to which British courts have become 'activist' on human rights issues on account of the subjectivity involved in distinguishing radical from standard judicial interpretations, it seems clear that British courts are by and large highly deferential to governments. In general, with the odd exception, courts with apparently weak powers of judicial review are only too aware of the sovereignty of Parliament and the danger to their standing and respect as exemplars of the rule of law. From the point of view of the critics of human rights judicial review, this is a welcome manifestation of judicial modesty and democratic propriety, which should encourage the critics to continue with their objections just in case the courts should routinely seek to intervene in the democratic process. However, from the point of view of those who see substantial human rights deficiencies in current government enactments and existing legislation and common law, the inaction and inefficacy or 'futility' of the dialogue model is a source of frustration and despair (Ewing and Tham 2008).

9.3.2 A Democratic Bill of Rights[1]

Despite the critical comments made the previous section, there are elements in and associated with the UK Human Rights Act, and in the Victorian and ACT human rights acts in Australia, that would appear to be in accordance with democratic assumptions. The creation of parliamentary human rights committees, the requirement that public authorities must seek to implement the European Convention on Human Rights, and the duty of government ministers to provide statements of human rights compatibility when proposing legislation, may all be seen as within the spirit of a traditional parliamentary style democratic government. The question with which this section is, very briefly, concerned is the extent to which these and similar mechanisms may be detached from the practice of human rights judicial review of legislation and yet have the sort of impact on human rights policies which those concerned about human rights violations would like to see in place (Hiebert 2006; JCHR 2006).

This alternative model, which I call a "democratic bill of rights", does not deny that there are human rights deficits of a particular type in actual democracies. Selfish majorities can unjustifiably oppress vulnerable minorities, just as powerful minorities can manipulate democratic processes and thereby disadvantage oppressed majorities. Democratic governments are motivated to some extent (as are all governments) to dissemble and lie to their people, to deprive opponents of their political rights, and to engage in short term political gain over long term national interests. Because of moral disagreement, cultural differences, economic self-interest, and limited rationality, democracy can go wrong in very many ways. All this is presupposed by the search for alternative ways of institutionalising effective and legitimate human rights mechanisms, the objective being to mitigate these deficits without unintentionally exacerbating them. Working out what is practicable and may be the most effective institutional arrangements best suited to promote a culture

[1] Since this chapter was written the Commonwealth of Australia has enacted the Human Rights (Parliamentary Scrutiny) Act 2011, along the lines proposed in this chapter. See Kinley and Ernst 2012.

in which rights can flourish depend a great deal on the nature of the society in question. The framework outlined below relate to what might be practicable and successful in the Australian context, without making any claim as to its universal applicability.

By a "democratic bill of rights" is meant a bill of rights that is institutionalised in ways that channel the legislative and governmental activities of the state, with the courts being involved only in the enforcement of such legislation as is enacted by the Parliament. The overall objective of a democratic bill of rights is to bring pressure on the system to make it more responsive to human rights considerations (Campbell 2006, 332–8). Ideally such a bill of rights would be entrenched to emphasis the depth and seriousness of the commitment to human rights. Its content would itself be a matter for democratic decision-making, but is likely to embody the existing human rights obligations that have been accepted under international law by the government in question, plus those fundamental value commitments that reflect that polity's particular understanding of what constitutes a human right. In Australia, the Report of the National Human Rights Consultation would suggest that this would mean a much greater emphasis on social and economic rights, in particular, the rights to an adequate standard of living' – including adequate food, housing and clothing, the right to the enjoyment of the highest attainable standard of physical and mental health, and the right to education' (Commonwealth of Australia 2009, 365–6).

This model involves political rather than judicial review, with the political forces in question being the Parliament and its committees working in cooperation with quasi-autonomous government bodies, human rights organisations within civil society and the operations of political parties. With a non-justiciable bill of rights the political focus of human rights would be on their moral import rather than their legal standing.

Such a bill would include an explicit obligation on governments to legislate for the realisation of human rights goals, a political obligation which is clearly present in the UN Universal Declaration of Human Rights and in the practice of most democratic governments. In particular there could be specifically identified "human rights legislation", either in separate acts of Parliament, such as anti-discrimination laws and basic health rights legislation, or in identified sections of ordinary legislation, such as a Crimes Act. This legislation, which is designed to give effect to the Bill of Rights and the human rights international treaty obligations which the state has endorsed.

While the provisions of the bill of rights would not be justiciable, such human rights legislation could have the special legal status that courts in common law countries give to fundamental common law rights, in that they cannot be repealed by implication through later legislation, only by explicitly worded amendments directly addressed to the rights in question. In addition, it is suggested that, building on existing Australian institutions, the already existing Human Rights and Equal Opportunities Commission be accorded a constitutionally protected and justiciable right to a status independent of government, a right to funding that enables the Commission to conduct enquiries into alleged human rights abuses brought to its attention by a political party with significant parliamentary representation, and a right to be consulted on the human rights implications of impending legislation.

The prime mechanism for furthering the objectives of a democratic bill of rights is the operation of a Joint Standing Committee on Human Rights, along the lines of the existing Senate Scrutiny of Bills Committee in Australia, and the Human Rights Committee in the UK, with membership from both the House of Representatives and the Senate, perhaps with some constitutionally guaranteed and justiciable powers, such as the power to delay legislation so as to ensure that there is opportunity for its views to be heard and its arguments properly considered. Parliamentary scrutiny could be guided by debate as to the proper content of human rights untrammelled by predictions of judicial interpretations. The focus could be on getting the laws right rather than judicially full-proofed, as the UK Joint Committee on Human Rights is currently seeking to do. (JCHR 2006; Tolley 2009).

In brief, the aim of a democratic bill of rights is to highlight the political obligations of governments and place the responsibility for articulating and promoting human rights where it belongs, within a wider democratic system. The institutional framework suggested is designed to bring pressure to bear on governments at key moments in the process of policy formulation, legislative drafting and parliamentary consideration, and legislative action and so to utilise and build upon the only sound basis on which human rights can flourish, namely the support of the politically concerned citizens of a country.

The obvious sceptical view of a democratic bill of rights is that, in the absence of judicial review, it would not be taken seriously and would simply be dominated by the government of the day. Everything, on this view, depends on the political process being carried out under the shadow of the courts. This is seen as unproblematic if the very idea of the rule of law involves the substantive moral values typically expressed in human rights declarations, such as equality, non-discrimination and respect for others. We have already considered the democratic objections to this approach, but perhaps a substantive conception of the rule of law is in principle compatible with democratic values provided that parliaments rather than courts have the responsibility of legislating in accordance with such an ideal. However, in the parlance of current constitutional politics a substantive rule of law model is associated with the idea of "legality", of which the courts are the proper institutional determinants. The counter view, recommended here, is to limit "legality" within a democracy to ensuring conformity to the formally good law as enacted by the elected Parliament. This approach represents not simply an optimistic view regarding the sense of justice and humanity to be found amongst the community of voters, but a democratic scepticism concerning the reliability of courts as moral leaders.

Certainly the efficacy of a democratic bill of rights will depend on the ways in which legislators can be held accountable to the public and on the formal as well as the substantive quality of the legislation to which that accountability gives rise. That in turn depends on: the quality of public debate; the available sources of information; the strength of organisations within civil society; the responsiveness of political parties; and the integrity of judiciaries. That the adequacy of all or any of these ingredients is often in doubt does not mean that there is a better way to go than seeking their improvement. Human rights judicial review has not been efficacious and cannot, I have argued, be expected to become so within a basically democratic culture, given its undemocratic nature. Treating courts as human rights authorities has given a false sense of moral legitimacy to often unconscionable government policies and diverted human rights from being a moral discourse with popular appeal into becoming a technical area of law divorced from ordinary political discourse. The suggestion is that human rights judicial review has been a set-back for the human rights movement, seen in broad terms as the efforts of concerned individuals and organisations seeking to moralise the often immoral outcomes of political process.

9.4 Conclusion

This essay discusses some of the key arguments concerning the legitimacy and effectiveness of bills of rights by highlighting the importance of distinguishing the different conceptions of the "rule of law" which are deployed by the contestants in this debate. Reference to the "rule of law" and "the principle of legality" feature centrally in the complex arguments as to the best means for articulating and implementing human rights. For some people, the "rule of law" means having an overriding moral duty to obey the law of the land in which we live, which means accepting what the courts understand the law to be. For others the "rule of law" means that there is no moral duty to obey a law which violates human rights. To bridge this chasm of misunderstanding, without abandoning the concept altogether, it is suggested that it is preferable to adopt a thin conception of the rule of law as having to do with governance through the medium of rules that are clear in their specification of which categories of person are forbidden, required or permitted to act in a particular way and what are the consequences to be imposed should they fail to conform.

The many advantages of such a system, which include the potential for the effective implementation of human rights, are dependent on general conformity to the law and its accurate application by impartial courts when there is nonconformity. Given that the laws in question, even if their source is a democratic process, may turn out to be seriously defective in terms of human rights, it is understandable to seek to improve on a democratic system with formal rule of law by adding an element of the substantive conception of the rule of law which incorporates the content of at least some fundamental human rights and encourages courts to exercise their moral muscle through powers of human rights judicial review. This, I have suggested, is a false promise, a threat to the human rights benefits of adhering to the formal conception of the rule of law, and an impediment to creating and sustaining an effective and democratic approach to the articulation and protection of human rights.

References

Allan, J. 2001. The effect of a statutory bill of rights where parliament is sovereign: The lesson from New Zealand. In *Sceptical essays on human rights*, ed. T. Campbell et al. Oxford: Oxford University Press.

Allan, J. 2006. The Victorian *charter of human rights and responsibilities*: Exegesis and criticism. *Melbourne University Law Review* 30(3): 906.

Allan, T.R.S. 2001. *Constitutional justice: A liberal theory of the rule of law*. Oxford: Oxford University Press.

Barendt, E. 1995. The separation of powers and constitutional government. *Public Law* 579.

Bellamy, R. (ed.). 2006. *Constitutionalism and democracy*. Aldershot: Ashgate.

Byrnes, A., et al. 2009. *Bills of rights in Australia: History, politics and law*. Sydney: UNSW Press.

Campbell, T. 1996. *The legal theory of ethical positivism*. Aldershot: Dartmouth.

Campbell, T. 2000. Democratic aspects of legal positivism. In *Judicial power, democracy and legal positivism*, ed. T. Campbell et al. Aldershot: Dartmouth.

Campbell, T. 2001. Incorporation through interpretation. In *Sceptical essays on human rights*, ed. T. Campbell et al. Oxford: Oxford University Press.

Campbell, T. 2004. *Prescriptive legal positivism: Law, rights and democracy*. London: Cavendish.

Campbell, T. 2006. Human rights strategies: An Australian alternative. In *Protecting human rights without a bill of rights: Institutional performance and reform in Australia*, ed. T. Campbell et al. Aldershot: Ashgate.

Charlesworth, H. 2002. *Writing in rights: Australia and the protection of human rights*. Sydney: University of New South Wales Press.

Charlesworth, H. 2006. Australia's First bill of rights: The Australian Capital Territory's *human rights act*. In *Protecting rights without a bill of rights: Institutional performance and reform in Australia*, ed. T. Campbell et al. Aldershot: Ashgate.

Christiano, T. 2008. *The constitution of equality*. Oxford: Oxford University Press.

Commonwealth of Australia. 2009. *National human rights consultation: Report*. Canberra.

Craig, P. 1997. Formal and substantive conceptions of the rule of law: An analytical framework. *Public Law* 467.

Debeljak, J. 2007. Parliamentary sovereignty and dialogue under the Victorian *charter of human rights and responsibilities*: Drawing the line between judicial interpretation and judicial law-making. *Monash University Law Review* 33(1): 9.

Dworkin, R. 1996. *Freedom's law*. Cambridge, MA: Harvard University Press.

Ely, J.H. 1980. *Democracy and distrust: A theory of judicial review*. Cambridge, MA: Harvard University Press.

Ewing, K., and J.C. Tham. 2008. The continuing futility of the human rights act. *Public Law* 668.

Fuller, L.L. 1969. *The morality of law*, 2nd ed. New Haven: Yale University Press.

Galligan, B. 1995. *A federal republic: Australia's constitutional system of government*. Melbourne: Cambridge University Press.

Galligan, B., and F.L. Morton. 2006. Australian exceptionalism: Rights protection without a bill of rights. In *Protecting human rights without a bill of rights: Institutional performance and reform in Australia*, ed. T. Campbell et al. Aldershot: Ashgate.

Gardbaum, S. 2001. The new commonwealth model of constitutionalism. *The American Journal of Comparative Law* 49: 707.

Gearty, C. 2004. *Principles of human rights adjudication*. Cambridge: Cambridge University Press.

Hart, H.L.A. 1961. *The concept of law*. Oxford: Oxford University Press.

Hiebert, J.L. 2006. Parliamentary bills of rights: An alternative model? *The Modern Law Review* 69(1): 7.

Hirschl, R. 2004. *Towards juristocracy: The origins and consequences of the new constitutionalism*. Cambridge, MA: Harvard University Press.

Hogg, P.W., and A.A. Bushell. 1997. The *charter* dialogue between courts and legislature: Or perhaps the *charter of rights* isn't such a bad thing after all. *Osgoode Hall Law Journal* 35: 75.

Joint Committee on Human Rights (JCHR). 2006. *The committee's future working practices.* Twenty-Third Report of Session 2005–2006, London.

Kavanagh, A. 2009. *Constitutional review under the UK human rights act 1998*. Cambridge: Cambridge University Press.

Kinley, D., and C. Ernst. 2012. Exile on main street: Australia's legislative agenda for human rights. *European Human Rights Law Review* 1:58.

Raz, J. 1977. The rule of law and its virtue. *Law Quarterly Review* 69: 781.

Sadurski, W. 2002. Judicial review and the protection of constitutional rights. *Oxford Journal of Legal Studies* 22: 275.

Scalia, A. 1997. *A matter of interpretation: Federal courts and the law*. Princeton: Princeton University Press.

Schauer, F. 1988. Formalism. *Yale Law Journal* 97: 509.

Thayer, J.B. 1893. The origin and scope of the American doctrine of constitutional law. *Harvard Law Review* 7: 129.

Tolley, M.C. 2009. Parliamentary scrutiny of rights in the United Kingdom: Assessing the work of the joint committee on human rights. *Australian Journal of Political Science* 44(1): 41.

Tomkins, A. 2011. Parliament human rights and counter-terrorism. In *The legal protection of human rights*, ed.T. Campbell et al. Oxford: Oxford University Press.

Tushnet, M. 1999. *Taking the constitution away from the courts*. Princeton: Princeton University Press.

Tushnet, M. 2003. New forms of judicial review and the persistence of rights-and-democracy based worries. *Wake Forest Law Review* 38: 813.

Tushnet, M. (ed.). 2007. *Bills of rights*. Aldershot: Ashgate.

Waldron, J. 1993. A rights-based critique of constitutional rights. *Oxford Journal of Legal Studies* 13(1): 18.

Waldron, J. 1999. *Law and disagreement*. Oxford/New York: Oxford University Press.

Williams, G. 2006. The Victorian *charter of human rights and responsibilities*: Origins and scope. *Melbourne University Law Review* 30: 880.

Williams, G. 2007. *A charter of rights for Australia*. Sydney: University of New South Wales.

Chapter 10
The Rule of Law, Validity Criteria, and Judicial Supremacy

Kenneth Einar Himma

10.1 Introduction

The concept of the rule of law and the ideals expressing its content are deeply contested. Theorists distinguish two broad conceptions: procedural rule of law and substantive rule of law. The former focuses largely on the procedures by which law is enacted and applied while the latter focuses on the content of the law. One might argue that both conceptions are somehow part of the very concept of law, but this much is clear: whether internal to law or not, the standards comprising the rule of law, procedural and substantive, are also standards of political legitimacy. Whether or not the exercise of coercive state authority is morally justified will depend in any given instance, in part, on whether or not it conforms to the standards comprising the procedural and substantive rule of law ideals.

This is not, of course, to say that these standards exhaust the conditions of moral legitimacy; the problem of legitimacy is far more complex than that. For example, the ideal of procedural rule of law can be roughly summarized by the formula "governance by law and not men." The general idea here is that procedural rule of law insulates citizens from being governed by whims of officials by requiring that laws be enacted, properly framed, and applied according to certain conditions (which frequently are thought to include Lon Fuller's so-called internal morality

K.E. Himma (✉)
University of Washington, School of Law, Seattle, WA, USA
e-mail: himma@wu.edu

I.B. Flores and K.E. Himma (eds.), *Law, Liberty, and the Rule of Law*, Ius Gentium: Comparative Perspectives on Law and Justice 18,
DOI 10.1007/978-94-007-4743-2_10,

of law). But, as H.L.A. Hart points out, these ideals are compatible with the enactment and enforcement of morally wicked laws. Further, the ideals of the rule of law are not generally thought to require any particular model of legislative decision-making – in particular, there is no requirement that governance be by democratic procedures, rather than some other procedures. Thus, the idea that a law (or a legal system generally) conforms to the standards of the procedural rule of law does not entail that the law (or legal system) is morally legitimate and may justifiably enforce the law by coercive means.

The converse is also true. The idea that a law (or a legal system) does not satisfy these procedural standards does not entail that the law (or legal system) is not morally legitimate. Fuller gets too little credit in legal philosophy for his work on what he took to be an internal morality of law with critics focusing somewhat unfairly on the idea that these formal standards constitute an internal morality. Construed as external standards of morality or as principles of efficacy, his work is seminal. As he correctly noted, it would take a wholesale failure to satisfy his eight conditions of law to vitiate a society's claim to having a legal system; it would take a similarly systemic failure to delegitimize a legal system. Indeed, as we will see, many legal systems include certain practices that seem inconsistent with these procedural ideals.

Although my concern in this essay is with the procedural ideals associated with the rule of law, I would like to hazard a few observations about the substantive ideals. First, an analysis of the substantive conception of the rule of law, usually expressing, at the most general level, that the content of the law is "right", "justified", or "just", by itself, tells us very little that would enable us to assess the legitimacy of any given system. Obviously, we would have to have a theory that provides substantive norms of legitimacy that covers the various areas of law: constitutional, criminal, tort, contract, *et cetera*. Should these theories be considered pieces of a theory of substantive rule of law? Moreover, there are similar concerns at the broadest level: should, say, the elements of Rawls's original position analysis be considered part of the theory of substantive rule of law. Finally, some laws that might not be ideally just might be legitimate because there is a consensus on its desirability that involves the voluntary waiver of citizens of rights that would otherwise have delegitimized the relevant laws.

In this essay, I give an analysis of those elements of the U.S. rule of recognition dealing with constitutional interpretation and judicial supremacy in order to evaluate them under procedural rule of law standards; as these elements are increasingly common among other legal systems, the conclusions I draw here will be applicable to these other legal systems.

Although the analysis presupposes a positivistic framework, I think that the same conclusions can be reached without making those assumptions – and shall indicate why. I will conclude that judicial supremacy seems to violate procedural rule of law standards, on the one hand, but suggest that it remains an open question, requiring consideration of other standards, as to whether judicial supremacy is morally illegitimate, a question I shall not consider here.

10.2 Conceptual Foundations of Positivism

10.2.1 The Concept of Validity Criteria

Fundamental to a conceptual analysis of law is the metaphysical thesis that, in any possible legal system, there are certain properties that *constitute* a norm as law (in exactly the way the instantiation of 'unmarriedness' constitutes a man as a bachelor). Any norm instantiating the appropriate properties is, for that reason, a law in that legal system; any norm not instantiating the appropriate properties is, for that reason, not a law in that legal system.

One consequence of this idea is that in every conceptually possible legal system there exist necessary and sufficient conditions for a norm to count as law. If *S* is a legal system and *P* is a statement that describes the properties that constitute a norm as law, then *P* states necessary and sufficient criteria of "legal validity" in *S*.

It should be noted that the Differentiation Thesis is a metaphysical thesis – and not an epistemological thesis. The Differentiation Thesis neither presupposes nor implies any claims about the extent to which the criteria of validity of a system can be identified.

10.2.2 The Separability Thesis

Understood here, the Separability Thesis denies Augustine's claim that unjust norms cannot be law. While Augustine believed that law must conform to moral principles, the Separability Thesis claims there can be legal systems with validity criteria not including conformity to moral principles. In other words, there *can* be both wicked legal systems and wicked laws – like Nazi Germany, apartheid South Africa, and antebellum United States.

Thus construed, the Separability Thesis does not deny necessary relations between law and morality; it simply excludes one particular necessary relation between law and morality – namely, a necessary connection between the criteria for determining what counts as law and moral principles. Positivists have frequently recognized other necessary relations between law and morality. H.L.A. Hart claims law must include "the minimum content of natural [moral] law" for law to conduce to its conceptual purpose of guiding behaviour. Joseph Raz argues that makes possible forms of social cooperation not otherwise possible among non-angels and hence performs a distinctively moral task.

10.2.3 The Conventionality Thesis

Fundamental to positivism is the idea that law is a social artefact all the way down. This entails not only that the laws governing citizens are manufactured by social processes but that the laws governing officials are also manufactured by social processes. In particular, it entails that the rule of recognition defining the validity criteria is also a social artefact.

The Conventionality Thesis explains the content and authority of the validity criteria in every conceptually possible legal system in terms of a social convention practiced by the persons who function as officials. As it functions here, the term "convention" is used to pick out what Hart calls a "social rule". Social rules have an "external aspect" and an "internal aspect". The external aspect consists in members of the group converging their behavior to a rule – so much so that it can be described as doing it "*as a rule*" (Hart 1994, 5, emphasis in original). The internal aspect consists in members of the group converging on a critical reflective attitude that constitutes them as *normative* in the sense that deviations from that rule are appropriately criticized.

According to the Conventionality Thesis, law exists when there is a social rule of recognition that results in efficacious regulation of citizen behaviour. As Hart puts the point, "those rules of behaviour which are valid according to the system's ultimate criteria of validity must be generally obeyed, and… its rules of recognition specifying the criteria of legal validity and its rules of change and adjudication must be effectively accepted as common public standards of official behaviour by its officials" (Hart 1994, 113).

It is important to note that the idea that legal systems have criteria of validity is not controversial; neo-natural law theorists and Ronald Dworkin disagree not on whether there are criteria of validity but rather on whether they are fully constituted by conventional practices of officials. Neo-natural law theorists believe that there are certain necessary moral constraints on the content of enacted law, while Dworkin views law as an interpretive enterprise that is necessarily governed by a norm that validates not only those rules duly promulgated by courts or legislatures but also those principles that show those rules in the best moral light. But it is equally crucial to note that no one would deny that the criteria of validity are partly defined by social processes; that norms enacted by the US government must be passed by both houses and signed by the President is clearly a criterion of validity that governs lawmaking in the US because of something resembling a convention or an agreement.

10.3 The Logical Relationship Between the Criteria of Validity and the Social Rule of Recognition

The terms "criteria of validity" and "rule of recognition" are not synonymous. Whereas the social rule of recognition is at least partly normative as one would expect of *rules*, the criteria of validity are purely descriptive in character. Indeed, criteria of validity (*i.e.* the criteria that distinguish law from non-law in a legal system) are usually expressed by biconditionals without any normative language:

> *Criteria of Validity Schema*: X is a law in S if and only if X conforms to the conditions set forth by the proposition *P*, where *P* is a set of properties.

A statement with this form is neither a norm nor has the resources to provide reasons for action because it lacks deontic language capable of providing such reasons.

In contrast, the rule of recognition is expressed in deontic terms describing or defining obligations and duties. Thus, recognition norms have the following form:

> *Recognition Rule Schema*: A president/legislator/judge has a duty (or ought) to perform X in the execution of her function as president/legislator/judge.

The Recognition Rule Schema, unlike the Criteria of Validity Schema, contains the logical resources – *i.e.* deontic notions – to define and express duties.

The *purely descriptive* criteria of validity are extrapolated from a study of the *normative* recognition rules, particularly those that require certain acts as a precondition for creating law. Clearly, the recognition norms that directly define duties with respect to recognizing, creating, and adjudicating law, as well as those that confer the power to do so, will determine the properties a norm must have to have the status of law.

Although "rule of recognition" and "criteria of validity" are closely related, it is important to distinguish the two, however, because, as we will see below, there are some recognition norms defining duties pertaining to how the Court interprets the Constitution that are, strictly speaking, not part of the criteria of validity. The two terms are related without being synonymous.

It is important to note that this point can be generalized to anti-positivist theories. The terms "rule of recognition" and "recognition norms" are usually understood to be technical terms of art in legal positivism, and avoided by rival theories. For example, Dworkin rejects the idea that the validity criteria are exhausted by a social rule of recognition of the type Hart describes. If we use the terms simply to denote rules that define norms on the part of judges and officials that define duties and powers in making, changing, and adjudicating law (the meaning at the most abstract level), then the distinction between the rule of recognition and validity criteria should apply uncontroversially across rival theories. Judges will have legal duties, as we will see, to interpret the Constitution according to certain interpretive principles, yet it would be incorrect to characterize these duties as forming part of the validity criteria.

10.4 Identifying the Criteria of Validity and Rule of Recognition

Hart's view that the existence and content of the rule of recognition are determined by official practice entails that what officials *self-consciously treat* as validity criteria *are* the validity criteria. While individual officials – including judges – can presumably have mistaken beliefs about the validity criteria, it is simply not possible, on the Conventionality Thesis, for officials of the legal system, *considered collectively*, to be *generally* mistaken about some *social* validity criterion. If officials all self-consciously recognize and treat norms satisfying *N* as valid law and *N's authority rests on acceptance*, then *N* determines a validity criterion in *S*. What officials collectively regard as the properties constituting norms as legally valid, as a conceptual matter, *are* the properties that are incorporated into the social rule of recognition defining the criteria of legal validity.

Each feature constituting a social rule is empirically observable. First, we can empirically ascertain convergence in behaviour. Second, we can empirically ascertain that conformity to the rule is encouraged and that deviations are criticized. Third, we can empirically ascertain that great social pressure is brought to bear on participants in the group to conform to the rule. Although it is possible to hide these features, legal systems, like the U.S., characteristically make no attempt to do so.

Accordingly, if Hart's Conventionality Thesis is true, then the project of identifying the validity criteria is empirical. The only way to identify the content of the social rule of recognition and the validity criteria is by empirical means. To identify the content of the validity criteria in any particular society, one must employ roughly the same sorts of empirical tools that are commonly utilized by sociologists to study the *behaviour* of officials. Thus, according to what I will call the Modelling Constraint, then, a correct description of the validity criteria in a legal system *S* must express those properties that, as a matter of observable empirical fact, officials collectively recognize as giving rise to legally valid norms they are obligated to enforce.

This feature also seems to be true of anti-positivist theories – although it will not be possible, on these other theories, to fully identify the criteria of validity by purely empirical observation. If, on the neo-natural law view, there are necessary moral constraints on the content of law, judges and legislatures might make a sufficient number of moral mistakes that it may seem that the relevant moral constraints are not functioning as validity criteria. But it might be possible to identify enough of the practices relevant to this paper through empirical means that the conclusions I draw about judicial supremacy and the rule of law under positivist assumptions can be extended to at least some anti-positivist theories.

10.5 The U.S. Supreme Court and the Nature of Final Authority

There is disagreement about whether the U.S. Supreme Court should have final authority to decide whether laws are valid under the Constitution but this much is clear: the Supreme Court *currently* has final authority to decide some constitutional issues. Indeed, one could not plausibly deny, as Ronald Dworkin aptly puts it, that the U.S. Supreme Court "has the last word on whether and how the states may execute murderers or prohibit abortions or require prayers in the public schools, on whether Congress can draft soldiers to fight a war or force a president to make public the secrets of his office."(Dworkin 1986, 2) Whether the U.S. adoption of the doctrine of judicial supremacy is legitimate (which is a normative issue), the U.S. courts clearly exercise judicial supremacy over the relevant issues.

10.5.1 The Capacity to Create Legal Obligations that Bind Other Officials of the System

A court has *authority* to decide a substantive legal issue only if its decision creates presumptive *obligations* on the part of other officials to accept its decision as law. To have authority is to be able to issue directives that are *authoritative* over some relevant class of individuals; and a directive is authoritative in virtue of its obligating the relevant class of individuals.

A court's authority to decide a substantive issue of law is *final* if and only if there is no *official* agency with authority to overrule the court's decision. As Dworkin puts this uncontroversial point: "[an] official has final authority to make a decision [when her decision] cannot be reviewed and reversed by any other official." (1977, 32) Accordingly, if a court has final authority over a decision, then its decision creates an obligation that binds officials in the jurisdiction; since there is no possibility of reversal, the obligation is final.

The obligations created by the decisions of a court with final authority are legal – if not *morally legitimate*. This has a very important consequence: *Insofar as a court has final authority to decide a substantive issue of law, it can legally bind officials in its jurisdiction, other things being equal, with either of two conflicting decisions on that issue.* For example, if a court has final authority to decide whether abortion rights can be restricted by legislation, then its decision creates legal obligations that bind other officials regardless of how the decision comes out – as long as the court reaches its decision in an acceptable way. Thus, the Supreme Court can legally bind other officials with a decision that is mistaken under the "correct" theory of interpretation (if such there be).

10.5.2 Final Authority and the Criteria of Validity

While it is natural to think that the holdings of the court with final authority are legally binding because they establish the content of the law, this is not necessarily true. It is both logically and causally possible for officials to be legally bound to enforce the content of a norm lacking the status of law – something that frequently happens in disputes that implicate the law of some other nation, state, or jurisdiction.

But this is not how officials in the U.S. understand the constitutional holdings of the Court. Although officials and citizens might disagree with a holding by the

Court, thinking it mistaken as a matter of interpretation, that holding is nonetheless treated and characterized as law. Even when a holding is widely thought mistaken, the state enforces the holding with the same coercive mechanisms used to enforce any other legal norm. The holdings of the Court *establish* the content of the law in the constitutional arena.

This should not be taken to mean that a Court holding declaring a statute unconstitutional *invalidates* the law in the sense that it removes a statute from the books or precludes a legislature from re-enacting the very same law to challenge the Court to reverse itself (which happens quite frequently with *Roe v. Wade*) (*vid. v.gr.* Adler and Dorf 2003). An explicit repeal by the legislature is required to remove the statute from the books, but there is little reason for that body to expend the energy after a statute is declared unconstitutional. The legal effect of a declaration of unconstitutionality and a legislative repeal is the same: the statute creates no enforceable rights or duties. And the same is true of a re-enactment – unless the Court reverses itself upon a subsequent legal challenge.

Officials and constitutional theorists disagree on how to characterize the effects of a declaration of unconstitutionality. Some theorists and judges argue that the effect of a declaration of unconstitutionality is to nullify the law. Indeed, in *Norton v. Shelby County*,[1] the Court declared, "an unconstitutional act is not a law; it confers no rights; it imposes no duties; it is, in legal contemplation, as inoperative as though it had never been passed." Others argue that such declarations might preclude state enforcement of the law by the parties to the decision, but go no further than that. Such decisions do not "nullify" the law – because the statute would take effect without other action by the legislature if the Court were to reverse itself.

None of this makes much difference because the Court's declaration of a norm as unconstitutional clearly renders the norm unenforceable and hence as lacking the force that partly constitutes an enacted bill as *law*; norms of a system *S* that may not be legally enforced are not properly characterized as "law" or as having the status of "legal validity" or "legality." Legal norms are backed up by the police power of the state. Once this latter feature is removed, their status as "law", as far as positivism is concerned, has for all practical purposes been removed – regardless of whether such norms remain on the books.

Indeed, as a matter of legal practice, other executive officials follows the holding and decline to enforce laws that are declared unconstitutional or laws with content that is sufficiently close to a law that is declared unconstitutional as to suggest a strong probability that it would be declared unconstitutional. This practice includes the President.

Although there are some constitutional scholars who believe there is no legal duty among such officials to refrain from enforcing such laws and presumably adopt this practice as some sort of professional courtesy or out of prudence, they are concerned with a different issue than the positivist. Constitutional scholars are

[1] 118 U.S. 425 (1886). For a defence of this view, *vid.* Alexander and Schauer (1997). For its part, the Court has not always adhered to this view. *Vid. U.S. v. U.S. Coin and Currency*, 401 U.S. 715 (1971), 741.

arguing a normative issue regarding the interpretation of the Constitution – namely, the issue of whether, under the proper interpretation of the Constitution and associated history, Supreme Court decisions *should* be construed as creating general obligations. This is a *normative* issue that is different from the purely *descriptive* issue with which the positivist is concerned – namely, whether the other officials converge on a social norm that requires them to refrain from enforcing such laws. If, as seems clear, the answer is "yes," then officials are taking the internal point of view towards a recognition norm that creates a legal obligation to refrain from enforcing such laws (*vid.* Kramer 2005).[2] That practice might change if and when constitutional theorists arguing the normative issue reach a general consensus that there is no such legal duty under the proper interpretation of the Constitution. But, until the practice itself changes, officials are treating the holdings as legally obligatory – especially if they would criticize, as seems reasonable to hypothesize, incidents where other officials utterly ignore the holding and enforce a law identical to the one declared unconstitutional by the Court. Constitutional theorists are concerned with the content of the proper interpretation of the Constitution and not the content of the rule of recognition, which are related but distinct rules.

From the standpoint of general jurisprudence – and this seems to be true no regardless of whether positivism is true or some form of anti-positivism is true – unconstitutional enactments are not properly characterized as "law" because they no longer are enforced as a general practice among officials and hence do not give rise to enforceable legal rights or obligations. This, at any rate, is how the terms "law" and "legal validity" should be understood here.

Indeed, lawyers are trained to regard the holdings of the court with final authority as establishing the content of the law. Every casebook in constitutional law in the U.S. contains excerpts from controversial Supreme Court cases that are widely considered mistaken. For example, there is not a comprehensive casebook or treatise on constitutional law in the U.S. not containing an excerpt or discussion of the *Roe* case. It is taken for granted among legal practitioners, students, and officials of the legal system that, for better or worse, the Court's decision in *Roe* established the content of the "law" (in the sense explained above) on abortion in the U.S.

It would seem, on any plausible general jurisprudential theory, U.S. officials, then, have a legal duty that requires them to treat the holdings of the court with final authority as establishing the content of the law on certain issues involving the Constitution – although this authority is, as we will see, limited in a number of ways. It is not just that officials happen to behave this way. Most, but not all, accept and practice this rule because they believe they are required to do so by fundamental principles governing the structure of the legal system. But some may accept the rule

---

[2] Kramer argues that the Supreme Court has usurped final authority, which should be taken back by the people. In any event, the descriptive claim, grounded in a comprehensive historical analysis, confirms that the official practice today confers final authority over the Constitution to the Supreme Court; the normative claim is that this is illegitimate. But the normative issue is not relevant for a positivist analysis of the content of the rule of recognition – although it is undeniably important.

for purely prudential reasons (say, to get ahead) and even believe it is not the best rule or required by such principles.

10.5.3 Final Authority and Official Disagreement

That officials are bound by a holding does not imply they have to agree with it; it merely implies they must comply with it with respect to acts within its scope. For example, a Senator might disagree with a holding that a legislative act is constitutional and vote against it believing it unconstitutional when it comes up for renewal. There is nothing in the claim that the Court has final authority to decide constitutional issues that implies that any official bound by it must *believe* it is correct.

Indeed, there is nothing in the idea that the Court has final authority that implies a Justice who dissents with a holding must abandon his or her dissent the next time the issue comes up. On the abortion issue, Justice Scalia has indicated that he will "continue to dissent from [the Court's] enterprise of devising an Abortion Code, and from the illusion that [the Court has] authority to do so."[3] This is not only consistent with the analysis offered up to this point; as we will see, it is arguably required of Scalia, given his views on the best theory of constitutional interpretation, by the recognition norm that the Justices converge in practicing (or to put it in jurisprudentially agnostic terms, by the legal duties that bind the Justices in interpreting the Constitution)!

The general practice is this: an official who refused to enforce some holding of the court with final authority believing it mistaken and hence not law would induce a cascade of criticism and a court order to enforce the holding. Insofar as these expectations are both institutional and normative, officials are practicing a recognition norm that makes certain court holdings determinative of the *content of the law* – a fact that determines the content of the criteria of validity.

A judicial decision is sufficient, but not necessary, for legality because officials might treat a duly enacted norm as law for an extended period without a judicial challenge. If citizens are diligent in conforming to the norm, then the norm is fairly characterized as "law" even without an official affirmation by the court with final authority. This feature of legal practice complicates the task of summarizing the necessary and sufficient conditions for law – and the reader should understand, at the outset, I have not resolved such issues.[4]

---

[3] *Hodgson v. Minnesota*, 497 U.S. 417 (1990), 480 (dissenting).

[4] So far I have focused on Supreme Court declarations that a law is unconstitutional; however, additional issues are raised by Court declarations that a law is constitutional. But it is important to be careful here. Just as a Court decision that one of the Justices believes mistaken does not preclude that Justice from dissenting the next time the issue comes up or require the Justice to change his or her vote, so too it does not require any official to enforce a law that he or she believes, contra the Supreme Court ruling, is unconstitutional. While as Frank Easterbrook points out, there is a longstanding practice among presidents to refuse to enforce statutes that they believe to be unconstitutional, there might very well be a practice among officials, including presidents, not to enforce statutes they believe the Court has mistakenly declared to be constitutional. On this *vid.* Easterbrook (1989–1990) and Paulsen (1994, 267 *et seq.*).

10.6 The Rule of Recognition and the Constitution

As may be evident from the preceding section, there is no straightforward relationship between rules of recognition and written constitutions. First, a legal system might not have a written constitution. Second, even if it does, officials might not view it as binding and ignore it. Third, a constitution's text must be interpreted, and there are many different theories of constitutional interpretation. To determine the role a written constitution plays in determining what counts as law, we have to observe all the relevant practices of officials in the system.

Many positivists have assumed the U.S. Constitution directly defines criteria of validity. Hart argues, for example, that the "criteria provided by the rule of recognition… may… be substantive constraints on the content of legislation such as the Sixteenth or Nineteenth Amendments to the United States Constitution" (Hart 1994, 250). Likewise, Brian Leiter states that "[a] rule is a valid rule of law in the United States if it has been duly enacted by a federal or state legislature and it is not inconsistent with the federal constitution" (Leiter 2001, 278–301).

Although quite common, this formulation does not jibe with official practice or the self-understanding of officials about their duties. The problem arises because officials frequently regard Supreme Court validity decisions as objectively mistaken – on moral grounds or on constitutional grounds. For example, the Court's holding in *Roe v. Wade* continues to be controversial – 35 years after it was decided! Many people believe the *Roe* decision is *incorrect* as a matter of constitutional law and interpretation. While some believe *Roe* is inconsistent with the Constitution's protection of a person's right to life, others believe it illegitimately created a new constitutional right. And such critics include congressional representatives, the attorney generals for several recent presidents, and Supreme Court Justices – the very officials whose practices determine the content of the validity criteria.

This means that officials characteristically treat such decisions as establishing what is legally valid – "legally valid" and "law" here being construed to express the idea that these decisions have the effect of creating, sustaining, or extinguishing *enforceable* legal rights and duties. Even when there is widespread disagreement among officials about whether a Court decision is "correct" as a matter of constitutional law, officials cooperate by treating the decision *as* the law. Enforcement agencies decline to enforce a law the Court has declared unconstitutional even if they think the decision mistaken. The relevant legislative bodies might re-enact the law, but it has no legal effect. Other courts dismiss as a matter of law any action grounded in an enactment declared unconstitutional by the Court.

This is not happenstance; as a matter of legal practice, officials generally regard one another as under an institutional duty to defer to the Court's validity decisions that fall within the scope of the Court's commonly accepted authority. In *Arizona v. Evans*, for example, the Court declared that "[s]tate courts, in appropriate cases, are not merely free to – they are bound to – interpret the United States Constitution…, [but] they are *not* free from the final authority of this Court."[5] Though the Court has found

[5] *Arizona v. Evans*, 514 U.S. 1 (1995), 8–9.

other occasions to affirm its authority over other officials, such reminders are rarely needed because officials always converge on expecting one another to accept the Court's decisions as establishing the law.

This has an important consequence: such behaviour indicates that officials are self-consciously practicing a recognition norm (or, to make the point in anti-positivist language, conforming to a legal duty) that confers upon the Court final authority to decide whether a duly enacted norm conforms to the substantive norms of the Constitution. Insofar as most officials regard themselves as bound by even mistaken Court decisions, it is because they are converging upon practicing a recognition norm that imposes a second-order duty to treat the Court's decisions as establishing the law (as the positivist understands that term).

Positivists and antipositivists agree on this. As Hart puts it, "[W]hen [the supreme tribunal] has said [what the law is], the statement that the court was 'wrong' has no consequences within the system: no one's rights or duties are thereby altered" (1994, 141). As Dworkin puts it, the Court "has the power to overrule even the most deliberate and popular decisions of other departments of government if it believes they are contrary to the Constitution, and it therefore has the last word on whether and how the states may execute murderers or prohibit abortions or require prayers in the public schools, on whether Congress can draft soldiers to fight a war or force a president to make public the secrets of his office" (1986, 2).[6]

But this means that the view that the criteria of validity are directly defined by the Constitution is incorrect as an empirical description of the validity criteria in the U.S. While this view purports to validate all and only duly enacted norms that conform to the substantive guarantees of the Constitution, officials characteristically recognize and treat as law even those Supreme Court validity decisions they believe are mistakenly decided *as matter of constitutional law*.

Another natural view goes too far in the other direction. John Chipman Gray, for example, argues that the law is, as a conceptual matter, what the highest court says it is: "To quote… from Bishop Hoadly: 'Nay, whoever hath an absolute authority to interpret any written or spoken law, it is He who is truly the Law Giver to all intents and purposes, and not the person who first wrote and spoke them.'"(Gray 1924, 125) On this view, final authority to decide what the law is logically entails "absolute authority" that cannot be legally constrained in any way.

Accordingly, Gray inferred the notorious claim that the law in the U.S. is what the Supreme Court says it is from the claim the Court has final authority to decide the validity of duly enacted norms. Since, on this line of analysis, the Court has unlimited authority to shape constitutional content, the validity criteria in the U.S. include the following norm:

> A duly enacted norm is valid if and only if it conforms to whatever the Supreme Court decides is asserted by the substantive guarantees of the Constitution.

This makes the Court the standard and denies that the Constitution might genuinely constrain the Court in some way.

---

[6] Of course, many theorists believe that, as a matter of political morality, the Court ought not to have this authority. *Vid. v.gr.* Waldron (1999).

Hart explicitly rejects Gray's view as applied to the U.S. Constitution on the ground that the Court's legal authority over validity decisions is always constrained by the determinate meanings of the Constitution: "At any given moment judges, even those of a supreme court, are parts of a system the rules of which are determinate enough at the centre to supply standards of correct judicial decision" (Hart 1994, 145). On Hart's view, then, Gray's view overlooks the fact that the Court is legally bound to ground its validity decisions in the language of the Constitution and hence that the Court is legally constrained to *interpret* the Constitution.

Hart is correct that there are limits to the range of constitutional interpretations that officials are prepared to accept as establishing what is and is not legally valid in all existing legal systems. For example, a Court decision invalidating a federal speed limit on the ground that it violates the Second Amendment right to bear arms would likely provoke a constitutional crisis unprecedented in U.S. history. Moreover, a Court decision invalidating the legality of paper money on an originalist theory would probably be ignored and viciously criticized. If so, Gray's view of the validity criteria in the U.S. legal system is incorrect.

At this point, then, we can identify the beginnings of a recognition rule (and hence a legal norm) that defines the duties of officials to abide by the Supreme Court's decisions that satisfy certain constraints that is inconsistent with Gray's view but reflects the fact that the U.S. Supreme Court has final authority over the interpretation of the Constitution: Officials in the U.S. have (1) a duty to treat as legally valid duly enacted norms upheld by the Court as conforming to an interpretation of the Constitution that is rationally grounded in the text of the Constitution; and (2) a duty to treat as not legally valid duly enacted norms struck down by the Court as not conforming to an interpretation that is rationally grounded in the text of the Constitution.

It is reasonable to think there are other interpretive limits on the Court's discretion than just the requirement that constitutional interpretations be rationally grounded in the text. Though we can't begin to understand the Constitution without understanding the ordinary meanings of its terms, those ordinary meanings cannot dictate a particular outcome in any validity case likely to be entertained by the Court. And this means that the ordinary meanings of the constitutional language in "hard cases" always leaves the Court free to choose either a "yes" answer or a "no" answer to the question of whether a particular duly enacted norm is legally valid.

Consider whether the Court should uphold a duly enacted norm that prohibits virtual child pornography. It is true that the Court cannot understand the First Amendment without understanding the ordinary meanings of such terms as "abridge" and "speech," but this does little to constrain the Court in reaching a particular outcome; for merely putting together the ordinary meanings of "Congress", "shall", "make", "no", "law", "abridging", "freedom", "of", and "speech" tells us almost nothing about whether the First Amendment prohibits a ban on virtual child pornography. Since the ordinary meanings of the First Amendment are indeterminate with respect to the permissibility of a ban on virtual child pornography, these meanings leave the Court free to uphold or to strike down the statute as it sees fit.

Accordingly, the idea that interpretation be rationally grounded in the meanings of the text really doesn't amount to much in determining the *outcome* of validity cases. There are always two logically possible outcomes in any case challenging the validity of a duly enacted norm: the Court can either uphold the norm or strike it down. While ordinary meanings of constitutional terms preclude a very large number of irrational interpretations of the constitutional text, the text will leave in any "hard" case one rational interpretation that would justify upholding the norm and one rational interpretation that would justify striking it down; for, by definition, a case is "hard" when existing law fails to dictate a unique outcome. Given that any validity case likely to reach the Supreme Court is hard in this sense, just considering the ordinary meanings of terms will never eliminate a sufficiently large set of interpretations to rule out, as a logical matter, one of the two conflicting decisions. In essence, then, the linguistic constraints operate to constrain the Court in *justifying* its decisions in hard validity cases, but it does not operate to limit the *outcomes* available to the Court.

Existing legal practice is difficult to reconcile with the idea that the only limit on the Court's discretion is a duty to rationally ground its decisions in some plausible interpretation of the Constitution. The Court's validity decisions are always based on interpretative standards that demand considerably more than just a minimally rational connection to the ordinary meanings of the constitutional text. Each of the prevailing approaches to constitutional interpretation, such as evolutionism, originalism, and textualism, purport to identify the best interpretation of the text and hence one that is superior to any interpretation bearing only a minimal connection to ordinary meanings of the text.

This suggests that an accurate statement of the validity criteria must also take account of the role that these substantive interpretive standards play in constraining judicial determinations of what counts as law. As Kent Greenawalt points out (2009, 655–6, emphasis added):

> Whether every standard of interpretation that constrains judges should be characterized as a "legal" standard is doubtful. Some standards of interpretation, such as that ordinary words should be accorded their natural meaning absent some reason to do so, are general and fundamental to all interpretation of language; but other standards are distinctly legal. Whether standards are distinctly legal or not, *so long as judges are bound to follow them in deciding what the Constitution means, the standards need to be accorded some place among ultimate or derivative criteria for determining law.*

Greenawalt believes that the rule of recognition and criteria of validity must acknowledge the role that legal principles of interpretation, like originalist or textualist standards, play in determining what counts as law in the U.S.

Not surprisingly, Greenawalt affords "prevailing" interpretive standards a prominent place in determining what counts as law in the U.S. in his description of the validity criteria. As puts the matter in his own description of the U.S. rule of recognition: "On matters not clear from the text, the prevailing standards of interpretation used by the Supreme Court determine what the Constitution means" (2009, 659).

Although a major step in the direction of adequately capturing the Court's authority with respect to deciding issues of constitutionality, Greenawalt's formulation is at odds with the empirical practices of the other officials. As Greenawalt himself points out (2009, 656–7):

> [To] say that whatever standards are now prevailing… are part of the ultimate rule of recognition… could be misleading… [A]ll Justices believe it is sometimes appropriate to alter previously prevailing standards of interpretation…

It is not just that Justices sometimes *believe* it is appropriate to alter those standards. Rather, the point is that the Court *has authority* to alter interpretive standards in making validity decisions; should the Court decide to interpret the Constitution based on the popular understanding, I would hypothesize that other officials would accept those holdings and enforce them. But if the Court is not legally bound by just the "prevailing" standards, then it follows that the Court, as an empirical matter, has legal authority to depart from those standards.

But this seems fatal to Greenawalt's view. If, as an empirical matter, the Court has authority to bind officials with validity decisions that explicitly depart from prevailing standards, it is because officials are practicing a norm that requires them to treat those decisions as establishing what is legally valid. But since, according to positivism, what officials collectively recognize as legally valid on the ground that it satisfies a general criterion *is* legally valid, it follows that the Court's departures from prevailing standards in making validity decisions establish what is legally valid.

At this point, it would be helpful to attempt to determine where the Supreme Court Justices themselves draw the line with respect to what *they* are prepared to do. Given that it is the Court's obligations with which we are concerned, we might make more progress by attempting to identify the limits imposed by the standards that the Justices themselves accept as constraining the Court's discretion in constitutional cases.

The Justices clearly employ a number of interpretive standards that constrain the discretion of the Court beyond the limits defined by the ordinary meanings of the terms. A Justice who accepts one of these standards, then, will regard herself as duty-bound to decide validity cases in accordance with the constitutional interpretations that satisfy that standard.

Nevertheless, the task of identifying the relevant recognition norm is complicated by the fact that Justices frequently disagree about which interpretative standards are appropriate. If, in contrast, each Justice regarded originalism as the only legitimate standard of constitutional interpretation, the Justices would be practicing a norm requiring them to decide validity cases on an originalist understanding. But this, of course, is not the case: while some Justices favour an originalist approach, others favour an approach that views the Constitution as a "living document"; still others favour a pragmatic approach, adopting elements of different strategies as circumstances warrant. Insofar as the Justices regard the Court's decisions as binding on the other officials regardless of which of these favoured principles ultimately provides the justification, a description of the relevant recognition norm should not uniquely favour one of the interpretive principles.

It is worth noting Justices routinely criticize one another for their choice of prevailing interpretive strategies. Originalists, for example, frequently criticize living document theorists for inappropriately reading their political preferences into the Constitution, while living Constitution theorists criticize originalists for adhering to an understanding of constitutional text that lacks contemporary relevance. In every such case, however, the criticism is that the particular interpretation, even if plausibly grounded in some prevailing interpretive standard, is not grounded in what – in some sense – is the *best* interpretation of the Constitution.

This kind of criticism suggests that Justices are practicing a recognition norm (or, to put in theory-neutral terms, following a legal duty) requiring the Court to ground validity decisions in the best interpretation of the Constitution. The most coherent explanation for the fact that Justices criticize each other for failing to produce the best interpretation of the Constitution is that they regard themselves as bound by the best interpretation in making decisions and are practicing a norm that makes this the standard.

Something more, of course, should be said about the relevant sense of "best". What is "best" might, for example, be determined from a policy standpoint; or it might be determined from the standpoint of personal ambition. Thus, while the claim that the Justices regard themselves as under a duty to ground their validity decisions in the best theory of constitutional interpretation should seem eminently plausible, we cannot understand exactly what it amounts to without an explanation of what is meant by "best."

Somewhat surprisingly, we can look to the work of positivism's most influential critic for a theoretically viable account of the sense that is employed in the Court's validity practice – something that helps confirm the point that the thesis of this essay applies across the positivist/anti-positivist divide. Dworkin makes a number of empirical claims about what judges "characteristically" do in deciding hard cases. Dworkin observes that judges, as a general matter, experience themselves as constrained by morally normative considerations of political legitimacy.[7] Hard cases of any kind, on his view, are typically decided on the strength of moral considerations – and not the sort of policy considerations that ground legislative decisions. Judges in this legal system take an interpretive attitude towards law that requires them to interpret the law in a way that shows it in the best moral light.

These empirical claims are quite plausible. Supreme Court opinions and dissents "characteristically" suggest that the Justices are trying to interpret the Constitution in a way that legitimizes the legal system and its official monopoly of the police power. These opinions and dissents frequently challenge each other's arguments and interpretive principles on grounds of political morality.

The range of interpretive strategies that might fall under the rubric of "morally best" is quite wide. For example, it would embrace a purely result-oriented theory that simply attempts to reach the morally best outcome, regardless of all other considerations – including considerations of legitimacy having to do with democracy. It would also embrace Dworkin's own moral reading of the Constitution, which requires that putatively moral terms in the Constitution be interpreted as incorporating the corresponding moral norms. But it would also embrace purely historicist theories, like originalism, which *precludes recourse to objective morality* in deciding a case in favour of an interpretation based on a historical understanding of the terms; originalists, like Scalia, typically believe that originalism is justified on the basis of considerations of moral legitimacy. Indeed, it would embrace consequentialist-driven

[7] Here it is important to remember that the notion of legitimacy is a *moral* notion that is concerned with the extent to which the state is *morally* justified in using its coercive force.

interpretations – or, for that matter, any hybrid method consisting of various pieces of this. At the end of the day, it seems reasonable to think that Justices are all concerned to reach ground their decisions in the morally best interpretation of the Constitution – and there are many different views about how to reach this.

In *Planned Parenthood v. Casey*,[8] for example, the Court argued that considerations of legitimacy required it to reaffirm *Roe*:

> [T]he Court's legitimacy depends on making legally principled decisions under circumstances in which their principled character is sufficiently plausible to be accepted by the Nation… There is… a point beyond which frequent overruling would overtax the country's belief in the Court's good faith… The legitimacy of the Court would fade with the frequency of its vacillation.[9]

In response, Justice Scalia argues that the majority's claim that "the Court must adhere to a decision for as long as the decision faces 'great opposition' and the Court is 'under fire' acquires a character of almost czarist arrogance."[10]

It is no accident that majority and dissenting Justices criticize each other in terms of what is legitimate. At a deeper level, the Justices' views on constitutional interpretation are usually based on normative views about moral legitimacy. Proponents of more conservative textualist and originalist approaches typically reject more liberal theories of constitutional interpretation as being inconsistent with moral principles emphasizing the legitimacy of majoritarian decision-making. Scalia's disdain for living Constitution approaches is unmistakably moral in character:

> This is not to say that I take issue with [the claim] that the problem of judicial rewriting of democratically adopted texts is 'deeply rooted in our history' and that 'judges have exercised that sort of presumably *undemocratic authority* from the very beginning'. To acknowledge that is simply to acknowledge that there have always been, as there undoubtedly always will be, *willful* judges who bend the law to their wishes. But acknowledging *evil* is one thing, embracing it is something else… (Scalia 1997, 131–2; emphasis added.)

It is clear Scalia believes Court decisions that modify the Constitution violate democratic ideals of legitimacy: allowing judges to "exercise undemocratic authority" is an "evil" that threatens "the existence of democratic government".

Liberal theorists are no less likely to ground their conceptions of what the Court is legally bound to do in substantive considerations of political morality. William Brennan rejected originalism as "arrogance cloaked in humility" and argued for an interpretative norm that protects the individual rights to which human dignity gives rise (Brennan 1986, 19–20):

> In general, problems of the relationship of the citizen with government have multiplied and thus have engendered some of the most important constitutional issues of the day. As government acts ever more deeply upon those areas of our lives once marked "private," there is an ever greater need to see that individual rights are not curtailed or cheapened in the interest of what may temporarily appear to be the "public good."

---

[8] 505 U.S. 833.

[9] 505 U.S. 866.

[10] 505 U.S. 999.

Whereas Scalia's view of legitimacy emphasizes the significance of majoritarian decision-making and hence requires a non-moral purely historicist interpretation of the Constitution, Brennan's view emphasizes the significance of respecting individual rights. Like Scalia, Brennan formulates the Court's legal duty in terms of protecting certain substantive ideals of political morality and advocates interpreting the Constitution in the light of evolving moral standards.

Such empirical observations suggest that the Justices are practicing the following second-order recognition norm:

> *Duty to Find the Best Interpretation Standard* (DutBest): Supreme Court Justices are obligated to decide the validity of duly enacted norms according to what is, as an objective matter, the morally best interpretation of the Constitution.

As their writings indicate, Justices attempt to (1) conform their behaviour to a norm that obligates them to decide cases according to the morally best interpretation of the Constitution and (2) take the internal point of view towards that standard as governing their behaviour as officials.

The other officials also seem to take the internal point of view towards *DutBest* – though, strictly speaking, the only duties defined by *DutBest* are owed by the Supreme Court. Like Supreme Court Justices, the other officials of the legal system tend to ground their views about how the Court ought to decide cases in standards of constitutional interpretation that are based on more general views about the Court's morally legitimate role in a democratic society. When other officials criticize mistaken Court decisions, such criticism is immediately grounded in these views about how to interpret the Constitution and ultimately grounded in the underlying moral views about the scope of the Court's legitimate authority under democratic ideals. Accordingly, the attitude and behaviour of both the Court and the other officials seem to converge on *DutBest*.

On the strength of such considerations, then, one might think that the objectively best interpretations of the constitutional norms directly define validity criteria. On this line of analysis, the following is a validity criterion in the U.S.:

> *Objectively Best Interpretation Formulation* (OBIF): A duly enacted norm is legally valid if and only if it conforms to what is, as an objective matter, the morally best interpretation of the substantive norms of the Constitution.

If the officials in the U.S. accept *DutBest* as defining the Court's duties in making validity decisions, then it must straightforwardly give rise to a validity criterion.

OBIF violates the Modeling Constraint by understating the Court's authority to bind other officials with its decisions. While the other officials will criticize the Court for not producing the objectively best interpretation, those officials will nonetheless continue to treat mistaken decisions as binding law. Since the Court thus has characteristic authority to bind other officials by either of two conflicting interpretations of the relevant provisions, a norm can be legally valid even if its content is, as a matter of fact, inconsistent with the objectively best interpretation of the Constitution. It follows, then, that the *objectively* best interpretations of the substantive provisions of the Constitution, if such there be, do not directly determine what counts as law in the U.S. – though it is true that they function to constrain the Court's decision-making in validity cases.

Given that officials will accept *any* Supreme Court decision that and is grounded in what a majority of Justices take to be the morally best interpretation of the Constitution, it appears that the relevant recognition norms *DutBest* and therefore that the relevant recognition norm defining the duties of officials in the U.S. should be formulated as follows:

> *Final Authority* (FinAuth): Officials in the U.S. have (1) a duty to treat as law those duly enacted norms until struck down by the Court as failing to conform to what they collectively have decided is, as an objective matter, the morally best interpretation of the Constitution and satisfies the Acceptability Constraint; and (2) a duty to treat as not being law those duly enacted norms that are struck down by the Court as not conforming to what they collectively take to be the interpretation that is, as an objective matter, the morally best interpretation that satisfies the Acceptability Constraint.

FinAuth coheres more tightly with empirical legal practice because it acknowledges that officials will accept the Court's decisions about what is the morally best interpretation of the Constitution.

Accordingly, a more accurate statement of the ultimate validity criterion will look something like this:

> *Court's Best Interpretation Formulation* (CBIF): A duly enacted norm is legally valid unless declared unconstitutional according to what a majority of the Justices decide is, as an objective matter, the morally best interpretation of the substantive norms of the Constitution.

Again, it should be emphasized that there are many issues to which the Court's authority does not extend – such as to issues that involve political questions – but the Court has final authority to decide whether an issue is a political question. If, on the one hand, the Court declines to address an issue on the ground that it decides it is a political question, this is consistent with *CBIF*. If, on the other, it mistakenly decides a case that presents a political question, then officials are bound by that holding – which is also consistent with *CBIF*.

10.7 Conclusions: The Rule of Law and Judicial Supremacy

Insofar as the procedural rule of law ideal is concerned to ensure governance by law, instead of by men, by limiting the discretion of officials in making, changing and adjudicating law, it appears that this ideal will not be fully satisfied in any legal system which affords judicial supremacy to courts over any class of legal issues. In particular, any legal system which affords final authority to the courts to decide the constitutionality of duly enacted norms will necessarily fall short to the extent that officials put themselves under a duty to abide by the judicial decisions of the relevant courts on constitutionality – if, as is usually the case, the relevant courts have the authority to bind other officials with their mistaken decisions.

Of course, it is important to note that such systems do not utterly fail with respect to these ideals, whether conceived of as internal or external to the notion of law. As long as judges must rationally ground their interpretations in the text of the Constitution (or in other relevant texts), their decisions will be sufficiently constrained to warrant characterizing their decisions as rule by law, rather than men.

It, thus, remains an open question whether the practice of judicial supremacy in the U.S. is morally legitimate and hence morally justified. As anyone familiar with the literature on the justification of judicial supremacy can attest, rule of law considerations do not dominate the discussion. The question is frequently framed in terms of whether the practice is compatible with democratic ideals or, if not, whether the practice is compatible with values that outweigh the democratic ideals. It would be theoretically naïve to think that an issue of such complexity and import could be resolved by simply considering rule of law considerations.

And, again, although I have taken legal positivism as an organizing principle for the discussion, I believe these results apply to anti-positivist theories as well. It is unlikely, for example, that Dworkin would take the position that, say, the *Defense of Marriage Act* is not legally valid because it violates the Dworkinian position that laws should include those principles and norms that show the law in the best moral light. However, while he might claim it illegitimate on substantive rule of law ideals, he must make a case for whichever he take the substantive rule of law ideals to be. It is simply not obvious and requires a good bit of theoretical analysis to produce a plausible defence of any substantive (or content-based) theory of legitimacy.

Complicating matters further here is the issue of whether these substantive ideals must be assumed as objectively true, rather than subjective or intersubjective/conventional. If the relevant ideals are regarded as objectively true, then no one, as Jeremy Waldron points out, has privileged access to these moral ideals and hence cannot infallibly decide such questions.

To conclude, the nature of law nearly assures that some official body will be awarded final authority over the content of enacted law, and hence raises difficult issues regarding procedural and substantive rule of law, as well as other difficult issues regarding political legitimacy. This is not surprising: insofar as law is a social artefact, human beings will be making the law with all their fallibility and lack of complete command over the language. The issue of political legitimacy will always go much deeper than rule of law ideals.

References

Adler, M.C., and M.D. Dorf. 2003. Constitution existence conditions and judicial review. *Virginia Law Review* 89: 1105.

Alexander, L., and F. Schauer. 1997. On extrajudicial interpretation. *Harvard Law Review* 110: 1359.

Brennan, W.J. 1986. Speech. In *The great debate: Interpreting our written constitution*, ed. W.J. Brennan. Washington, DC: Federalist Society.

Dworkin, R. 1977. *Taking rights seriously*. Cambridge, MA: Harvard University Press.

Dworkin, R. 1986. *Law's Empire*. Cambridge, MA: Harvard University Press.

Easterbrook, F.H. 1989–1990. Presidential review. *Case Western Law Review* 40: 905.

Gray, J.C. 1924. *The nature and source of law*. New York: The MacMillan Company.

Greenawalt, K. 2009. How to understand the rule of recognition and the American constitution. In *The rule of recognition and the U.S. constitution*, ed. K.H. Himma and M.C. Adler. Oxford: Oxford University Press.

Hart, H.L.A. 1994. *The concept of law*, 2nd ed. Oxford: Oxford University Press.

Kramer, L. 2005. *The people themselves: Popular constitutionalism and judicial review*. Oxford: Oxford University Press.

Leiter, B. 2001. Legal realism and legal positivism reconsidered. *Ethics* 111: 278.

Paulsen, M.S. 1994. The most dangerous branch: Executive power to say what the law is. *Georgetown Law Journal* 83: 217.

Scalia, A. 1997. *A matter of interpretation*. Princeton: Princeton University Press.

Waldron, J. 1999. *Law and disagreement*. Oxford: Oxford University Press.

Chapter 11
Retroactive Application of Laws and the Rule of Law

Juan Vega Gómez*

11.1 Introduction

I will try and make one main claim in this paper: issues of retroactivity have to be dealt within a two stage process, one dealing with a formal test of retroactivity and a second one that involves issues of justification. The reason for this is that when analyzing problems of retroactive application of laws, I think confusion is prone to occur when these sorts of problems are concentrated entirely on issues of justification, *i.e.* when dealing with these sorts of issues we tend to go directly into a justification process, so my idea is that a clearer understanding of the problem of retroactivity might be advanced and more analytical headway can be obtained if the problem is divided into these two stages.

Section 11.2 of the paper deals with the first stage of the process and develops a possible formal test for retroactivity, the formal test is a consequence of adopting

*I have acquired many debts in the various stages of writing this paper, but would specially like to thank Brian Bix and Michael Giudice for detailed comments, discussions and corrections. Thanks are also due to Enrique Cáceres, Keith Culver, Julie Dickson, Imer Flores, Iwao Hirose, Rodrigo Ortiz Totoricaguena, Joseph Raz, Yanara Suenaga, René G. de la Vega, Wil Waluchow, and Benjamin Zipursky. Earlier drafts of the paper were presented at several conferences, but my special gratitude is for audiences at the Jurisprudence Discussion Workshop at the Legal Research Institute at UNAM, Mexico City (Mexico); the Department of Philosophy at York University, Toronto, Ontario (Canada); and the Department of Philosophy at McMaster University, Hamilton, Ontario (Canada). Of course all remaining errors are entirely my fault. I also benefited from leave and thanks are due to UNAM and the Faculty of Law at University of California at Los Angeles (USA) and Mark Greenberg for providing me with an ideal atmosphere to work on my research. The idea of writing on retroactivity problems first came to mind while commenting on a then recent Mexican Supreme Court decision, *vid.* Vega Gómez (2006).

J. Vega Gómez (✉)
Legal Research Institute, National Autonomous University of Mexico (UNAM),
Mexico City, Mexico
e-mail: jvegagom@unam.mx

I.B. Flores and K.E. Himma (eds.), *Law, Liberty, and the Rule of Law*,
Ius Gentium: Comparative Perspectives on Law and Justice 18,
DOI 10.1007/978-94-007-4743-2_11,

Raz's idea of a formal conception of the "rule of law", I think that issues of retroactivity are best seen within this framework. At one point while developing the ideas for a formal conception of the "rule of law", Raz states that: "A law is either retroactive or not" (1979, 215). I will try and flesh out this idea due to the fact that I think this demands a formal test – a yes or no answer for retroactivity problems. Section 11.3 of the paper explains the second stage of the process and tries to argue in favor of the two stage process main claim; Sect. 11.4 deals with some objections to the main points put forward; and finally, Sect. 11.5 presents a conclusion.

Before beginning I must clarify that I will only deal with issues strictly related to retroactivity in legislation, *i.e.* I will not deal with issues of retroactivity in adjudication,[1] but hope that this focus on retroactive legislation will help explain issues on retroactive judge-made law. I should also add that I make an interchangeable use of *a retroactive law* and *a retroactive application of a law*, the main point of the paper is to know when we have a retroactive law, I use retroactive application of a law because my background in testing these claims is a judge trying to answer these questions in a concrete case of application of legislation.

11.2 Formal Conception of the Rule of Law and First Stage in the Process

First I will develop some basic ideas around this formal conception and its relation to retroactive application of laws and highlight the importance of law's capability to guide the behavior of its subjects: As Raz states, the formal conception of the rule of law is not the rule of the good law (1979, 211), we must not confuse this formal conception with an idea that thinks that complying with the rule of law entails that the law in question is good law, *i.e.* that the rule of law promotes morally sound directives and helps maintain a democratic system. Or that the concepts of rule of law and the promotion of human rights entail each other. The formal conception of the rule of law warns us that this is not necessarily the case, this formal conception does not say much regarding the attributes that have to be met by the people who make the law or the kinds of laws that they will promulgate. Let me quote a passage from Raz's essay on the rule of law and its virtue (1979, 211):

> A non-democratic legal system, based on the denial of rights, on extensive property, on racial segregation, sexual inequalities, and religious persecution may, in principle, conform to the requirements of the rule of law better than any of the legal systems of the more enlightened western democracies. This does not mean that it will be better than those western democracies. It will be an immeasurable worse legal system, but it will excel in one respect: in its conformity to the rule of law.

[1] I should also add that at this moment I will not deal with how this basic framework corresponds with legal decisions within a comparative perspective, *i.e.* in civil and common law traditions.

It is important not to over exaggerate this passage: the formal conception of the rule of law by itself does not necessarily entail the rule of good law, we have a better understanding of the notion of the rule of law if we do not conflate it with issues of moral importance, conflating these latter issues calls for a "complete social philosophy" as Raz says (1979, 211). So what is the core idea underlying this formal conception if not the notion of good and democratic law if the rule of law is to be followed? The idea is this: law must be capable of guiding the behavior of its subjects (1979, 214), digging a bit deeper and having in mind other elements of Raz's theory of law we can say that authorities attempt to have a mediating role between subjects and right reasons that they are supposed to correctly follow (1986, specially Chapter 3). Authorities' directives claim to guide our actions and claim to determine those right reasons (or in fact determine the right reasons if we are talking of legitimate authorities). The point to keep in mind here is that this mediating role authorities play and the directives issued by the authority claim to guide our conduct and this makes sense only if the law has the capability of guiding the behavior of its subjects.

This is the basic intuition – as Raz calls it – from which the doctrine of the rule of law derives, and from this basic intuition several principles are derived from it, the one which concerns us is the one that states that one cannot be guided by a retroactive law (1979, 214), why? The answer is pretty much straightforward in this formal conception of the rule of law: because we have to know beforehand what an authoritative directive requires from us to be able to be guided by it,[2] it would be odd for an authority to demand conformity to a directive that I had no prior knowledge of its existence and content, unless some kind of fortune telling capacity is expected from me, which of course is not the case.

So the question I want to turn to is the following: how do we determine when we have a retroactive application of a law according to this formal conception? How can we answer this question considering the basic intuition from which the doctrine of the rule of law derives? *i.e.* that law must be capable of guiding the behavior of its subjects. Let me turn to a minimum test I have in mind in order to answer the question of retroactivity, one that emphasizes law's guidance function, and counterfactual tests.

I think much of the issues on retroactivity implicitly or explicitly deal with counterfactual tests, and one way that might help us to get a straightforward answer to the issue of retroactivity and make sense of Raz's statement that "either a law is retroactive or not" can be by using counterfactuals, this way we can start envisioning a yes or no answer regarding retroactive application of laws.

[2] The other seven principles are: laws should be relatively stable; the making of particular laws (particular legal orders) should be guided by open, stable, clear, and general rules; the independence of the judiciary must be guaranteed; the principles of natural justice must be observed; the courts should have review powers over the implementation of the other principles; the courts should be easily accessible, and the discretion of the crime-preventing agencies should not be allowed to pervert the law.

Let us imagine a straightforward case of retroactivity, for example as Fuller says, an easy case of a statute which purports to make criminal an act that was perfectly legal when it was committed (Fuller 1964, 59). The case we can think of is a statute enacted in 2010 that prohibited and made it a crime to smoke inside a car with the presence of children. Orlando is and was a heavy smoker and in 2008 he smoked several times inside his car and in the presence of his children. With the new 2010 statute he is being called into court for his behavior and actions that took place in 2008. This is a case of retroactive application of the law due to the fact that the new statute was enacted after Orlando's acts of smoking in the car with his children, an act that was perfectly legal at that time.

To get a straightforward answer to this straightforward case of retroactivity a counterfactual test might apply. The counterfactual test would ask: "If Orlando had known that this statute was going to be enacted, *would* he have acted differently"? If the counterfactual test yields a *yes* answer we have a retroactive application of a law, if it yields a *no* answer, we do not have a case of retroactivity.

What are the features of this counterfactual. *First*, are we to ask this counterfactual in relation to Orlando or the person involved in the possible retroactive application of the law? Let us consider this first possibility: This is one way to deal with the issue and consider the intentions of the person under the possible application of a retroactive law, *v.gr.* ask what Orlando's intentions would have been had he known that this statute was going to be enacted. But as straightforward as this possibility might be in getting a good answer, in this analysis of retroactivity we have to consider two main issues. First, if I were to ask the person involved, *i.e.* Orlando, would you have acted differently? the answer most certainly will be *yes*, I would have done a different thing, considering that this way he might just get out of problems regarding the new law that prohibits smoking in the car in the presence of children, so we have to stay away from this quite obvious reply; and secondly and most importantly, I think we have to employ a more abstract question and person regarding this counterfactual, because in a concrete adjudication case in court if we were to ask the person involved or every person involved in the possible retroactive application of the law this would ensue an indeterminate answer regarding the law. This last point makes us aware of another important requirement of the law, *i.e.* law's generality trait and precisely because of this we need to look for a test and a person who encompasses many cases, therefore the test for our counterfactual has to be asked regarding a hypothetical person, and ask this hypothetical person if she would have acted differently considering the new statute that has been enacted.[3]

And *secondly*, what are the conditions that have to be met by this hypothetical person: one possibility is to ask just about anyone who may or may not have an

[3] The idea of using counterfactuals regarding hypothetical persons was brought to my attention by Andrei Marmor's book (2005, especially Chapter 2). I should add that Marmor considers this possibility in a different context, *i.e.* regarding legal and other types of interpretation.

important consideration for what the law instructs. Consider the possibility of asking a person who has no respect for the law whatsoever, respect in the sense of guiding his conduct according to law's directives. From this point of view it would be impossible to come to a conclusion about what the law demands, this person does not consider the law in any action guiding way, so if this person is asked why did you do this? The answer can't be for example: at that time it was the law that I could smoke inside the car in front of my children, this person just does not care, and does not take any of the law's standards as guiding her conduct. So we must also move away from this point of view and consider the point of view of the person who *does* consider law's directives as giving her reasons to guide her conduct. If I were to ask this person: Why did you do that? We can assume that an answer would be: at that time the law did not prohibit smoking in the same car in the presence of children.

The conclusion is that we must disregard asking this counterfactual to the person or persons actually involved in the possible retroactive application of the law and we must also eliminate asking this question from the perspective of the person not interested in law's directives as action guiding. For this formal test to have some plausibility we should consider the internal point of view, the person who uses expressions as the ones stated by Hart: expressions such as: "It is the law that…", expressions of "…ordinary men living under a legal system, when they identify a given rule of the system" (Hart 1961, 99).

Therefore, the counterfactual test I am trying to advance asks the following: If X had known that this statute was going to be enacted, X *would* have acted differently. In this case X is a hypothetical person who adopts the internal point of view and considers law's directives as action guiding.

Let us consider our counterfactual regarding the example of a statute enacted in 2010 that prohibited and made it a crime to smoke inside a car in the presence of children. As we considered before, Orlando is and was a heavy smoker and in 2008 smoked several times in his car and in the presence of his children. With the new 2010 statute he is being called into court for his behavior and actions that took place in 2008. In the counterfactual: If X had known that this statute was going to be enacted, *would* X have acted differently? We then ask this from the internal point of view and if the counterfactual test yields a *yes* answer then we have a retroactive application of the law. The answer in this imagined case is *yes*, a person who considers laws directives as action guiding *would* have acted differently in this scenario, she would have acted differently because she – supposedly and contrary to fact – knows that smoking inside the car in the presence of children is a crime punished by law.

At this point I would like to address a couple of important objections on why this test might prove to be too simple of a test.

The *first* and very important objection leveled at this idea is that with this formal test*: every change in the law would count as a retroactive application of the law*, this is *why* it is too simple of a test and probably an otiose test at the end because this seems counter to most changes, amendments, reforms, etcetera that take place in the law. Fuller has this very idea in mind when he states the following (1964, 60):

> Laws of all kinds, and not merely tax laws, enter into men's calculations and decisions. A man may decide to study for a particular profession, to get married, to limit or increase the size of his family, to make a final disposition of his estate- all with reference to an existing body of law, which includes not only tax laws, but the laws of property and contract, and perhaps, even, election laws which bring about a particular distribution of political power. If every time a man relied on existing law in arranging his affairs, he were made secure against any change in legal rules, the whole body of our laws would be ossified forever.

This point is a crucial one. Of course the idea of the formal test cannot go against a basic and important point regarding our legal systems, *i.e.* the existence of secondary rules of change that solve the problem of a static quality of a pre-legal system (Hart 1961, 93). We have these secondary rules that allow changes in the law and also allow for the elimination of unneeded statutes and modifications and amendments called upon by our legal system. The objection that I think Fuller and others have in mind is that for every action I take there cannot be a freeze-frame of the law valid at that time. This is true and I agree, but the question employed in the objection is too broad of a question to ask: what exactly does *changes in the law mean*? Our formal test and the counterfactual are not trying to rule out every change in the law, it deals with changes in the law regarding a specific action that the law is trying to regulate *ex post facto*. The directives instruct us to ϕ or not to ϕ, regarding *this* is that we have to analyze the question of "changes in the law" leveled by the objection. It is not the case that retroactive problems have to deal with everything that has a consequence regarding ϕ-ing. With the formal test and the counterfactual we are not ruling out future events of enacted statutes, just ex post facto consequences that it purports to have, this is what retroactivity is all about, changes in the law to regulate future behavior is inevitable and is not to be confused with cases of retroactivity.

A *second* and also very important objection claims that all retroactive cases analyzed with our counterfactual test will yield a yes answer. I want to resist this conclusion with two scenarios. One is when we have indeterminate cases of legal questions:[4] sometimes the law might not provide a definite answer for the counterfactual test, in these cases the counterfactual test does not make sense due to the fact that in the counterfactual: If X had known that this statute was going to be enacted, he would have acted differently, we cannot make sense of what the law demands, even if we ask this from the internal point of view. In other words, we cannot make sense of our antecedent in the conditional because we have unsettled law that has to be developed and settled via adjudication at the court level.[5]

And a second scenario where the counterfactual would not necessarily yield a yes answer becomes apparent if we consider the case where there is a change in the law via a statute, but this statute is more beneficial to the person, in these cases it is possible that a no answer would be the result of the counterfactual. For example and to use a special

---

[4] This is an important point made by Hurley regarding retroactivity questions (*vid.* 1990).

[5] I am still trying to avoid the issues and questions raised by problems of retroactivity in adjudication.

tax case, consider an action that took place in 2000, that action –let us say a monetary transaction– was taxed with a 15% amount, there is a new statute in 2010 where that same action is being taxed with a 10% amount, if the new statute is being considered in our counterfactual it would yield a no answer, i.e., in the question: *If X had known that this statute was going to be enacted, would he have acted differently?,* not necessarily, in this case he would have acted the same, he would have made the same monetary transaction, due to the fact that the new statute is even more beneficial to his action. This is what I make of legal systems that do not consider ex post facto changes in the law that are more beneficial to the persons as retroactive applications of a law.

To return to the issue of: Is this formal test too simple? I consider that indeed this is a simple test, but it is a simple test that constitutes just one part of the issue of retroactivity, a second important test is still pending. But it is not too simple of a test because it encompasses all changes in the law and neither because the formal test and counterfactual will *always* yield a yes answer.

This is the more modest claim that I want to make in this paper, why? Because I am aware that these kinds of counterfactuals have their own difficult and intricate issues and I don't think I am capable of sorting these out at the moment, but I do want to make two points here: one, that independently of the fact that these kinds of counterfactuals have their own problems in philosophy, I think legal reasoning engages in these tests in everyday adjudication problems, *v.gr.* when a court is trying to interpret a statute or constitutional provision it is not uncommon that they ask themselves a counterfactual test, something like the following: if the framers had known about these unexpected future problems, what would have they decided on this case at hand.[6] I do not think these tests are entirely ignored by judges and it seems to appeal to common practice in the law. And second: maybe further issues have to be figured out in order to come to a definite answer *re*: this kind of counterfactual test, but we do need some test that has to yield a yes or no answer to the issue of retroactivity. This is why this claim is a modest one.

If the idea of a formal test has some plausibility, and I am correct to assume that we need a yes or no answer regarding these cases of retroactive application of laws, then we can summarize the possibilities that we so far have in analyzing retroactive application of laws: (1) retroactive, if the counterfactual yields a yes answer, (2) not retroactive, if the counterfactual yields a no answer, and (3) it is neither retroactive nor not retroactive, these are cases of indeterminacy or uncertainty in the law.

11.3 Second Stage

Now to return to my main claim: The two stage process in dealing with problems of retroactivity I am trying to advance puts at a second stage the reasoning and justification of the case at hand, by justification and reasoning I mean reasoning that

---

[6] On counterfactual tests as a legal interpretation technique, *vid.* Alexander (1995), Marmor (2005), and doubts raised by Stoljar (2001, 447–65).

involves issues of legal, moral and political concerns, reasoning that will definitely decide if a retroactive application of a law is justified on certain moral and political grounds, or maybe that a retroactive application of a law is not justified according to a constitutional provision that explicitly states that retroactive application of laws is prohibited. But the point is this: these issues of justification can be handled better if we first determine if we have a case of retroactive application of a law, why? (1) on many occasions if these issues of retroactivity are analyzed going straightforwardly into a justification process, the issue of whether we have a case of retroactivity or not gets confused with the reasons we have for applying or not applying a law retroactively, and (2) we can have a clearer view of what kind of reasons I need to put forward in order to justify certain case if prior to that I have a clear knowledge if it is either retroactive or not considering the formal test that would yield a yes or no answer.

And I do think that we need a yes or no answer to this question, issues of retroactivity viewed within a formal conception of the rule of law enable us to have a clearer picture of the whole problem, and helps us consider retroactivity within these two important stages.

The benefits of the two stage process analysis of retroactivity can be highlighted if we consider another of Fuller's interesting insights on retroactivity mentioned in a discussion regarding a tax law first enacted in 1963 imposing a tax on financial gains realized in 1960 at a time when such gains were not yet subject to tax. Such a statute – according to Fuller – "may be grossly unjust, but it cannot be said that it is, strictly speaking, retroactive" (1964, 59).

We should add that Fuller's argument also states: "To be sure, it bases the amount of the tax on something that happened in the past. But the only act it requires of its addressee is a very simple one, namely, that he pays the tax demanded. This requirement operates prospectively. We do not, in other words, enact tax laws today that order a man to have paid taxes yesterday, though we may pass today a tax law that determines the levy to be imposed on the basis of events occurring in the past" (1964, 59).

Of course Fuller is right in the sense that the requirement operates prospectively and of course the tax law does not order a man to have paid taxes yesterday. But the problem with Fuller's insight is his notion of strictly speaking not retroactive. If we have a category of "strictly speaking not retroactive", we also need another one that labels the problem as broadly speaking not retroactive, and so forth. This is precisely what my analysis wants to avoid, while at the same time contribute to sharpen the boundary of these important concepts. We can avoid this problem if in this tax example we ask whether there is an impairment of law's capability to guide behavior and the answer is yes, if the man had known about this latter statute he would have acted differently, considering most importantly his gains he rightly acquired before the statute.

What I think is happening with Fuller's point is that indeed many legal systems consider tax laws not subject to a retroactive application scrutiny and this is why they consider them not retroactive applications of the law. But with the ideas here advanced we have to come to the conclusion that in this tax law example we *do* have a retroactive application of the law according to our counterfactual test, but maybe this retroactive application of the law is justified on political, economical and moral grounds. This is what I am trying to argue, we consider many cases of retroactive application of laws justified so we go on and say something like Fuller: "strictly speaking this is not retroactive", when indeed it is retroactive and maybe justifiably so, but it is retroactive and adding "not strictly retroactive", I insist, does not help.[7]

Someone sympathetic to Fuller's account might conclude that the idea I have regarding a formal test and a justification stage process will consider many cases of application of laws retroactive, when in practice these are not seen as retroactive. This is true, but it shows not a weakness with my account but a strength: If the formal test and justification process yields many cases as retroactive we are better off, this places the burden of justification to the legislature, courts and administrative bodies, they are the ones that have to come up with important moral and political reasons to justify a retroactive application of a law, this is a task *they* are called to perform. My point is that going straight to the conclusion that an application of a statute is not retroactive law is hiding many of these important justification discussions, it settles the debate without having a debate about the justification of a retroactive law. My counterfactual test addresses the moral and political issues of justification clearly instead of hiding, as Hart said, "the true nature of the problems with which we are faced" (1983, 77).[8]

With this in mind and the two stage process properly explained we now have more possibilities in analyzing retroactive application of laws: (1) retroactive if the counterfactual yields a yes answer, but justified, (2) retroactive if the counterfactual yields a yes answer and not justified, (3) not retroactive, if the counterfactual yields a no answer, and (4) it is neither retroactive nor not retroactive, these are cases of indeterminacy or uncertainty in the law.

11.4 Possible Objections

Maybe I am getting things completely wrong here and I am arriving to a false conclusion. It just might be that drawing on a formal conception of the rule of law, using counterfactuals and relying on law's guidance function to properly address retroactivity issues might suggest that law's guidance function is being overstated and that retroactive issues have to be seen as a matter of degree and not as I suggested a problem that beforehand needs to yield a yes or no answer. This is what is

[7] Fuller goes on to consider various responses to his argument regarding the tax law, but in the end he unfortunately cuts the dialogue short and leaves the issue unresolved (*vid.* 1964, 61).

[8] Thanks again to Mike Giudice for helping me state this idea more clearly.

suggested by Charles Sampford in a thorough and detailed analysis of *Retroactivity and the Rule of Law* (2006, 9 and 81).[9]

Sampford argues that the guidance function argument "is neither overwhelming nor unequivocal. Reliance weighs against retroactivity in many cases, but it (or the principles underlying it) actually justifies retroactive legislation in others. This has important consequences for the traditional concepts of the rule of law and even suggests a complete *reconceptualization* of the ideal." (2006, 7) And Sampford argues for this relying heavily on the formal conception of the rule of law. Even if I am tempted to say right from the start that Sampford's arguments are confusing the two stage process of retroactivity and that he is going directly to the justification process, I think his ideas regarding the guidance function of law need to be addressed.

Let us first assume that Sampford and I have the same idea in mind when talking about law's guidance function. Sampford develops two lines of arguments to claim that law's guidance function is being overstated. *First* is the idea that the use of retroactive law may be an important source of guidance, for example, the use of retroactive laws can guide people in cases of loopholes or mistakes made by the legislature, the use of retroactive law guide people by providing a warning to citizens not to rely on existing law and that taking advantage of these loopholes and unintended effects of the legislature is probably going to be penalized through retroactive law. Sampford argues (2006, 81):

> Retrospective laws which close "loopholes" and "unexpected interpretations and consequences" reinforce the guidance of primary laws. Thus the retroactive law does not itself provide guidance but assists other laws to provide guidance. "Prospective retrospectivity" (that is, clear guidelines for retrospective rule making can generate an expectation that retroactive law will be applied in the future to prevent actions) is extremely important for this purpose.

But is this right? First of all how can retroactive law provide guidance in the sense of signaling a warning to citizens not to rely too closely on the details of existing law, because the question then is: why do we have law at all? Obviously people reasonably guide their conduct or accept the consequences of their actions based on what the law provides, not on what the law *could* provide.

[9] Sampford suggests using the term retrospectivity and then goes on to define it as: "retrospective laws are laws which alter the future legal consequences of past actions and events" (2006, 22). I am not sure what to make of various ideas here, especially the idea of "alter future legal consequences", but then he goes on to say that the common picture of retrospectivity is that of a person performing a discrete and completely lawful action on one day, and on the next having a sanction attached to their action despite the fact that it is already in the past. If this is what he means by retrospectivity, then we agree and my use of retroactivity instead of retrospectivity to address his ideas does not have any impact on the arguments made. I will only use retrospective when quoting his ideas literally. But I acknowledge that there is room for much conceptual work to be done regarding types of retroactivity or retrospectivity, this paper is an attempt to clarify *some* of the problems. I became aware of Sampford's book after some of these ideas were developed, this is why I am considering them at the end of the article and as a possible objection, a possible objection due to the fact that as will become apparent Sampford's conclusions are radically different from mine.

Sampford argues among other things that retroactive law provides a warning to citizens not to rely too closely on the details of existing law *especially in cases of mistakes made by the legislature and effects that laws have and that were not intended by these legislative bodies*. But I think mistakes made by legislative bodies and unforeseen effects is not an all uncommon consequence of legislative practice, remember H.L.A. Hart's powerful insight regarding the handicaps that permeate the activity of regulating conduct in advance, *i.e.* a relative indeterminacy of aim and a relative ignorance of fact in which "possible combination of circumstances which the future may bring" are impossible to be foreseen by the legislator (1961, 125), the legislator will legislate having one or two specific problems in mind and will try and regulate those specific actions, but once the law has been enacted you never know what other facts may arise and then questions of whether those facts apply to the statute or not is where interpretation and creativity play an important role, trying to minimize the need for interpretation and creativity in adjudication was an assignment that formalism tried to accomplish but with little success (1961, 126 *et seq.*).

One other comment that must be mentioned regarding Sampford's first line of argument against the guidance function is the following: Sampford argues for "'Prospective retrospectivity' (that is, clear guidelines for retrospective rule making can generate an expectation that retroactive law will be applied in the future to prevent actions) and its importance for this purpose" (2006, 81), but if we have clear guidelines regarding the use of retroactive legislation and how and when it must be used then I do not think that we are talking of a retroactive law at all, if citizens are aware of when and how these kind of laws will be enacted then notice of the law is met and I do not see how we can still label the problem as one of retroactive laws.

Concerning this last comment Sampford might reply that what these clear guidelines for "prospective retrospectivity" do is signal a warning that a law *might* be enacted and promulgated, not that it specifically determines how and when these kinds of laws will be enacted. At one point he puts the point this way: "the use of retrospective laws – or the knowledge that they might be used – can itself provide guidance of a useful and socially desirable sort" (2006, 82). Sampford continues arguing that with these kinds of retrospective laws "those who have been warned that the rule might be changed between action and adjudication take a risk in so acting and they cannot complain if the risk materializes" (2006, 252). But this is even more problematic. Imagine an action guiding directive that says: "I *might* issue this directive", in this case when I ask this authority should I ϕ or not ϕ, the response is: "I might ask you to ϕ and I might ask you not to ϕ. What kind of an authority is this? I am not sure what is Sampford's idea of an authority, but this is not a good example of an authority, even less so a good example of the authority of law.

Aside from the above arguments and most importantly, this notion of "prospective retrospectivity" might advance an all encompassing concept of non-retroactivity, if a legal system clearly states when and how a retroactive law may be enacted then no laws will count as retroactive because the citizen has the opportunity to guide their behavior according to these general guidelines of "prospective retrospectivity", and this seems to go to the other extreme, with general guidelines on retroactive law then we do not have a retroactive law at all.

A *second* line of argument explored by Sampford to claim that law's guidance function is being overstated is one that argues that not all laws, *i.e.* each and every law needs to have as an objective to guide behavior – or be capable of guiding behavior – there are several types of laws that serve several purposes, but guiding behavior is not one of them (2006, 83). Sampford says that we can think of various examples of non-normative laws that do not have this purpose of guidance. For example, a law which mandate that violently psychotic people be locked away, or that sick people can be quarantined. Sampford states (2006, 86):

> In each case, there is no guidance to the individual involved. If an individual is contagious or psychotic to the relevant extent, there is nothing they can actively do, on the basis of the law's guidance, to avoid incarceration. Yet we would not say that laws against incarceration of psychotic or contagious individuals are, to that extent, not laws – or not justifiable laws. They serve a public welfare agenda. So, it is false that laws must always serve as a guide to behavior.

Regarding this second line of argument, a couple of considerations may be put forward: First of all we agree that law's guidance function does not entail that each and every law has to be capable of providing guidance,[10] but while these examples of non-normative laws *may* prove an important point regarding law's guidance function and the nature of law, the point does not tell us much regarding the problem of retroactivity, because the issue here is not to find a law that is not capable of providing guidance, these laws will rarely be considered as retroactive, the key issue is to find examples of laws that purport to guide the behavior of it subjects and are still not considered as a retroactive application of law.

I mentioned before that it was important to assume that in this discussion Sampford and I have the very same idea in mind when talking about law's guidance function, *i.e.* law as issuing reasons that purport to guide our conduct and purport to make a practical difference in our deliberations on what we should do, I think this is the best way to understand Sampford's claims about overstating the guidance function though these claims do not succeed.

Unfortunately it is not at all clear what Sampford has in mind with the notion of guidance function, at one point he states that the guidance function relies not on the content of the law, but on intentions and principles behind the law (2006, 262–3), he thinks that law's guidance function is better understood within the domain of the integrity of what the law represents to ordinary citizens, due to the fact that citizens accept the laws that govern them because they think laws are morally justified by morally worthy principles and goals (2006, 263).

---

[10] Regarding Sampford's claim, I am putting aside the fact that he states that the claim that all laws must be capable of guiding behavior is a "normative claim" and attributes this to Raz and offers this counterargument against it. First of all this is not what is claimed by a proponent of law's guidance function, it is not a claim regarding *all* laws, *i.e.* each and every law, and secondly, those who consider the law's guidance function important to explain in a rendering of law's nature do not necessarily hold this from a normative stance. *Vid.* Sampford's claim (2006, 82–3). Jules Coleman also attributed to some proponents of legal positivism the claim that each and every law must make a practical difference, *vid.* Coleman (2001, 143).

This second way of understanding law's guidance function that at some points is suggested by Sampford makes his support of the formal conception of the rule of law a futile one, this implies not only a difference in understanding the rule of law, but a totally different standpoint in topics such as the content of the law. If this second way of understanding law's guidance is the correct one to appreciate Stampford's claims then we need to discuss many questions prior to the issue of retroactivity, questions such as: how is it possible to be guided by intentions and principles "behind" the law? (2006, 262–3) and do citizens really morally justify the law that guide their conduct? And then ask what happens with citizens that do not morally justify the law? Obviously these questions go beyond the scope of this paper. In this discussion on retroactivity I just want to place serious doubts on Stampford's objective of balancing a defense of a formal conception of the rule of law with these latter claims on how to understand law's guidance function.

11.5 Conclusion

In any case and to return to our main issue of retroactivity and the rule of law, I argued that a formal conception of the rule of law helps us understand the issues raised by retroactive application of the law, this entails that we explain the notion of retroactivity as demanding also a formal test that yields a yes or no answer, then continue to a second stage of justification where moral and political arguments can be advance to justify a retroactive application of a law. Another way to put my main claim is that much analytical headway can be obtained if retroactivity is analyzed in this two stage process way.

Sampford suggests one way of going about this, but his *reconceptualization* of the ideal of the rule of law suggests not only a reconceptualization of the formal notion of the rule of law – which he tries to defend – but also a reconceptualization of many other issues entailed by this formal conception. I tried to advance one way of fleshing out a notion of retroactivity within the confines of a formal conception of the rule of law.

References

Alexander, L. 1995. All or nothing at all? The intentions of authorities and the authority of intentions. In *Law and interpretation, essays in legal philosophy*, ed. A. Marmor. Oxford: Clarendon.

Coleman, J. 2001. *The practice of principle*. Oxford: Oxford University Press.

Fuller, L.L. 1964. *The morality of law*. New Haven: Yale University Press.

Hart, H.L.A. 1961. *The concept of law*. Oxford: Clarendon.

Hart, H.L.A. 1983. Positivism and the separation of law and morals. In *Essays in jurisprudence and philosophy*, ed. H.L.A. Hart. Oxford: Clarendon.

Hurley, S. 1990. Coherence, hypothetical cases, and precedent. *Oxford Journal of Legal Studies* 10: 221.

Marmor, A. 2005. *Interpretation and legal theory*, 2nd ed. Oxford: Hart Publishing.

Raz, J. 1979. *The authority of law*. Oxford: Oxford University Press.
Raz, J. 1986. *The morality of freedom*. Oxford: Oxford University Press.
Sampford, C. 2006. *Retrospectivity and the rule of law*. Oxford: Oxford University Press.
Stoljar, N. 2001. Vagueness, counterfactual intentions, and legal interpretation. *Legal Theory* 7: 447.
Vega Gómez, J. 2006. Retroactividad de la ley: Comentarios a la aplicación retroactiva del artículo 289 bis del Código Civil, en *Decisiones Relevantes de la Suprema Corte de Justicia de la Nación*, México: Suprema Corte de Justicia de la Nación–Instituto de Investigaciones Jurídicas, Universidad Nacional Autónoma de México.

About the Contributors

Brian H. Bix is the Frederick W. Thomas Professor of Law and Philosophy at the University of Minnesota. He is author of numerous articles on jurisprudence, contract law and family law, and also of *Jurisprudence: Theory and Context* (6th ed., 2012), *Contract Law: Rules, Theory, and Context* (2012), *A Dictionary of Legal Theory* (2004), and *Law, Language, and Legal Determinacy* (1993).

Brian Burge-Hendrix is a Professor and Faculty Tutor in the Humanities at Quest University. He is author of several articles on legal philosophy, ancient legal theory, and the philosophy of music, and also of *Epsitemic Uncertainty and Legal Theory* (2008). He was a member of the Cambridge Forum for Legal and Political Philosophy while a Junior Research Fellow at Churchill College, Cambridge.

Tom Campbell is a Professorial Fellow in the Centre for Applied Philosophy and Public Ethics (CAPPE) at Charles Sturt University and formerly Professor of Law at the Australian National University and of Jurisprudence at University of Glasgow. He is author of *The Legal Theory of Ethical Positivism* (1996), *Rights: A Critical Introduction* (2006), and *Justice* (2010), and also a Fellow of the Royal Society of Edinburgh and of the Academic of Social Sciences in Australia.

Imer B. Flores is a Professor-Researcher at the Legal Research Institute and at Law School, National Autonomous University of Mexico (UNAM). He is author of several articles on jurisprudence, legal and political philosophy, and constitutional law and theory. He is also founder of the Journal *Problema. Anuario de Filosofía y Teoría del Derecho*, and Visiting Professor of Law at Georgetown University Law Center (2012–2013).

Courtney Taylor Hamara completed her M.A. in philosophy in 2009 at McMaster University under the supervision of Professor W.J. Waluchow. She is currently working towards a combined B.C.L./LL.B. at McGill University, and once she completes her law degree intends to pursue a Ph.D.

I.B. Flores and K.E. Himma (eds.), *Law, Liberty, and the Rule of Law*,
Ius Gentium: Comparative Perspectives on Law and Justice 18,
DOI 10.1007/978-94-007-4743-2, © Springer Science+Business Media Dordrecht 2013

Kenneth Einar Himma is teaching at the University of Washington School of Law. He is author of numerous articles on jurisprudence, information ethics and law, philosophy of religion, philosophy of mind, and applied ethics. He is also associate editor of *The Oxford Handbook of Jurisprudence and Philosophy of Law* (2004), and editor of *The Nature of Law: Philosophical Issues in Conceptual Jurisprudence and Legal Theory* (2011).

Andrzej Maciej Kaniowski is Professor of Ethics and Social Philosophy at the University of Lodz. His teaching and research interests range from social philosophy (especially Jürgen Habermas and Immanuel Kant) to ethics and bioethics. He is author of several articles on social philosophy, ethics, politics, critical theory, and Kantian practical philosophy.

Conrado Hübner Mendes completed a Ph.D. in legal theory at the University of Edinburgh and a Ph.D. in political science at the University of São Paulo. He is author of several articles on constitutional theory and public law. He is currently a Humboldt Foundation Georg-Forster Post-Doctoral Fellow at the Wissenschaftszentrum Berlin.

Gülriz Uygur is an Associate Professor in Philosophy of Law at the Ankara University, Law School, General Secretary of the Turkish Philosophy Society and Head of the department of Legal Philosophy. She is author of several articles on law and ethics, legal ethics, violence against women, social justice, and focuses on how the law protects and promotes human dignity. She is also member of the UNESCO Human Rights Committee.

Juan Vega Gómez is a Professor-Researcher at the Legal Research Institute, National Autonomous University of Mexico (UNAM). He is author of articles on jurisprudence, legal philosophy and theory. He is also founder and chief-editor of the Journal *Problema. Anuario de Filosofía y Teoría del Derecho*.

Printed by Printforce, the Netherlands